MODERN BAND METHOD

Teacher Ed

A Beginner's Guide for Group or Private Instruction

Scott Burstein
Spencer Hale
Mary Claxton
Dave Wish

Book 1

Contributors:

Tony Sauza, Clayton McIntyre, Lauren Brown, Joe Panganiban

ISBN 978-1-5400-8438-5

Visit Hal Leonard Online at
www.halleonard.com

Contact us:
Hal Leonard
7777 West Bluemound Road
Milwaukee, WI 53213
Email: info@halleonard.com

In Europe, contact:
Hal Leonard Europe Limited
42 Wigmore Street
Marylebone, London, W1U 2RN
Email: info@halleonardeurope.com

In Australia, contact:
Hal Leonard Australia Pty. Ltd.
4 Lentara Court
Cheltenham, Victoria, 3192 Australia
Email: info@halleonard.com.au

GRAPHIC KEY

 Full Band   **Guitar**   **Keyboard**   **Bass**   **Drums**

Text and notation that appears in this format is content that is exclusive to the teacher version of this series. All other text is as it appears in the student instrument books. We've included the page numbers of the sections as they appear in the student books, placed next to their respective graphics. Also, while there is no accompanying audio and video with the teacher edition, we've included the respective icons as a reference in relation to the student books.

Introduction

Welcome to Modern Band, a series designed to help music teachers of all backgrounds bring Modern Band into their practice.

Modern Band is a category of school music programs that uses contemporary popular music as its repertoire, such as pop, rock, hip-hop, R&B, electronic dance music, and other contemporary styles as they emerge. Modern Band also utilizes (but is not limited to) the musical instruments that are common to these genres: guitar, keyboard, bass, drums, voice, and other technology.

The *Modern Band* method series gives you a sequential, skills-based, standards-aligned curriculum that will help you take your students from complete beginners to proficient music-makers. Just as importantly, this method series will also provide you with the tools and techniques necessary to welcome *new students* into your Modern Band program *at any time*.

Let's take a look at the four elements of Modern Band. We call them the Four "Rs" for short.

1. Repertoire
2. Reading
3. Recital (Decision Making)
4. 'Riting (Composition/Improvisation)

1. Repertoire for Modern Band

Modern Band repertoire is primarily selected by students. In a Modern Band classroom, most of the musical repertoire is chosen by the students. This is possible because so many students come to the Modern Band classroom with a familiarity and taste for different forms of music. Though students select the majority of the repertoire, teachers can and should at times offer pieces to expose students to new and relevant music.

Modern Band repertoire is culturally responsive. By having students select most of the repertoire, Modern Band allows children to bring familiar songs and styles into their classes and ensures that they can see themselves reflected in their curriculum.

Modern Band repertoire evolves at the speed of popular music. Popular music moves quickly. New songs become smash hits and then are quickly forgotten as other favorites emerge. This presents special challenges and opportunities for the Modern Band repertoire. It also makes it as dynamic as the culture that your students are living in.

You will find tips for selecting student-selected repertoire in Appendix B.

2. Reading for Modern Band

Modern Bands often use a combination of iconic and standard staff notation. Iconic notation is simply the representation of music using drawings, pictures, lines, numbers, and other visual devices, all intended to help students play a piece of music. Iconic notation has been around since the middle ages. It was the preferred means of teaching the lute and vihuela, two older precursor instruments to the guitar. Today, iconic notation is broadly used in popular music education.

The use of iconic notation aligns with the National Core Arts Standards, as they consistently use the language, "use standard and/or iconic notation," when delineating each standard and the anticipated student skill needed to achieve it. (*http://nationalartsstandards.org/sites/default/files/Music%20at%20 a%20Glance%20rev%202-6-15.pdf*)

The iconic notation used in this series is explained in the instrument introductions (pg. 7) and throughout the series as it is introduced. Standard notation accompanies this iconic notation as a reference for the instructor and is introduced in the student books as their familiarity and comfort with their instrument grows.

3. Reciting in Modern Band

In a Modern Band recital, students' musical decision-making and musical agency are key parts of and can be actively taught and encouraged. Have you ever seen a band take a song request from the audience? They often jump and play a request without the use of any sheet music or song charts. How do the musicians even know what to play? The answer is simple: The band members know how to comp on their instruments.

Musicians comp when they make decisions about what to play during a performance as they support their fellow musicians. Comping is the term that is used to describe the spontaneous or practiced selection of rhythm patterns, chord voicings, and melodic riffs that musicians use to support a musical performance.

Comping can be as simple as varying a strum pattern on the guitar between the verse and chorus of a song, or it can be far more complex, like making up complex drum fills, intricate bass lines, or horn riffs. With this in mind, let's consider how these simple patterns work together in the context of an actual tune.

Below are the first six bars of "Someone Like You" by Adele, as it might appear in a song book, with some highlighted features.

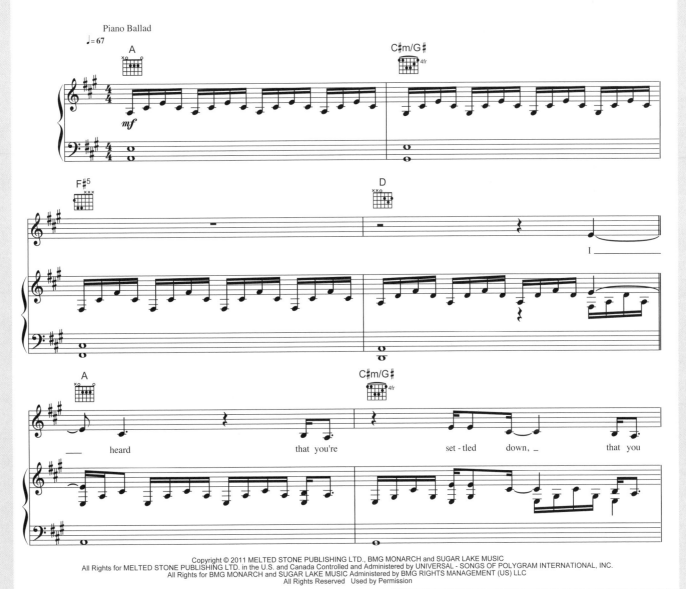

This score provides at least four invaluable insights on how musicians in a band might use comping as they performed the piece:

- **Tempo**: This gives information to all the musicians on how they'll approach their comping choices. For example, the drummers may have a few beats they favor for slower tempo pieces like ballads. Harmonic instrumentalists might have comping patterns they prefer for ballads.

- **Chords**: The chords are shown two ways here. First, they are named by letter above the staff. They are also spelled out on the staff in standard notation. In a Modern Band setting, guitarists, ukulele players, and keyboardists might look at the chord names like "C" and "Ami" and will know how to play one or more forms of these chords (root position, inversions, barre chords, etc.). They will play the chords together in ways that make sense for their instruments and will try various strumming patterns, choosing one or more that have the right sound and feel for the piece. Although this arrangement is a piano score, the comping keyboardist might also rely on the chord names rather than the written piano part. This provides them the flexibility to adjust their performance based on what the musicians around them are playing.

- **Bass Line**: A bass player or keyboardist might use the bass line as written here, but more likely, they would look at the chord names written above the staff, the same ones used by players of harmonic instruments like guitars or pianos. From those chord names, a bass player would likely comp a bass line that centered around chord tones especially around the root of each chord, but also possibly the 3rd and 5th.

- **Melody**: In a band setting, this melody would almost always be sung by a vocalist who would likely know the melody by ear and from memory.

In Appendix E of this teacher's edition, we include a bank of chord diagrams and drum icons which you and your students can use to learn the Full Band Songs they want to perform.

4. 'Riting in Modern Band

Once a student can comp using chords and rhythms, they now have one of the more foundational sets of tools for song writing. When a music-maker comps through a song, they *create* an arrangement of the tune. When they put chords together in an order they like, they *create* a chord progression. If they put words to paper, they *create* lyrics. When they set those lyrics over a chord progression or beat, they *create* a song. You will find composition activities throughout this series.

What You Will Find in This Book

This book contains complete Modern Band scores, individual excerpts for each instrument, and exercises to teach and learn comping, soloing, composition, instrument technique, music literacy, and reading comprehension. While this book does not intend to be a definitive, all-encompassing text, it will serve as a resource to guide in creating and refining student-centered Modern Band ensembles.

This book is divided into 12 sections, each containing four to six subsections based on the instrumental skills. The pacing of the sections is up to you as the instructor and may vary based on the age of students, length and frequency of classes, and familiarity and comfort with Modern Band techniques and music. At the conclusion of the sections, there is a glossary of key terms, key to iconic notations, and alignment with National Core Arts Standards in Music.

GUITAR 🎸 4

Introduction

Welcome!

If you are reading this, you have already made the decision to learn to play guitar so you can play some of your favorite songs. One of the best things about playing in a Modern Band is that you don't need much time to start jammin', but there are plenty of skills to learn and master over time too. Most popular musicians are able to perform in a wide variety of musical styles by playing chords with different rhythms to accompany a vocalist. They often add memorable riffs, or short melodic phrases, that stay in your head all day. This method book is designed to teach you skills to play guitar and create music in a variety of popular music styles—pop, rock, R&B, funk, hip-hop, and more. Let's get started!

Jam Tracks 🔊 and Video Lessons ▶️

Use the audio Jam Tracks throughout this book to practice the songs and exercises. Also be sure to watch the included video lessons that demonstrate many of the techniques and concepts. To access all of the audio and video files for download or streaming, just visit *www.halleonard.com/mylibrary* and enter the code found on page 1 of this book.

Parts of the Guitar

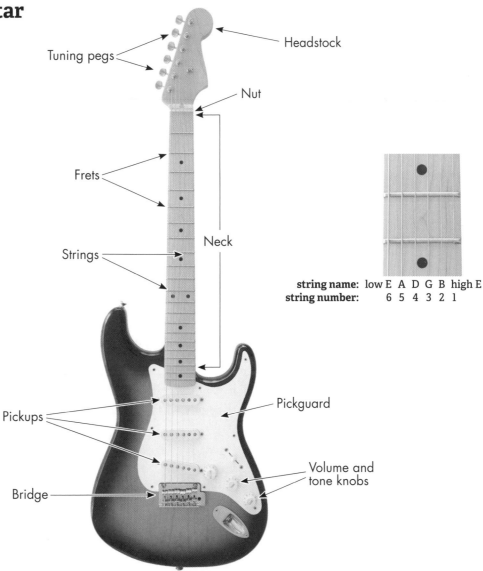

Headstock

Tuning pegs

Nut

Frets

Neck

Strings

string name: low E A D G B high E
string number: 6 5 4 3 2   1

Pickguard

Pickups

Volume and tone knobs

Bridge

Tuning ▶

Even if you're using perfect technique, your guitar won't sound right if it's not in tune. Be sure to watch the video and tune your guitar before you start playing.

Basic Technique ▶

If you're playing a right-handed guitar, hold the neck of the guitar in your left hand and rest the body of the guitar on your lap. If you're standing, you should use a strap to hold the instrument and adjust it to a comfortable height. If you're using a left-handed instrument, use the opposite hands.

You play notes by strumming or plucking the strings with a guitar pick.

Hold the pick between your thumb and index finger. Grip near the tip of the pick so that you will have more control, but not so close that your fingers are hitting the strings. Then strum through all the strings up and down.

Notation ▶

Here are a few graphics that will show up throughout each section. The first is the **chord diagram**. The numbers refer to the left-hand fingers used to press down the strings (for a right-handed guitar player). The open circles tell you to play a string **open**, or without holding down any frets. If you see an "X" over a string, it means to not play that string.

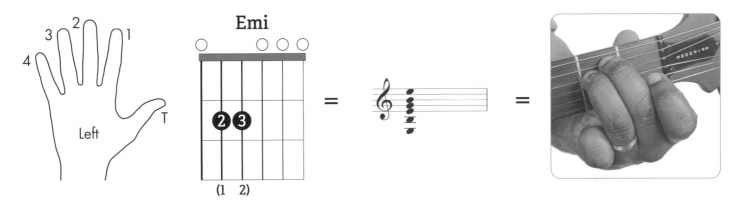

Strumming

Next, let's look at how we notate rhythms. Count these numbers steadily, "1, 2, 3, 4, 1, 2, 3, 4...," and strum down on the black numbers. Strumming on the numbers is called playing the "on-beats."

1	2	3	4

1	2	3	4

The "+" signs (spoken as "and") between numbers are called "off-beats." When playing these, strum up through the strings rather than down.

1	2	3 + 4

1 + 2 + 3	4

Learning rhythms and chords will improve your ability to "comp." **Comping** means using your musical knowledge to make up rhythms over a chord progression that fit a song's style.

This book is designed for you to learn alongside other Modern Band musicians so you can jam with your friends and classmates, but it can also be used as a stand-alone book to learn to play guitar. Though some of the skills that you will be working on during each section will be different from those of the other instruments, all of the Full Band Songs 🎸 are designed to be played by a whole band together. Now, let's start playing some music!

Introduction

Welcome!

If you are reading this, you have already made the decision to learn to play keyboard so you can play some of your favorite songs. One of the best things about playing in a Modern Band is that you don't need much time to start jammin', but there are also plenty of skills to learn and master over time too. This method book is designed to teach you skills to play keyboard and create music in a variety of popular music styles—pop, rock, R&B, funk, hip-hop, and more. Let's get started!

Jam Tracks 🔊 and Video Lessons ▶

Use the audio Jam Tracks throughout this book to practice the songs and exercises. Also be sure to watch the included video lessons that demonstrate many of the techniques and concepts. To access all of the audio and video files for download or streaming, just visit *www.halleonard.com/mylibrary* and enter the code found on page 1 of this book.

The Keyboard

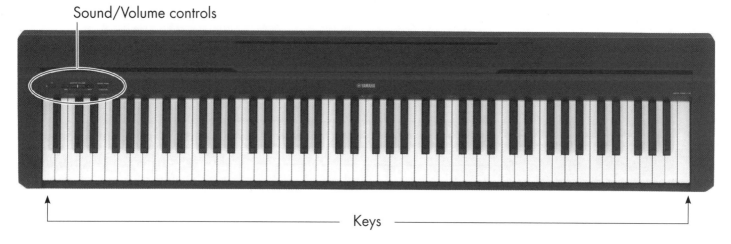

Sound/Volume controls

Keys

Some keyboards come with simple controls that allow you to increase and decrease your overall volume. Others are more complex, with several buttons, knobs, dials, and switches that allow you to shape the tone of the instrument. In this book, you only need to use a basic, natural sound of a real piano. However, if you happen to have a keyboard with several options to work with, then feel free to experiment in the songs throughout the book!

Basic Technique

You can sit or stand to play the keyboard. The keyboard stand and bench (if you're sitting) should be adjusted for your height.

The musical alphabet uses seven different letters, from A to G, and then repeats. You can easily find these on the white keys of our keyboard. On the keyboard, we have consistent numbers for the fingers:

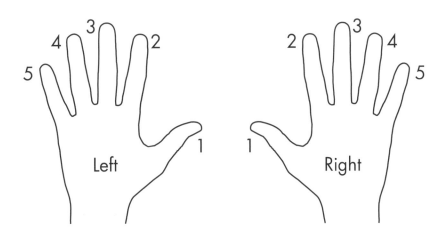

Iconic Notation ▶

Here are a few graphics that will show up throughout each section. The first is a chord diagram showing the white and black keys. The keys that are shaded in are the keys that should be played to perform the labeled chord. You can press down at the same time to play a full chord or play them in different combinations to create various **comping** patterns (improvised rhythmic accompaniment to a melody), which we will discuss later in the book. This first graphic is the E minor (Emi) chord. The numbers below each shaded key refer to your finger numbers:

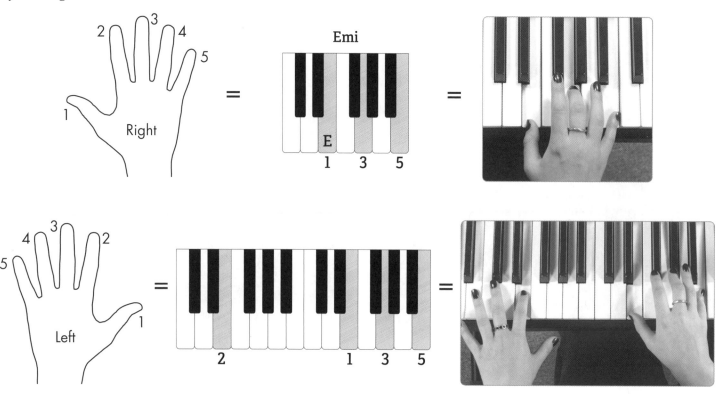

Rhythms in **iconic notation** are read left to right. All of the music used in this book is counted in groups of four. Count these numbers steadily ("1 + 2 + 3 + 4 +"). The "+" sign stands for the word "and." The black dots represent the three notes of the chord. The white dot represents a single bass note.

In the case of the Emi chord, for example, your right hand would play all three notes on every beat while your left hand only plays the note E on beat 1.

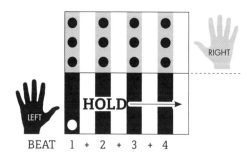

Here's how the chord diagrams and rhythm notation work in tandem:

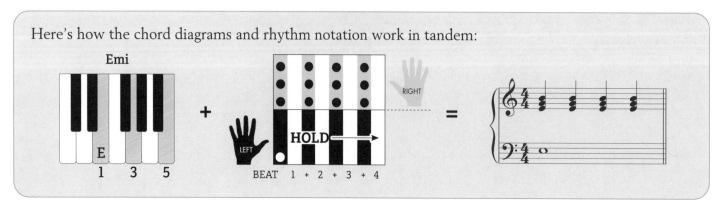

This iconic notation will aid you in your comping. **Comping** means using your musical knowledge to make up rhythms over a chord progression that fits a song's style. Throughout this book, we will give examples of these rhythms to increase your comping vocabulary.

This book is designed for you to learn alongside other Modern Band musicians so you can jam with your friends and classmates, but it can also be used as a stand-alone book to learn to play the keyboard. Though some of the skills that you will be working on during each section will be different from those of the other instruments, all of the Full Band Songs are designed to be played by a whole band together. Now it's time to start playing some music!

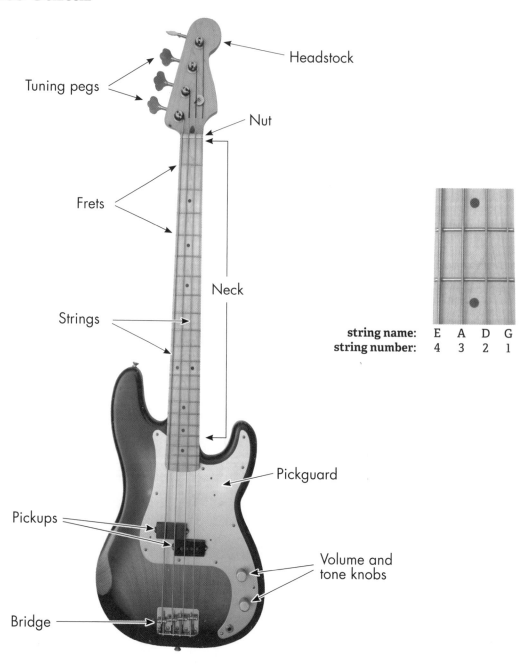

Introduction

Welcome!

If you are reading this, you have already made the decision to learn to play bass so you can play some of your favorite songs. One of the best things about playing in a Modern Band is that you don't need much time to start jammin', but there are plenty of skills to learn and master over time too. Most popular musicians are able to perform in a wide variety of musical styles by playing grooves with different rhythms to accompany a vocalist. They often add memorable riffs, or short melodic phrases, that stay in your head all day. This method book is designed to teach you skills to play bass and create music in a variety of popular music styles—pop, rock, R&B, funk, hip-hop, and more. Let's get started!

Jam Tracks 🔊 and Video Lessons ▶

Use the audio Jam Tracks throughout this book to practice the songs and exercises. Also be sure to watch the included video lessons that demonstrate many of the techniques and concepts. To access all of the audio and video files for download or streaming, just visit *www.halleonard.com/mylibrary* and enter the code found on page 1 of this book.

Parts of the Bass Guitar

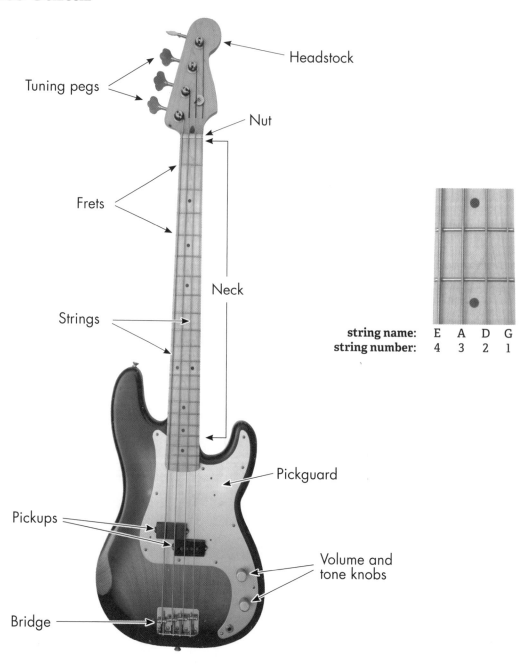

string name:	E	A	D	G
string number:	4	3	2	1

Tuning ▶

Even if you're using perfect technique, your bass won't sound right if it's not in tune. Be sure to watch the video and tune your bass before you start playing.

Basic Technique ▶

If you're playing a right-handed bass, hold the neck of the bass in your left hand and rest the body of the bass on your lap. If you're standing, you should use a strap to hold the instrument and adjust it to a comfortable height. If you're using a left-handed instrument, use the opposite hands.

The two most common ways to play the bass are fingerstyle and picking. Which technique you use is entirely up to you. Some players use different techniques for different styles of music.

With fingerstyle, you do not use a pick. Instead, place your right-hand thumb on the bass' pickup and alternate using your index and middle finger to play the strings, like two legs walking. Your fingers should fall into the thumb (when playing the low E string) or the next lower string (when playing any other string). When using a pick, place the pick between your thumb and index finger and pluck the string with the pick. Throughout this book, the term "picking" will refer to either technique.

Many students' natural tendency is to thumb the bass. When thumbing the bass, press down on the string, rather than pulling the string up or snapping it out. This can be an accommodation for younger students or students will smaller hands.

Notation

The following bass graphics will be used throughout the book. The first is the **note diagram**. An open circle above the diagram tells you to play a string **open**, or without holding down any frets. If you see an "X" over a string, it means to not play that string. In this example, the note diagram tells you to play the 4th string open.

Open E
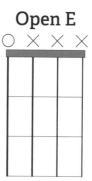

Another version of this graphic includes dots on the neck of the instrument. This shows you where to press down your finger on the neck of the instrument. In this example, the note diagram tells you to play the 3rd string while pressing down at the 3rd fret.

C

Next, let's look at how we notate rhythms. This is read left to right. Count these numbers steadily, "1, 2, 3, 4, 1, 2, 3, 4...," and play a note on the black numbers.

1	2	3	4

1	2	**3**	4

Here's what that note and rhythmic notation would look like in tandem:

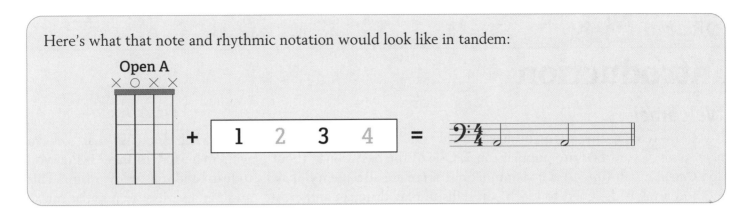

Learning rhythms and notes will improve your ability to "comp." **Comping** means using your musical knowledge to make up rhythms over a chord progression that fit a song's style.

This book is designed for you to learn alongside other Modern Band musicians so you can jam with your friends and classmates, but it can also be used as a stand-alone book to learn to play bass. Though some of the skills that you will be working on during each section will be different from those of the other instruments, all of the Full Band Songs 🎹 are designed to be played by a whole band together. Now, let's start playing some music!

Introduction

Welcome!

If you are reading this, then you have already made the decision to learn to play the drums so that you can play some of your favorite popular songs. One of the best things about playing in a Modern Band is that you don't need much time to start jammin', but there are also plenty of skills to learn and master over time. This method book is designed to teach you skills to play drumset and create music in a variety of popular music styles—pop, rock, R&B, funk, hip-hop, and more!

This book is designed for you to learn with other Modern Band musicians so you can jam with your friends and classmates, but it can also be used as a stand-alone book to learn how to play the drumset. Though some of the skills that you will be working on during each section will be different from those of the other instruments, all of the Full Band Songs 🎹 are designed to be played together by an entire Modern Band.

Jam Tracks 🔊 and Video Lessons ▶

Use the audio Jam Tracks throughout this book to practice the songs and exercises. Also be sure to watch the included video lessons that demonstrate many of the techniques and concepts. To access all of the audio and video files for download or streaming, just visit *www.halleonard.com/mylibrary* and enter the code found on page 1 of this book.

The Drumset

Below is a typical drumset. Your drumset might have more or fewer instruments:

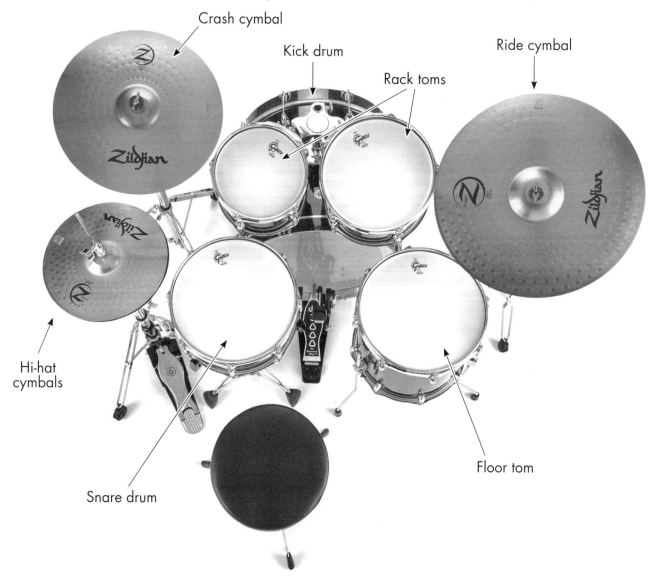

- Crash cymbal
- Kick drum
- Rack toms
- Ride cymbal
- Hi-hat cymbals
- Floor tom
- Snare drum

Basic Technique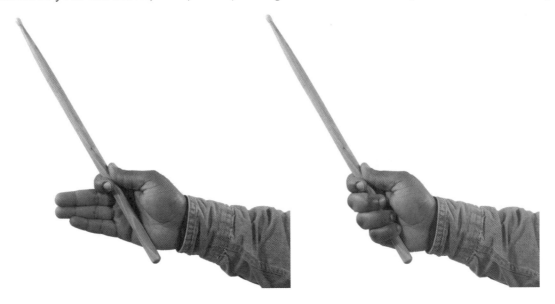

To hold the drumsticks, grab them between your thumb and index finger, approximately one third of the way up from the base of the stick. Then, wrap the rest of your fingers gently around the stick. Make sure you don't have any tension in your shoulders, arms, wrists, or fingers. You should always feel relaxed while playing.

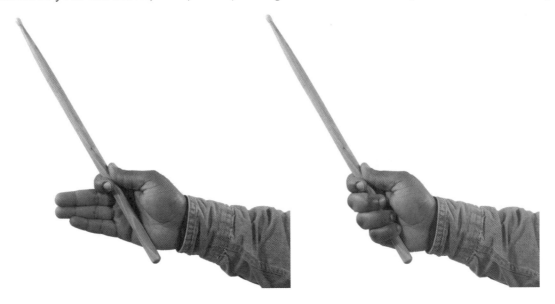

Both sticks are held the same way in each hand. This is called **matched grip**:

As a starting point, most drummers play with the right hand on the **hi-hat cymbals** and their left hand on the **snare drum**:

When it comes to using the feet, the natural placement that works along with the hand assignments is to put the right foot on the bass drum pedal and the left foot on the hi-hat pedal:

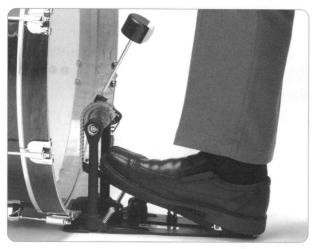 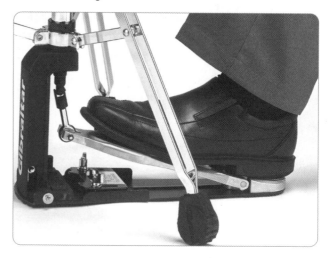

Iconic Notation

To show drum grooves, we will use **grid** or **iconic notation**. These figures, which we will call **drumbeat diagrams**, are read left to right, and the counting is written below. Anything that lines up in a vertical column is played at the same time, like the bass drum and hi-hat on beat 1. Here is an example:

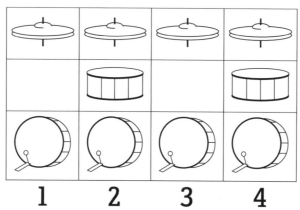

Here is another example where the grid shows an eighth-note subdivision:

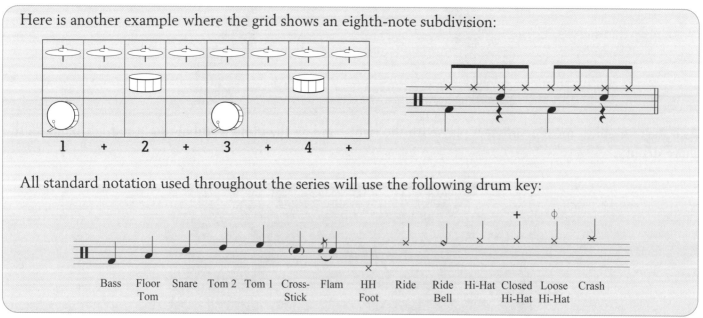

All standard notation used throughout the series will use the following drum key:

| Bass | Floor Tom | Snare | Tom 2 | Tom 1 | Cross-Stick | Flam | HH Foot | Ride | Ride Bell | Hi-Hat | Closed Hi-Hat | Loose Hi-Hat | Crash |

Playing in a Modern Band

When playing with a band, you should observe and listen to the rhythms and chords being played by your friends. Learning these rhythms and chords will improve your ability to comp. **Comping** means using your musical knowledge to make up rhythms and create grooves that fit a song's style.

The basic techniques and diagrams explained above will greatly help you in learning how to play the drumset. Now, let's start playing some music!

Comping: The whole ensemble can begin playing as a band right away with a One-Chord Jam. The Emi chord uses open strings on the guitar and bass, so no fretting is required, and it's all white keys on the piano. Drummers can either play steady quarter notes on the hi-hat or try to incorporate the snare drum on beats 2 and 4. Bass, guitar, and keyboard will then go on to learn two more chords/notes: C and G.

Improvisation: Using just two notes (A and C), student can begin composing original solos and exploring rhythmic and melodic improvisatory ideas.

Music Theory: A common way songs are notated in *Modern Band* is with song charts, which shows how the chords change over the measures of the songs. Students will read a basic, two- or four-bar repeating chord chart in this section to learn several songs.

Composition: Using their song chart reading skills and the chords they know, students will compose an original chord progression.

Full Band Song: Full Band Songs are intended to be songs that students spend more time learning, creating an arrangement for, and using as a means to practice instrumental and musical skills, such as playing chords, performing comping patterns, soloing, and singing.

Playing Chords/Lines; Instrument Technique: One-Chord (Note) Jam and Two-Handed Drumbeat

MU:Pr4.2.2

a) Demonstrate knowledge of music concepts (such as tonality and meter) in music from a variety of cultures selected for performance.

For our first warm-up, students can jam as a group using basic musical concepts that have already been mentioned in the introductions of each student book. A beginning warm-up is shown below in both standard notation (teacher's score) and iconic notation (for students).

For older and more advanced guitar students, it is encouraged that they use full open chords right away. An index of the full chord diagrams can be found in Appendix C.

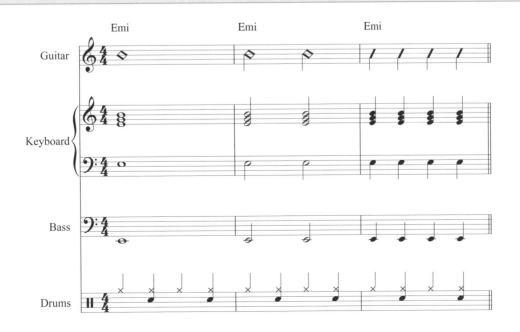

As a warm-up, play Emi and choose between the first, second, and third rhythms.

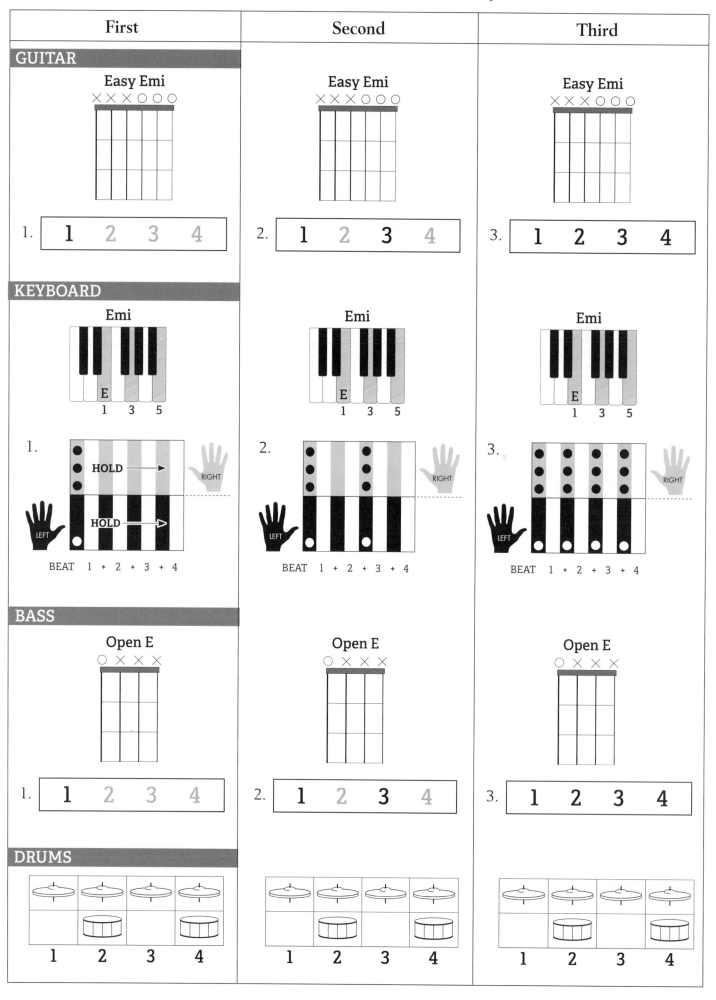

Now try the activity with another chord/note:

GUITAR	KEYBOARD	BASS

Easy G

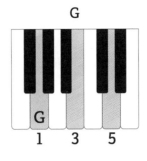

You can also try the activity with this chord/note:

GUITAR	KEYBOARD	BASS

Easy C

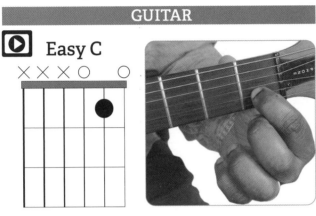

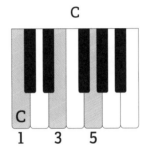

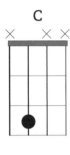

To help students focus on playing the chords rather than strumming just three strings (as to avoid the thicker ones) try using a sponge, folded paper, or tape to fully mute or dampen the strings.

Extensions and differentiation of warm-up:
- Each group (by instrument) plays each rhythm four times.
- Call out different numbers corresponding to each rhythm to check for understanding and as a means to assess progress.
- Have each instrument play a different rhythm (e.g., guitar on whole notes, keyboard on half notes, bass on quarter notes, etc.).
- Teacher-led "Repeat After Me": Play a new rhythm and have students can play it back (drums stay on their steady beat).
- Have students improvise their own rhythms.
- Have students lead in further call and response activities.

Improvisation/Instrument Technique: Two-Note Solo/Two-Handed Groove

| 🎸 7 | 🎹 7 | 🎸 7 | 🥁 7 |

MU:Pr4.1.2

a) Demonstrate and explain personal interest in, knowledge about, and purpose of varied musical selections.

MU:Pr4.1.E.5

a) Select varied repertoire to study based on interest, music reading skills (where appropriate), an understanding of the structure of the music, context, and the technical skill of the individual or ensemble.

MU:Pr5.3.E.5

a) Use self-reflection and peer feedback to refine individual and ensemble performances of a varied repertoire of music.

MU:Pr4.2.H.5

a) Identify prominent melodic and harmonic characteristics in a varied repertoire of music that includes melodies, repertoire pieces, and chordal accompaniments selected for performance, including at least some based on reading standard notation.

MU:Pr6.1.2

a) Perform music for a specific purpose with expression and technical accuracy.

MU:Pr6.1.E.5

a) Demonstrate attention to technical accuracy and expressive qualities in prepared and improvised performances of a varied repertoire of music.

MU:Pr6.1.H.5

a) Perform with expression and technical accuracy in individual performances of a varied repertoire of music that includes melodies, repertoire pieces, and chordal accompaniments, demonstrating understanding of the audience and the context.

The Two-Note Solo

Improvisation is an important skill for a modern band musician. There is harmonic improvisation, known as **comping**, and melodic improvisation, used for **soloing**. Often times, when the guitarist, keyboard player, or vocalist **solos**, the other instruments **comp**.

Here are steps you can take to practice the Two-Note Solo with your class:

- Once students learn their two notes, let them explore using them over a Jam Track or other music.
- Teacher-led "Repeat After Me": Play a one-bar riff and have students either respond with their own unique riff or repeat the riff you just played. Make sure to start with an easier riff and repeat it several times so they can figure it out.
- Have each student solo for a bar each, going around the room from student to student.
- Have students lead call and response activities.
- Singing solos can be a great way to have students internalize pitch, improvise ideas, and sing in their head voice. The Two-Note Solo allows students who are uncomfortable singing in front of their peers by allowing them to replicate an instrument instead of singing in their natural voice.
- The Two-Note Solo can be used as a vocal improvisation exercise as well. Repeat any of the previous activities with a student singing instead of playing.

Students can practice this solo/groove over the chords they just learned. In pairs, one student can practice playing C, G, or Emi chords while another student plays the two-note solo.

Improvisation: Two-Note Solo 🔊 ▶

The two notes shown here can be used to take a solo—the open 1st string, which is the note E, and the 3rd fret on the 1st string, which is the note G. Unlike the chord diagrams, this image shows two notes that you can play on the guitar, but not at the same time.

Improvisation: Two-Note Solo 🔊 ▶

These two notes, E and G, can be used to take a solo. Unlike the chord diagrams, this image shows two notes that you can play on the keyboard, one after the other:

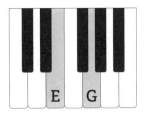

Here are some sample riffs to play on guitar and keyboard using the two solo notes:

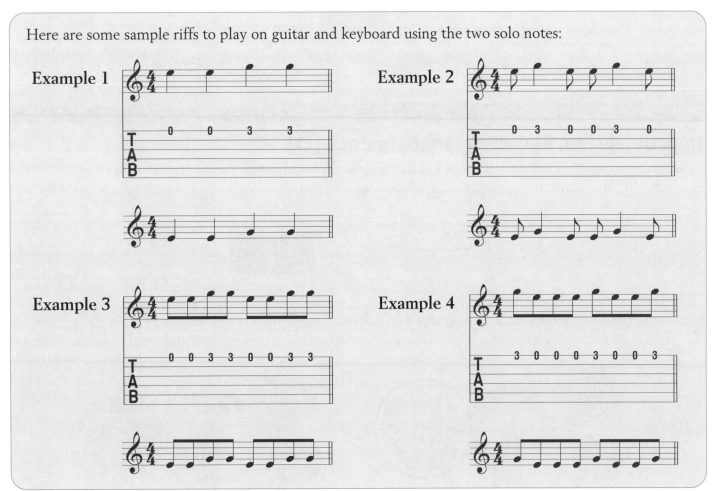

25

Improvisation: Two-Note Groove

The two notes shown here can be used to play a groove:

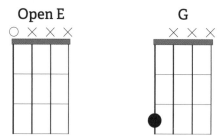

Open E   G

Here are some examples of bass grooves your students can play:

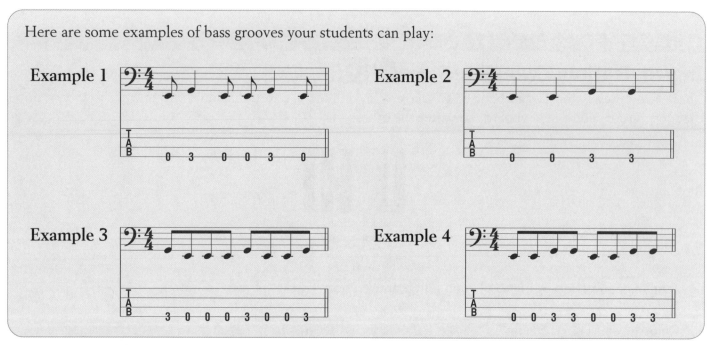

DRUMS

Improvisation: Switching Instruments

Now, we are ready to explore more areas of the drumset. The next two pieces are the **ride cymbal** and the **floor tom**. In the drumbeat diagram, their symbols look like this:

Move your right hand to the ride cymbal and your left hand to the floor tom, and then play the same pattern you previously used for the hi-hat and snare drum. You can try this with any two instruments on your drumset:

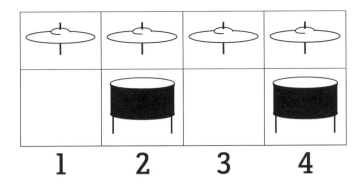

Music Theory: Doubling the Hi-Hat

When you play drums, you will often play the hi-hat cymbals closed. This means that your left foot will hold the hi-hat pedal down in the closed position, keeping the two cymbals close together to play a short sound.

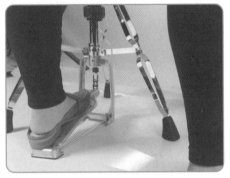

Closed hi-hat pedal

Closed hi-hat

Open hi-hat

Try playing the hi-hat twice as fast now. Count "1, 2, 3, 4," but this time, add an "and" in between the numbers. We use a "+" sign to represent "and" in the drumbeat diagram. Count "1 + 2 + 3 + 4 +…" out loud as you play:

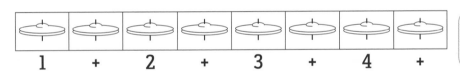

Now, add your snare drum hits back to the groove on beats 2 and 4:

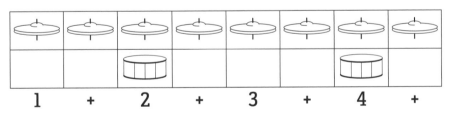
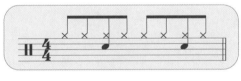

Music Theory: The Song Chart ▶

One way music is written is with a **lead sheet**. A lead sheet tells a musician how to play the chords of a song. The lead sheet example below has four **measures** (or **bars**), which are divided by vertical lines (**bar lines**). Each measure is made up of four beats, shown by the diagonal lines, or **slashes** (/). You can play any four-beat strum patterns over those four beats. The measures are repeated over and over again, indicated by the **repeat bar**.

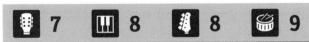

27

The next part of the lead sheet is the notes. The song below uses G for four beats (one measure), then an E for four beats, a C for four beats, and finally another E for four beats. For now, just try playing one note at the beginning of each measure.

 CAN'T STOP THE FEELING!

Justin Timberlake

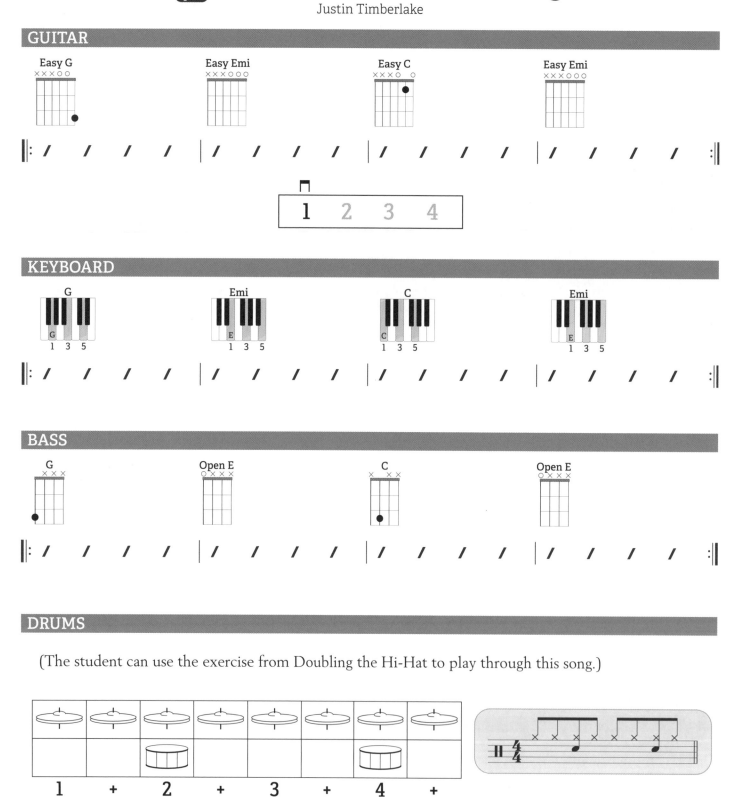

DRUMS

(The student can use the exercise from Doubling the Hi-Hat to play through this song.)

G   Emi
I've got this feeling inside my bones.

C   Emi
It goes electric, wavy when I turn it on.

G   Emi
All through my city, all through my home,

C   Emi
We're flying up, no ceiling, when we in our zone.

G   Emi
I got that sunshine in my pocket, got that good soul in my feet.

C   Emi
I feel that hot blood in my body when it drops, ooh.

G   Emi
I can't take my eyes up off it, moving so phenomenally.

C   Emi
Room on lock the way we rock it, so don't stop.

from TROLLS
Words and Music by Justin Timberlake, Max Martin and Shellback
Copyright © 2016 by Universal Music - Z Tunes LLC, Tennman Tunes, DWA Songs, MXM and KMR Music Royalties II SCSp
All Rights for Tennman Tunes Administered by Universal Music - Z Tunes LLC
All Rights for DWA Songs Administered by Universal Music Corp.
All Rights for MXM and KMR Music Royalties II SCSp Administered Worldwide by Kobalt Songs Music Publishing
International Copyright Secured   All Rights Reserved

Here are some songs that use the same three chords, Emi, G, and C.

Some of these songs have been transposed from their original keys.

WITHOUT YOU

David Guetta ft. Usher

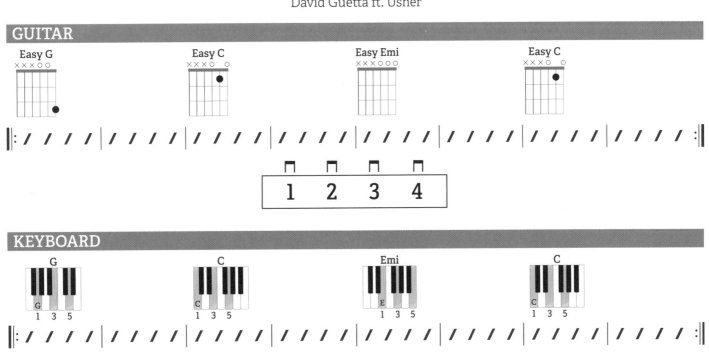

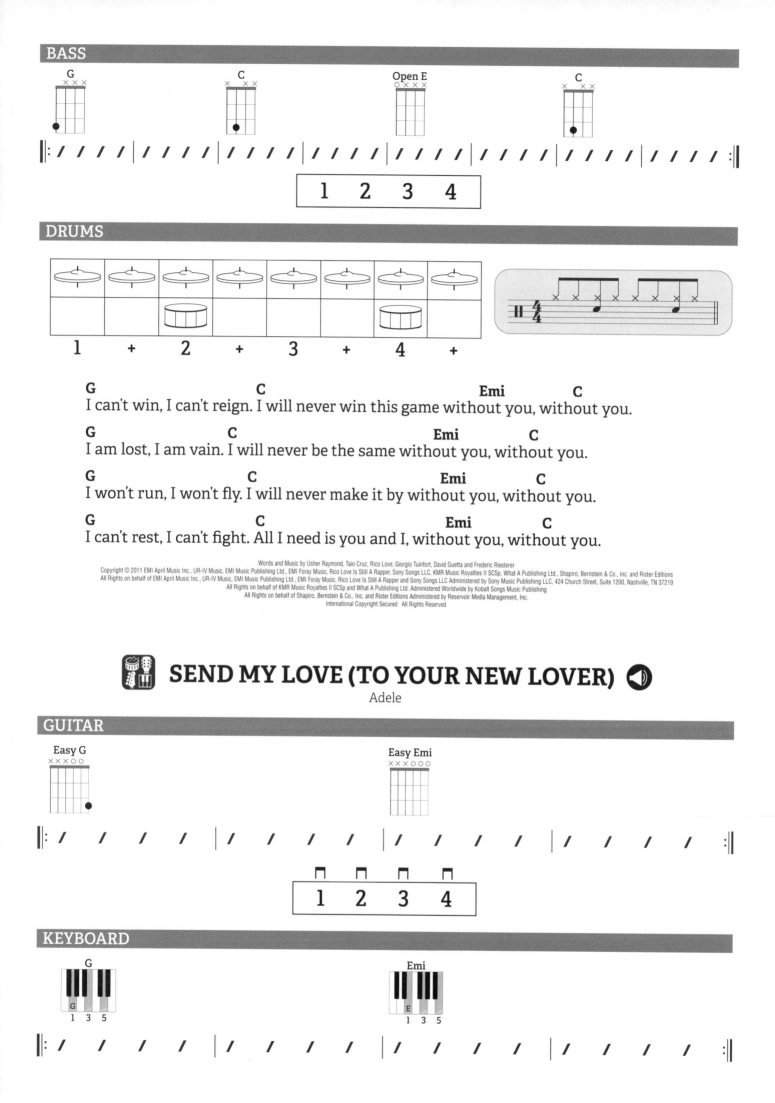

BASS

G   C   Open E   C

|: / / / / | / / / / | / / / / | / / / / | / / / / | / / / / | / / / / | / / / / :|

1   2   3   4

DRUMS

1   +   2   +   3   +   4   +

G   C   Emi   C
I can't win, I can't reign. I will never win this game without you, without you.

G   C   Emi   C
I am lost, I am vain. I will never be the same without you, without you.

G   C   Emi   C
I won't run, I won't fly. I will never make it by without you, without you.

G   C   Emi   C
I can't rest, I can't fight. All I need is you and I, without you, without you.

Words and Music by Usher Raymond, Taio Cruz, Rico Love, Giorgio Tuinfort, David Guetta and Frederic Riesterer
Copyright © 2011 EMI April Music Inc., UR-IV Music, EMI Music Publishing Ltd., EMI Foray Music, Rico Love Is Still A Rapper, Sony Songs LLC, KMR Music Royalties II SCSp, What A Publishing Ltd., Shapiro, Bernstein & Co., Inc. and Rister Editions
All Rights on behalf of EMI April Music Inc., UR-IV Music, EMI Music Publishing Ltd., EMI Foray Music, Rico Love Is Still A Rapper and Sony Songs LLC Administered by Sony Music Publishing LLC, 424 Church Street, Suite 1200, Nashville, TN 37219
All Rights on behalf of KMR Music Royalties II SCSp and What A Publishing Ltd. Administered Worldwide by Kobalt Songs Music Publishing
All Rights on behalf of Shapiro, Bernstein & Co., Inc. and Rister Editions Administered by Reservoir Media Management, Inc.
International Copyright Secured   All Rights Reserved

SEND MY LOVE (TO YOUR NEW LOVER)
Adele

GUITAR

Easy G   Easy Emi

|: / / / / | / / / / | / / / / | / / / / | / / / / | / / / / :|

1   2   3   4

KEYBOARD

G   Emi
G 1 3 5   E 1 3 5

|: / / / / | / / / / | / / / / | / / / / | / / / / | / / / / :|

BASS

To count the rhythm in this next song, say "1, 2 and, 3, 4 and." Pick on the numbers and on the "ands," shown by "+" symbols in the notation.

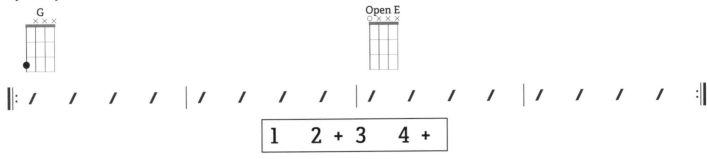

DRUMS

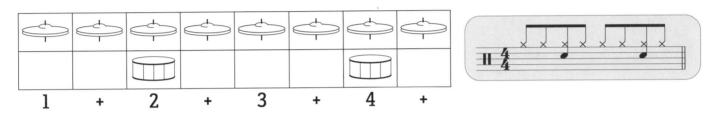

G
This was all you, none of it me. You put your hands on, on my body and told me, **Emi**
   you told me you were ready

G
For the big one, for the big jump. I'd be your last love, everlasting, you and me. **Emi**
   That was what you told me.

G
I'm giving you up, I've forgiven it all. You set me free. **Emi**

G
Send my love to your new lover, treat her better.

Emi
We've gotta let go of all of our ghosts. We both know we ain't kids no more.

G
Send my love to your new lover, treat her better.

Emi
We've gotta let go of all of our ghosts.
   We both know we ain't kids no more.

WAKE ME UP 🔊

Avicii ft. John Legend

GUITAR

In this song, the Emi and C chords are played for two beats each, and then G is played for four beats.

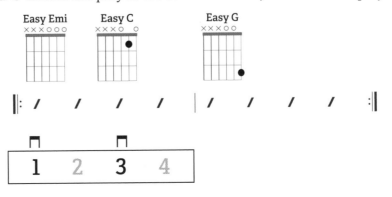

KEYBOARD

In this next chart, the first two chords last two beats each while the chord that follows last for four beats.

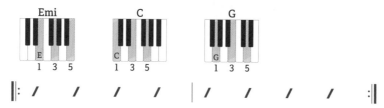

BASS

In this song, the E and C notes are played for two beats each, and then G is played for four beats.

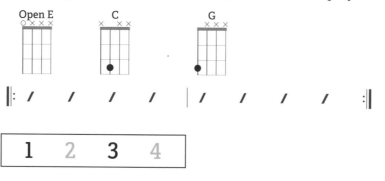

DRUMS

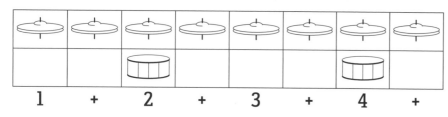

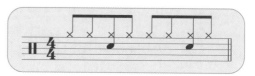

Emi   C   G
Feeling my way through the darkness,

Emi C   G
Guided by a beating heart.

Emi C   G
I can't tell where the journey will end,

Emi C   G
But I know where to start.

Emi   C G
They tell me I'm too young to understand.

Emi   C   G
They say I'm caught up in a dream.

Emi   C   G
Well, life will pass me by if I don't open up my eyes.

Emi   C G
Well, that's fine by me.

       Emi C G
So wake me up when it's all over,

      Emi C   G
When I'm wiser and I'm older.

     Emi C   G
All this time I was finding myself

Emi   C   G
And I didn't know I was lost.

Words and Music by Aloe Blacc, Tim Bergling and Michael Einziger
Copyright © 2011, 2013 Aloe Blacc Publishing, Inc., EMI Music Publishing Scandinavia AB, Universal Music Corp. and Elementary Particle Music
All Rights for Aloe Blacc Publishing, Inc. Administered Worldwide by Kobalt Songs Music Publishing
All Rights for EMI Music Publishing Scandinavia AB Administered by Sony Music Publishing LLC, 424 Church Street, Suite 1200, Nashville, TN 37219
All Rights for Elementary Particle Music Administered by Universal Music Corp.
All Rights Reserved Used by Permission

Composition: Compose a Chord Progression

MU:Cr1.1.2

a) Improvise rhythmic and melodic patterns and musical ideas for a specific purpose.

b) Generate musical patterns and ideas within the context of a given tonality (such as major and minor) and meter (such as duple and triple).

MU:Cr2.1.2

b) Use iconic or standard notation and/or recording technology to combine, sequence, and document personal musical ideas.

MU:Pr5.1.1

b) With limited guidance, use suggested strategies in rehearsal to address interpretive challenges of music.

MU:Pr6.1.2

a) Perform music for a specific purpose with expression and technical accuracy.

MU:Cr3.1.K

a) With guidance, apply personal, peer, and teacher feedback in refining personal musical ideas.

MU:Cr3.2.K

a) With guidance, demonstrate a final version of personal musical ideas to peers.

MU:Cr3.2.E.5

a) Share personally-developed melodic and rhythmic ideas or motives—individually or as an ensemble—that demonstrate understanding of characteristics of music or texts studied in rehearsal.

MU:Cr3.2.H.5

a) Share final versions of simple melodies (such as two-phrase) and chordal accompaniments for given melodies, demonstrating an understanding of how to develop and organize personal musical ideas.

MU:Cr1.1.E.5

a) Compose and improvise melodic and rhythmic ideas or motives that reflect characteristic(s) of music or text(s) studied in rehearsal.

MU:Pr6.1.E.5

a) Demonstrate attention to technical accuracy and expressive qualities in prepared and improvised performances of a varied repertoire of music.

MU:Cr1.1.H.5

a) Generate melodic, rhythmic, and harmonic ideas for simple melodies (such as two-phrase) and chordal accompaniments for given melodies.

MU:Cr2.1.H.5

a) Select, develop, and use standard notation or audio/video recording to document melodic, rhythmic, and harmonic ideas for drafts of simple melodies (such as two-phrase) and chordal accompaniments for given melodies.

MU:Pr6.1.H.5

a) Perform with expression and technical accuracy in individual performances of a varied repertoire of music that includes melodies, repertoire pieces, and chordal accompaniments, demonstrating understanding of the audience and the context.

> One of the first building blocks of composition is finding chords that work well together. Either as a full class, small groups, or individuals, have students compose a progression for a composition using the chords and notes they just used.

Compose (write) a progression using the G, C, and Emi chords, and any of the comping patterns you have used so far. Place them in the song chart grid below to create a new song.

GUITAR

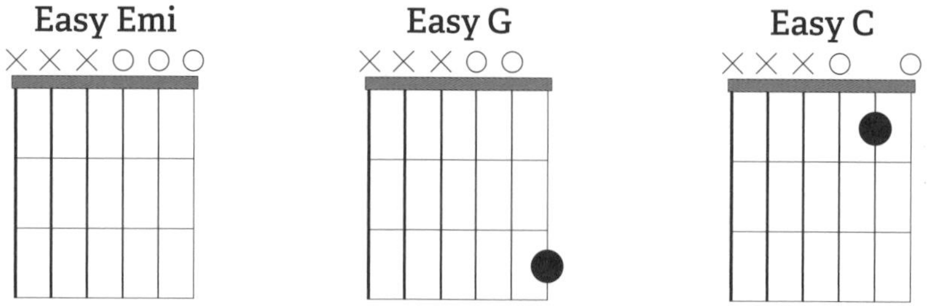

Easy Emi   Easy G   Easy C

Chords:

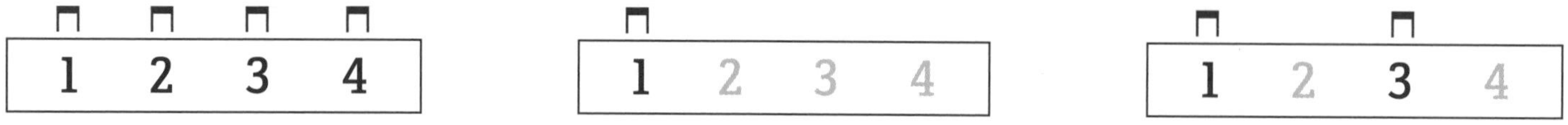

|: / / / / | / / / / | / / / / | / / / / :|

| 1 2 3 4 | 1 2 3 4 | 1 2 3 4 |

KEYBOARD

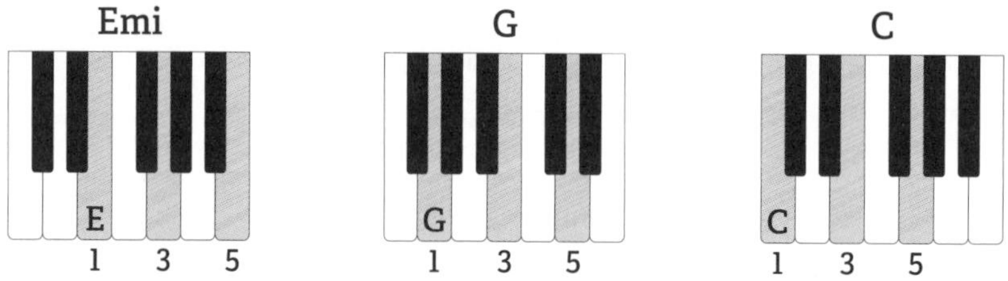

Emi   G   C

Chords

|: / / / / | / / / / | / / / / | / / / / :|

Comping Pattern

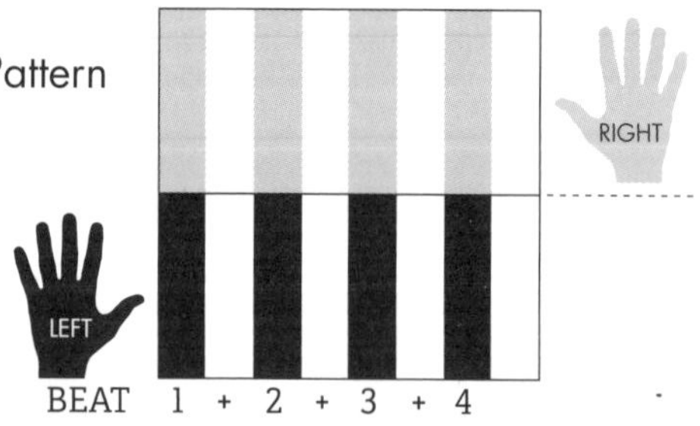

BEAT   1 + 2 + 3 + 4

34

BASS

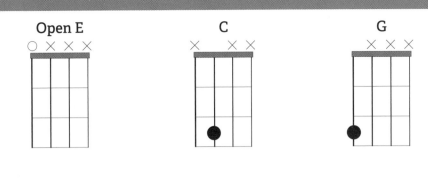

Bass Notes:

DRUMS

Great drummers are also composers. This means that they can write their own drumbeats. Rewrite the drumbeat you've already learned here:

1. Write out your steady, right-hand beat, and add the notes played on the snare drum on beats 2 and 4:

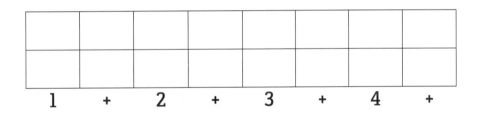

2. Now, you can add in one extra snare drum beat wherever you would like. Below is a grid if you want to write another:

3. You can now practice your new groove!

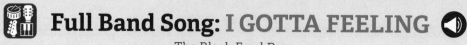
 11   11   11   12

MU:Pr4.2.2

a) Demonstrate knowledge of music concepts (such as tonality and meter) in music from a variety of cultures selected for performance.

MU:Pr4.1.2

a) Demonstrate and explain personal interest in, knowledge about, and purpose of varied musical selections.

MU:Pr4.1.E.5

a) Select varied repertoire to study based on interest, music reading skills (where appropriate), and an understanding of the structure of the music, context, and the technical skill of the individual or ensemble.

MU:Pr5.3.E.5

a) Use self-reflection and peer feedback to refine individual and ensemble performances of a varied repertoire of music.

MU:Pr4.2.H.5

a) Identify prominent melodic and harmonic characteristics in a varied repertoire of music that includes melodies, repertoire pieces, and chordal accompaniments selected for performance, including at least some based on reading standard notation.

MU:Pr6.1.2

a) Perform music for a specific purpose with expression and technical accuracy.

MU:Pr6.1.E.5

a) Demonstrate attention to technical accuracy and expressive qualities in prepared and improvised performances of a varied repertoire of music.

MU:Pr6.1.H.5

a) Perform with expression and technical accuracy in individual performances of a varied repertoire of music that includes melodies, repertoire pieces, and chordal accompaniments, demonstrating understanding of the audience and the context.

Performance Notes

This is the first Full Band Song through which we can approximate a more complete performance, singing and playing as a class. It works well for several reasons:

- The song has a repeating eight-bar chord progression that doesn't change. Once students have learned that, they have learned every chord.
- The chords in the original key of the song are chords students can play.
- The tempo is moderate for drummers.
- There is a step-wise melodic line in the Intro that keyboard players can play.
- It is likely a song most students will recognize.
- There is both singing and rapping in the song, which provides opportunities for more vocalists, even if they struggle to match pitch.

How does this chart differ from traditional song charts? Some of the basic skills of popular music are the ability to approximate, comp, and improvise. Included on this chart are suggested rhythm patterns to use for each instrument, based on previous knowledge, but the class is encouraged to think beyond the paper and to use their aural skills to create parts based on the original recording. Similarly, while there are no direct solos in the song, we encourage improvisation by including the Two-Note Solo scales, transposed to G major.

Here are a variety of ways to use this Full Band Song within your ensemble:

Can your students change chords at the appropriate times? If not:

- Play on the downbeat of the first measure, and then use beats 2, 3, and 4 to switch to the next chord.
- Split the chords up: Have the class divided into three sections so each student is only responsible for one chord or note. Students are responsible for counting and playing the chord when it is their turn.
- This song introduces melodic notation for the keyboard. Each letter represents an individual note. The vertical barlines help align the melodic notation to the harmonic notation. The contour of the letter shows the contour of the melody.
- If the drummer is struggling with the basic beat, split the drum set, with one student on the cymbals and another on the snare.

Adding vocals:

- Have all instrumentalists learn the Intro and Chorus vocal melodies and sing along in order to build their coordination of singing and playing simultaneously.
- Select singers to sing the Intro keyboard riff on a vowel/consonant combo, or a word, as a way to change up the instrumentation.
- Have the selected singers perform the rapped Verses and encourage them to create new lyrics as a classroom activity on composition and lyric writing.

Vary the texture in sections:

- Move from the hi-hat to the ride cymbal or even the floor tom to change the drum part in different sections of the song.
- Use a cymbal crash on a downbeat to signify large section changes such as the sung vs. rapped Verses.
- Have instrument groups enter and drop out, such as a section just for guitar, or just drum and bass.

Add new sections, utilizing dynamics and different rhythms:

- Have a guitarist or pianist take a two-note solo between the Chorus and Verse, or even over the Outro singing section.
- Play a large crescendo leading into the final Chorus.
- Add some stops or hits. For example, in the rap section, play a loud hit and cutoff on the downbeat of each measure, or on beats 1 and 2.

Completely change the feel of the song in a part:

- Go to a halftime feel by having the instruments play quarter notes instead of eighth notes, and the drummer can play quarter notes on the ride cymbal and snare hits only on beat 3.
- Make up a completely new rhythm, such as the dotted quarter–dotted quarter–quarter-note rhythm, which will give it a more Latin feel.

Suggestions for Similar Repertoire

- "Without You" by David Guetta ft. Usher
- "Can't Stop the Feeling" Justin Timberlake
- "Happier" by Marshmello and Bastille (without the Bridge)
- "Let Me Love You" by DJ Snake ft. Justin Bieber

These are just a few suggestions to teach a variety of musical skills with a single song. Success in Modern Band will be student-centered as well, so let the students offer input, try new things, and potentially vote on the version they would like to perform together. This can be done with a large ensemble performing together, or students can form mini-bands with their own versions that they can perform for each other.

Iconic Score

GUITAR

Easy G   Easy C   Easy Emi   Easy C

‖: / / / / | / / / / | / / / / | / / / / | / / / / | / / / / | / / / / | / / / / :‖

Use this rhythm for the Chorus:

And use this rhythm for the Verse
(V means to strum up):

KEYBOARD

Melody

‖: D D D D | C C B B | C C C C | C C C C | B B B B | B B B B | C C C C | C C C C :‖

G   C   Emi   C

‖: / / / / | / / / / | / / / / | / / / / | / / / / | / / / / | / / / / | / / / / :‖

BASS

G   C   Open E   C

‖: / / / / | / / / / | / / / / | / / / / | / / / / | / / / / | / / / / | / / / / :‖

Use this rhythm for the Chorus:

1	2	3	4

And use this rhythm for the Verse. To count this rhythm, say, "1 and, 2 and, 3 and, 4 and." Pick on the numbers and on the "ands," shown by "+" symbols in the notation.

DRUMS

We've left out the kickdrum part in the student book, but it appears in the standard staff score in case you have a student who is willing to try incorporating it into their playing.

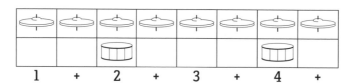

Standard Staff Score

INTRO/CHORUS

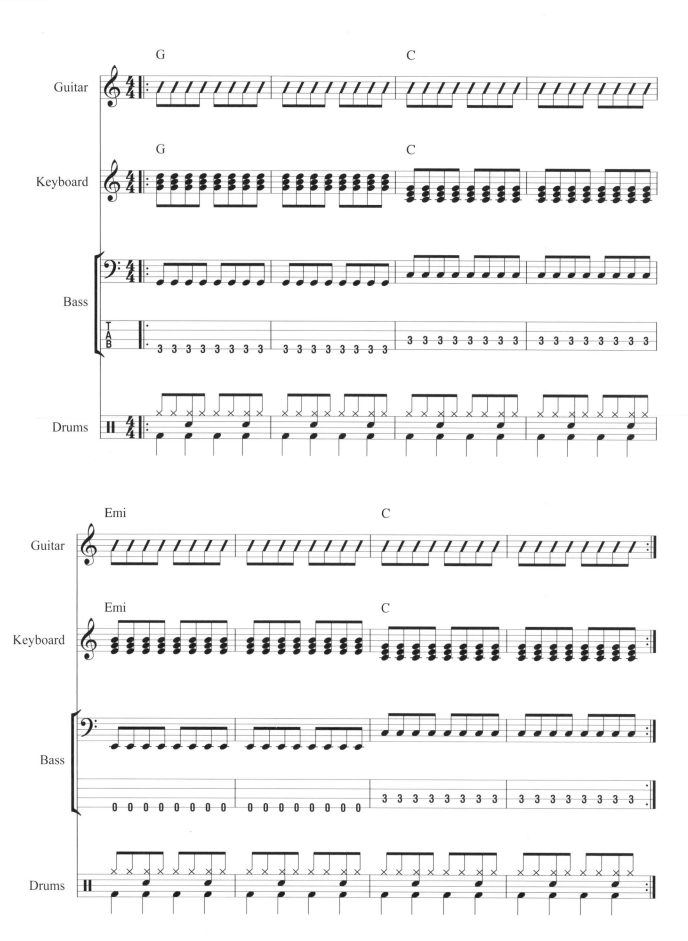

CHORUS

       G   C

I gotta feeling that tonight's gonna be a good night,

                      Emi   C

That tonight's gonna be a good night, that tonight's gonna be a good, good night.

VERSE

G   C

Tonight's the night, let's live it up. I got my money, let's spend it up.

Emi   C

Go out and smash it, like, oh my God. Jump off that sofa, let's get, get off.

VERSE

G   C

I know that we'll have a ball if we get down and go out and just lose it all.

          Emi   C

I feel stressed out, I wanna let go. Let's go way out, spaced out, and losing all control.

VERSE

G   C

Fill up my cup, Mazel Tov! Look at her dancing, just take it off.

Emi

Let's paint the town, we'll shut it down.

        C

Let's burn the roof, and then we'll do it again.

SECTION 1—SAMPLE RUBRIC					
Skill	**4**	**3**	**2**	**1**	**Next Steps**
GUITAR/ KEYBOARD Performing Chords	Student can play Ami, A, and E chords without use of diagrams as reference	Student can play Ami, A, and E chords with use of diagrams as reference	Student can play Ami, A, and E chords with use of diagrams and photo or model	Student cannot play Ami, A, or E chords	
GUITAR/ KEYBOARD/ BASS/ DRUMS Ensemble Performance	Student can consistently play in time with ensemble	Student can mostly play in time with ensemble	Student can sometimes play in time with ensemble	Student cannot play in time with ensemble	
GUITAR/ KEYBOARD/ BASS Melodic Playing	Student can perform selections learned from melodic notation in time	Student can play the notes in tablature (G/B) or melodic notation (K), out of time	Student can play the notes from tablature/melodic notation with few mistakes	Student cannot play notes from tablature/melodic notation	
GUITAR/ KEYBOARD/ BASS Rhythmic Performance	Student can perform and count whole and half notes and switch smoothly between them	Students can perform and count whole and half notes	Student can identify whole and half notes	Student cannot identify whole or half notes	
GUITAR/ KEYBOARD/ BASS Melodic Improvisation	Student can improvise a variety of four-beat phrases with the Two-Note Solo	Student can echo a variety of four-beat phrases with the Two-Note Solo	Student can play the two notes in the Two-Note Solo	Student cannot perform the notes in the Two-Note Solo	
DRUMS Technique	Student can perform two-handed backbeat at a variety of tempos	Student can perform steady eighth notes on the hi-hat with snare on beats 2 and 4	Student can perform steady quarter notes on the hi-hat	Student cannot play quarter-note patterns at a steady pulse	
DRUMS Arranging	Student can transfer drum patterns to a variety of different instruments in time	Student can perform two-handed drum patterns on different instruments	Student can perform each part of the two-handed beat in time, but not together	Student struggles to perform the two parts of the two-handed beat	
DRUMS Composition	Student can compose an original, two-part drum pattern	Student can modify and perform either part of a drum pattern	Student can modify and perform one part of a drum pattern	Student struggles to compose a two-part drum pattern	

Comping: "Low Rider" by War

Music Theory: Reading Tablature, Naming the Black Keys

Instrument Technique: The Kick Drum, Fingering Exercises

Comping: Crash on One, Ami and E Chords

Improvisation: Four-Note Solo

Music Theory: Whole and Half Notes

Full Band Song: "Heathens" by Twenty One Pilots

Playing Chords/Lines/Drumbeats: One-Chord/One-Note Song

 12   12   12   13

MU:Pr4.2.2

a) Demonstrate knowledge of music concepts (such as tonality and meter) in music from a variety of cultures selected for performance.

MU:Pr4.1.2

a) Demonstrate and explain personal interest in, knowledge about, and purpose of varied musical selections.

MU:Pr4.1.E.5

a) Select varied repertoire to study based on interest, music reading skills (where appropriate), and an understanding of the structure of the music, context, and the technical skill of the individual or ensemble.

MU:Pr5.3.E.5

a) Use self-reflection and peer feedback to refine individual and ensemble performances of a varied repertoire of music.

MU:Pr4.2.H.5

a) Identify prominent melodic and harmonic characteristics in a varied repertoire of music that includes melodies, repertoire pieces, and chordal accompaniments selected for performance, including at least some based on reading standard notation.

Here is another full-band warm-up. Each instrument can play together while learning the A chord and rhythm pattern.

Here are a few ways to practice this song as a group:
- Repeat the rhythm patterns as a whole group, making sure everyone plays in time.
- Teach students to sing (or whistle) the instrumental melody and have them work on singing it while playing the rhythm.
- Have instruments come in and out of the groove (e.g., no drums, just keyboard, guitar and bass, etc.).
- Work on dynamics, getting the group to play louder and softer without changing the tempo.
- Ask for a volunteer to make up a new rhythm pattern, and then have the class repeat it, changing the groove.
- Add a two-note solo to the groove with A and C notes.

LOW RIDER

War

Two-Note Solo Diagrams

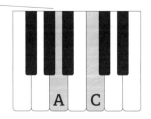

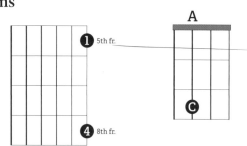

Music Theory: Reading Comprehension

🎸 12   🎹 12   🎸 12

MU:Pr4.2.2

b) When analyzing selected music, read and perform rhythmic and melodic patterns using iconic or standard notation.

MU:Pr5.1.2

b) Rehearse, identify, and apply strategies to address interpretive, performance, and technical challenges of music.

MU:Pr6.1.2

a) Perform music for a specific purpose with expression and technical accuracy.

MU:Pr4.1.H.5

a) Describe and demonstrate how a varied repertoire of music that includes melodies, repertoire pieces, and chordal accompaniments is selected, based on personal interest, music reading skills, and technical skill, as well as the context of the performances.

MU:Pr4.2.H.5

a) Identify prominent melodic and harmonic characteristics in a varied repertoire of music that includes melodies, repertoire pieces, and chordal accompaniments selected for performance, including at least some based on reading standard notation.

MU:Pr6.1.H.5

a) Perform with expression and technical accuracy in individual performances of a varied repertoire of music that includes melodies, repertoire pieces, and chordal accompaniments, demonstrating understanding of the audience and the context.

> This section includes a few songs to introduce melodic notation to students. The repertoire will differ from student book to student book. Some of the reading skills diverge here as well, with guitar and bass focused on tablature and keyboard reinforcing letter names. Students are encouraged to sing melodies they play. This will help them internalize and match pitch. It will also allow the students to express themselves musically without the inhibitions of being able to physically play a musical passage on the instrument. Then, students can work to replicate that phrasing on their instrument.

GUITAR

Music Theory: Reading Guitar Tab ▶

Tablature is another way to write music. It is used to write melodies and riffs. The tab staff has six lines and each line represents a string. The thickest string on the guitar is the lowest line on the tab.

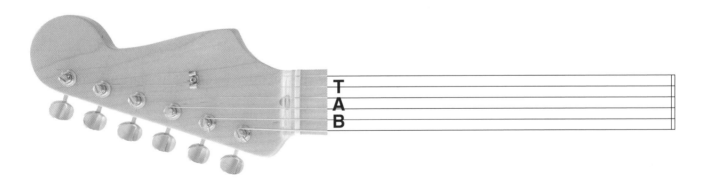

"Dark Horse" by Katy Perry has a riff played on the two thinnest strings of the guitar: strings 1 and 2. The numbers on the string tell us which fret to push down. For now, listen to the original song to get a sense of the rhythm to play.

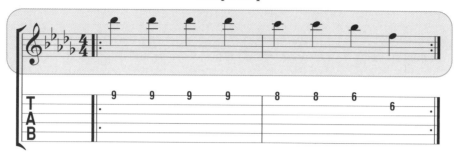

DARK HORSE

Katy Perry

This next riff is played on the lowest string of the guitar:

25 OR 6 TO 4

Chicago

KEYBOARD

Music Theory: Naming the Black Keys

Play the note C. Now play one black key to the *right*. This note is C-sharp (C♯). To name a black key, add "sharp" (♯) to the name of the white key just to its left.

Play the note D. Go one black key to the *left*. This note is D-flat (D♭). To name a black key, you can also add "flat" (♭) to the name of the white key just to its right.

Therefore, each black key has two names. C♯ and D♭ are the same note, but they have different names:

Now that you know some new notes, you can play this riff:

DARK HORSE

Katy Perry

Some songs are based on chords, some on riffs, and some use both.

Here is another riff that sounds best when played with the lower notes of the keyboard:

25 OR 6 TO 4
Chicago

Which fingerings work best for this riff? Since you are playing five different notes, you can use all five fingers. Start with your left-hand thumb (1) on A and your pinky (5) on E.

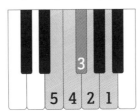

BASS

Music Theory: Reading Bass Tab ▶

Tablature is another way to write music. It is used to write melodies and riffs. The tab **staff** has four lines, and each line represents a string. The thickest string on the bass is the lowest line on the tab.

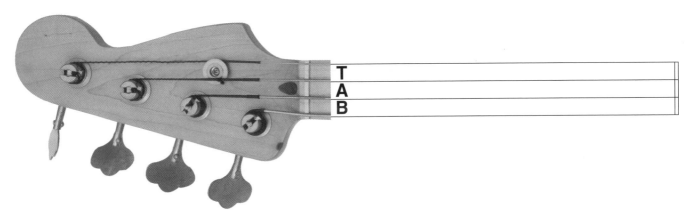

The next line up on the tab staff is the A string, which is the next string down on your bass guitar.

Here's a song you can use to practice playing the open E string evenly. Each "0" below tells you to pick the thickest string without holding down a fret with your left hand.

RUNNIN' WITH THE DEVIL 🔊
Van Halen

Words and Music by Edward Van Halen, Alex Van Halen, Michael Anthony and David Lee Roth
© 1978 MUGAMBI PUBLISHING, WC MUSIC CORP. and DIAMOND DAVE MUSIC
All Rights for MUGAMBI PUBLISHING Administered by ATLAS MUSIC PUBLISHING
All Rights Reserved   Used by Permission

Tablature can be used to learn new riffs. Numbers represent frets, not fingers. In the next example, the notes in the first measure are played on the 5th fret of the low E string; the notes in the second measure are played on the 3rd fret of the low E string, and so on.

Here are a couple riffs that just use the lowest string of the bass guitar. Listen to a recording of the songs for the rhythm.

25 OR 6 TO 4
Chicago

ONE NATION UNDER A GROOVE
Parliament Funkadelic

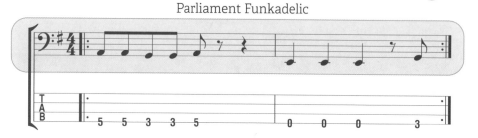

These next two examples also use the A string.

EX-FACTOR
Lauryn Hill

LET'S GROOVE
Earth, Wind & Fire

Instrument Technique and Music Theory

 13

Instrument Technique: The Kick Drum

Now that you can play the drumbeat with your hands, add in the **kick drum**. The kick drum is also known as the **bass drum**. Here is the symbol we will use in our drumbeat diagram:

Try these beats using the kick drum and the snare drum:

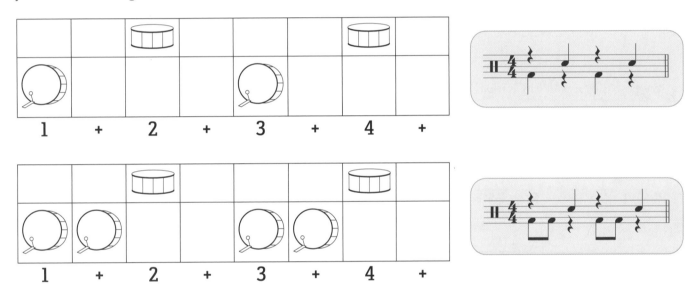

You can use this same beat to play "We Will Rock You" by Queen. Drumbeats rarely stay exactly the same throughout a whole song, so listen to each song carefully to find any variations.

 WE WILL ROCK YOU 🔊

Queen

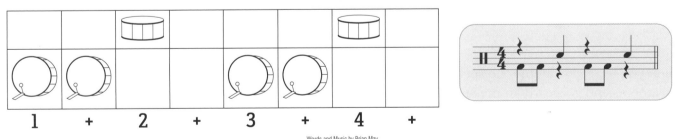

Putting Three Instruments Together

To play three instruments at the same time, you can start by playing your hi-hat on beats 1, 2, 3, and 4, your kick drum on beats 1 and 3, and your snare drum on beats 2 and 4:

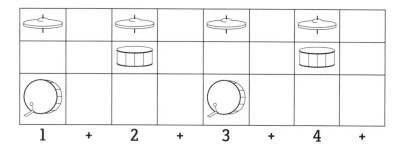

You can work up to this by playing just two parts at a time. Start with just the kick and snare:

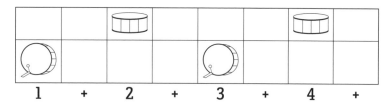

Now, try just the bass drum with the hi-hat:

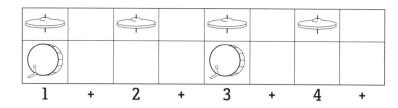
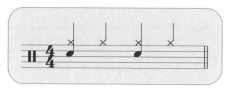

You can now put it all back together. Start slow to make sure everything is played at the correct point in time:

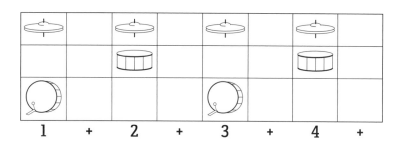

When you're ready, double the speed of your hi-hat by playing "1 + 2 + 3 + 4 +." Again, start with just two instruments and go slowly to make sure you're playing accurately:

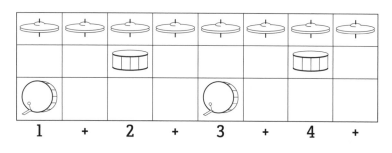
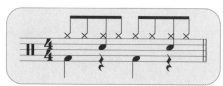

The drumbeat we just played features something that we call a **backbeat**. A backbeat refers to a groove that emphasizes beats 2 and 4, usually played on the snare drum. As you listen and play along, try playing the hi-hat on "1, 2, 3, 4" or "1 + 2 + 3 + 4 +" with the snare drum backbeat and see which sounds better:

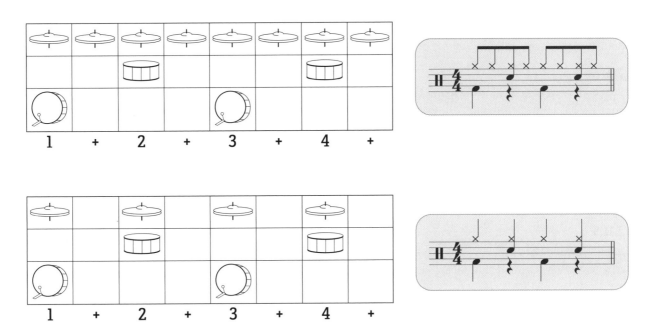

Music Theory: Quarter and Eighth Notes

When you played the hi-hat only on the beats, you were playing **quarter notes**:

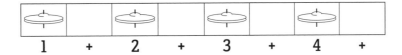

Using **standard notation**, that rhythm played in the drumbeat diagram above can be written like this:

When you played the hi-hat on "1 + 2 + 3 + 4 +," you were playing **eighth notes**:

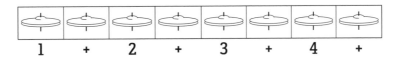

This rhythm can be written like this in standard notation:

51

Instrument Techniques

MU:Pr4.2.2

b) When analyzing selected music, read and perform rhythmic and melodic patterns using iconic or standard notation.

MU:Pr4.2.H.5

a) Identify prominent melodic and harmonic characteristics in a varied repertoire of music that includes melodies, repertoire pieces, and chordal accompaniments selected for performance, including at least some based on reading standard notation.

MU:Pr5.1.2

b) Rehearse, identify, and apply strategies to address interpretive, performance, and technical challenges of music.

MU:Pr6.1.2

a) Perform music for a specific purpose with expression and technical accuracy.

MU:Pr6.1.H.5

a) Perform with expression and technical accuracy in individual performances of a varied repertoire of music that includes melodies, repertoire pieces, and chordal accompaniments, demonstrating understanding of the audience and the context.

MU:Pr5.3.E.5

a) Use self-reflection and peer feedback to refine individual and ensemble performances of a varied repertoire of music.

> These next **technique tips** include different exercises for each instrument. These tips are important for developing instrument-specific skills. These exercises are opportunities for student-centered instruction because they demand instrumental groups to work independently and understand notation. Instructors can facilitate learning by checking on instrument groups one at a time.

GUITAR

Instrument Technique: Strengthening Your Fingers

Tablature is also useful for notating exercises. Try the exercise below for moving between fingers 1 and 2. Repeat this exercise with different fingers and on different frets.

Instrument Technique: Balancing the Fingers 🔊 ▶️

It's important that your fingers are equally as strong to play all types of music. To help get you there, you can play the following exercises starting with just one hand at a time and then together:

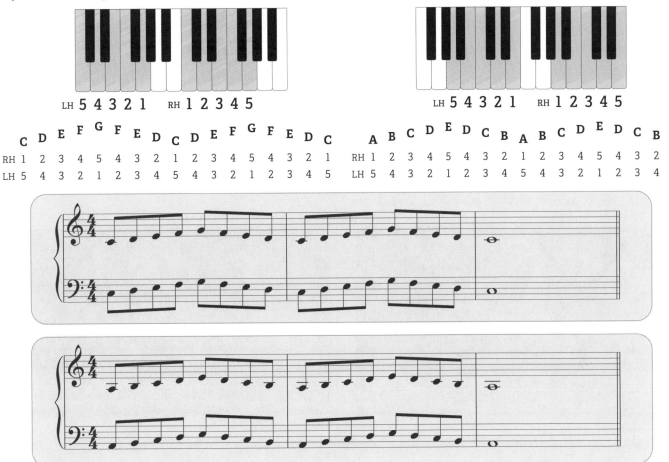

Begin slowly, and then speed up. Go back and forth until you can play each note clearly.

Instrument Technique: Strengthening Your Fingers 🔊 ▶️

In order to be able to play a variety of riffs and grooves, you must have strong and flexible fingers. Try different combinations of fingerings along with the video. (Try finger 1 or finger 2 for the notes on the 2nd fret in the first example; try fingers 1 and 4, or fingers 2 and 4 for the second example.)

Now, in the next exercise, focus on getting a clear sound out of each note while playing along with the Jam Track.

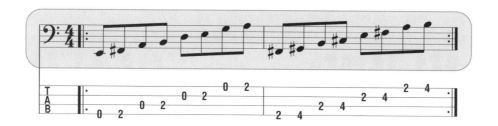

Instrument Technique: Heel Up and Heel Down

There are two common ways to play your kick drum:

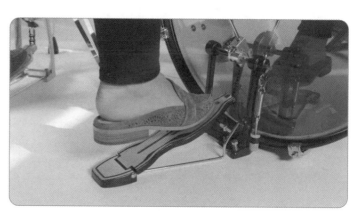

Both techniques are correct. Pick the one that works best for you. You might want to use different techniques depending on the music you are playing.

Playing Chords/Music Theory/Instrument Technique: Ami and E

MU:Pr4.2.2

a) Demonstrate knowledge of music concepts (such as tonality and meter) in music from a variety of cultures selected for performance.

MU:Pr4.1.2

a) Demonstrate and explain personal interest in, knowledge about, and purpose of varied musical selections.

MU:Pr4.1.E.5

a) Select varied repertoire to study based on interest, music reading skills (where appropriate), an understanding of the structure of the music, context, and the technical skill of the individual or ensemble.

MU:Pr5.3.E.5

a) Use self-reflection and peer feedback to refine individual and ensemble performances of a varied repertoire of music.

MU:Pr4.2.H.5

a) Identify prominent melodic and harmonic characteristics in a varied repertoire of music that includes melodies, repertoire pieces, and chordal accompaniments selected for performance, including at least some based on reading standard notation.

Playing Chords: Easy Ami

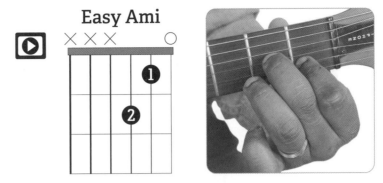

Easy Ami

The easy A minor chord (Ami) uses two fingers and is similar to the C chord. Try switching between the two chords with the song "Shout" by the Isley Brothers. Keep your pointer finger on the 1st fret of the 2nd string to make switching between these chords simple and smooth.

SHOUT
The Isley Brothers

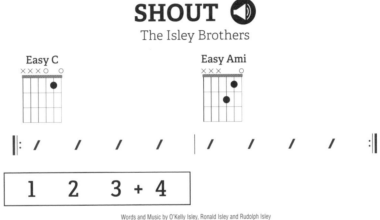

Easy C   Easy Ami

| 1 | 2 | 3 + 4 |

Playing Chords: Easy E

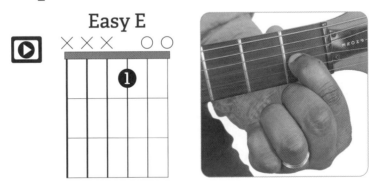

Easy E

You can change between the C and E chord by moving your first finger up or down one string.

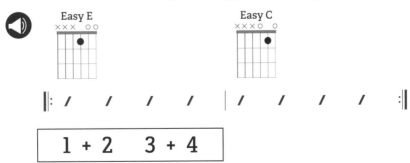

Easy E   Easy C

| 1 + 2 | 3 + 4 |

Music Theory: Minor vs. Major

Compare the Ami and A chord. What is different?

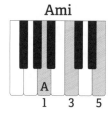

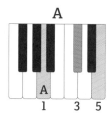

What is the difference in sound? How would you describe it?

The A chord's full name is really "A major" (it's assumed that a chord is a major chord unless told otherwise). All major chords have a similar quality of sound, and all minor chords do, too. Moving between them is always the same: the middle note moves one key to the left to go from major to minor.

Try playing a bar of each chord using these suggested rhythm:

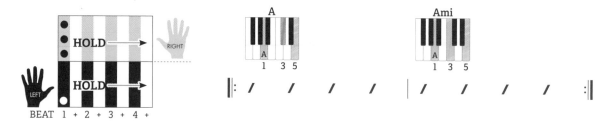

Here is another song where you can practice moving from a major chord to a minor chord:

SHOUT 🔊
The Isley Brothers

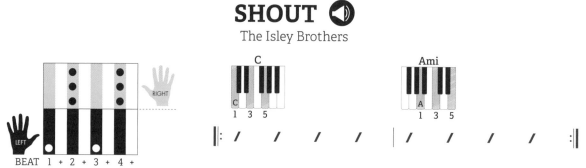

Instrument Technique: Muting Strings ▶

The length of a bass note can change the feel of a song. You can change the length of a bass note by **muting** it. To mute a note, lightly touch the string with your right or left hand to stop the string from vibrating. Try playing the notes in "Shout" by the Isley Brothers both muted and unmuted:

SHOUT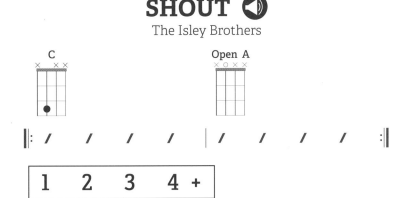
The Isley Brothers

Improvisation: The Four-Note Solo/Groove; Applying the Backbeat

🎸 14	🎹 14	🎸 14	🥁 16

MU:Cr1.1.2

a) Improvise rhythmic and melodic patterns and musical ideas for a specific purpose.

b) Generate musical patterns and ideas within the context of a given tonality (such as major and minor) and meter (such as duple and triple).

MU:Cr2.1.2

b) Use iconic or standard notation and/or recording technology to combine, sequence, and document personal musical ideas.

MU:Pr5.1.1

b) With limited guidance, use suggested strategies in rehearsal to address interpretive challenges of music.

MU:Pr6.1.2

a) Perform music for a specific purpose with expression and technical accuracy.

MU:Cr1.1.E.5

a) Compose and improvise melodic and rhythmic ideas or motives that reflect characteristic(s) of music or text(s) studied in rehearsal.

MU:Pr6.1.E.5

a) Demonstrate attention to technical accuracy and expressive qualities in prepared and improvised performances of a varied repertoire of music.

MU:Cr1.1.H.5

a) Generate melodic, rhythmic, and harmonic ideas for simple melodies (such as two-phrase) and chordal accompaniments for given melodies.

MU:Cr2.1.H.5

a) Select, develop, and use standard notation or audio/video recording to document melodic, rhythmic, and harmonic ideas for drafts of simple melodies (such as two-phrase) and chordal accompaniments for given melodies.

MU:Pr6.1.H.5

a) Perform with expression and technical accuracy in individual performances of a varied repertoire of music that includes melodies, repertoire pieces, and chordal accompaniments, demonstrating understanding of the audience and the context.

> This next improvisation section will build on the previous skills by adding the next two notes of the pentatonic scale. Like last time, this works best with a variety of examples: jamming over a song, teacher or student-led call and response, "Repeat After Me," trading measures, etc. As with the two-note solo, students can be encouraged to sing their four-note solos. See the Two-Note Solo on page 24 to revisit activity ideas.

Improvisation: Four-Note Solo

You can expand the two-note solo to four notes by playing the same frets on the next string. Try improvising using these four notes. Another musician can play the Ami chord along with you and the Jam Track.

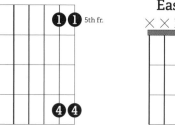 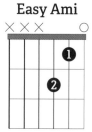

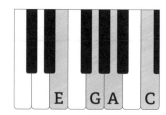

Improvisation: Four-Note Solo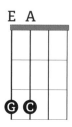

Improvise with these four notes:

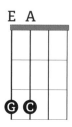

You can try lots of fingerings here based on which notes you are using for your solo. For instance, if you want to use all four notes in a row, then try playing E with 1, G with 2, A with 3, and C with 5, all with the right hand. However, if you want to alternate quickly between the A and C and then move down to E and G, you might use 1 and 3 for both and move your hand up and down the range of the keys.

Improvisation: Four-Note Groove

You can expand the two-note groove to four notes by playing the same frets on the next string. Try improvising using these four notes:

Here are a few examples of some bass grooves using the four notes, E, G, A, and C:

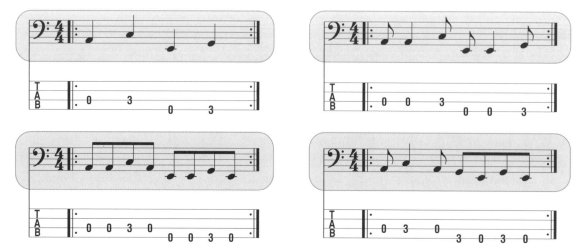

58

Drumbeat Variations: Playing the Crash Cymbal

It's now time to introduce another piece of the drumset: the **crash cymbal**. We use this symbol in our drumbeat diagram:

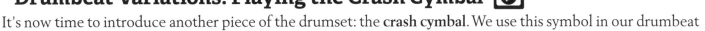

Here is a picture showing where the crash cymbal is usually placed in a drumset configuration:

The crash cymbal is often played on beat 1 at the beginning of a section of music. You can play the crash instead of the hi-hat on that particular beat:

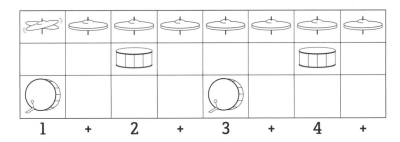

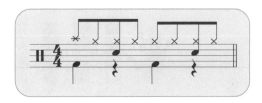

If you want to simplify that beat, then play this variation:

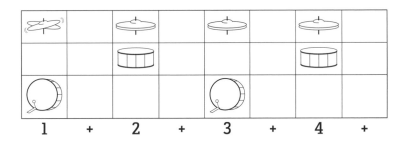

Music Theory: Whole Notes and Half Notes; Ear Training

MU:Pr4.2.2

b) When analyzing selected music, read and perform rhythmic and melodic patterns using iconic or standard notation.

MU:Pr5.1.2

b) Rehearse, identify, and apply strategies to address interpretive, performance, and technical challenges of music.

MU:Pr6.1.2

a) Perform music for a specific purpose with expression and technical accuracy.

MU:Pr4.1.H.5

a) Describe and demonstrate how a varied repertoire of music that includes melodies, repertoire pieces, and chordal accompaniments is selected, based on personal interest, music reading skills, and technical skill, as well as the context of the performances.

MU:Pr4.2.H.5

a) Identify prominent melodic and harmonic characteristics in a varied repertoire of music that includes melodies, repertoire pieces, and chordal accompaniments selected for performance, including at least some based on reading standard notation.

MU:Pr6.1.H.5

a) Perform with expression and technical accuracy in individual performances of a varied repertoire of music that includes melodies, repertoire pieces, and chordal accompaniments, demonstrating understanding of the audience and the context.

GUITAR, KEYBOARD, AND BASS

Music Theory: Whole Notes and Half Notes

In each measure of music so far, you have counted four beats. If you play a note once and let it ring for four beats, it lasts the whole measure. That is called a **whole note**. If it is cut in half, it becomes two **half notes**. Each whole note is four beats long, and each half note is two beats long.

Below, whole and half notes in traditional notation are shown along with their corresponding picking pattern.

> Guitar and Bass students can use the same iconic rhythmic notation, while Keyboard students will use the comping diagrams directly below.

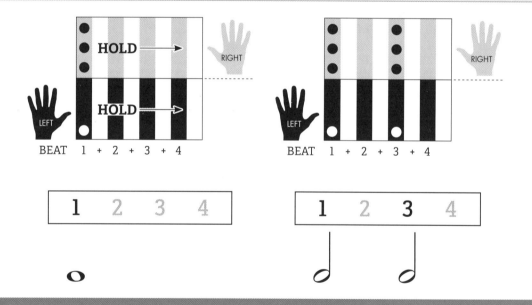

DRUMS

Music Theory: Using Your Ears and Your Voice

In "Heathens" by Twenty One Pilots, the drummer plays a backbeat with one bass drum hit moved away from beat 3. Here's a drumbeat diagram with the second bass drum beat removed:

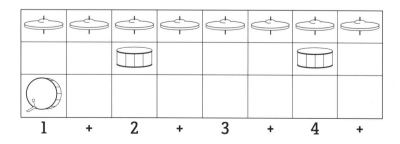

60

Beatboxing to Transcribe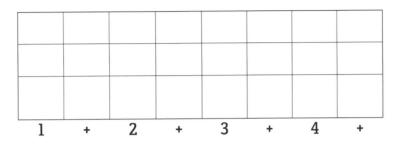

Transcribing music is a big part of being a musician, and drummers often use **beatboxing** to learn parts from a recording. Beatboxing is a way that you can use your voice to replicate the sounds of the drumset. You can use the words "boots" (bass drum) and "cats" (snare drum) to beatbox drum sounds. You can make them sound better by emphasizing the beginning of each word and not pronouncing the end. The sounds will be more like "buh" and "kah."

Can you beatbox to find where the removed bass drum beat goes in "Heathens?"
1. Listen to the recording, and try beatboxing just the bass and snare drum.
2. Try counting the beats out loud. The bass drum comes after which number?
3. Write where you hear the kick drum in the drumbeat diagram below.

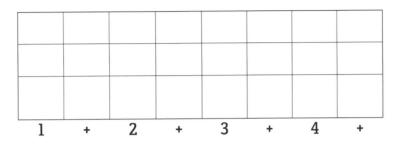

Does your drumbeat look like this one?

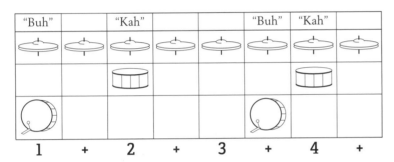 

You will use this beat in the Full Band Song "Heathens" by Twenty One Pilots.

Full Band Song: HEATHENS
Twenty One Pilots

MU:Pr4.2.2
a) Demonstrate knowledge of music concepts (such as tonality and meter) in music from a variety of cultures selected for performance.

MU:Pr4.1.2
a) Demonstrate and explain personal interest in, knowledge about, and purpose of varied musical selections.

MU:Pr4.1.E.5
a) Select varied repertoire to study based on interest, music reading skills (where appropriate), and an understanding of the structure of the music, context, and the technical skill of the individual or ensemble.

MU:Pr5.3.E.5
a) Use self-reflection and peer feedback to refine individual and ensemble performances of a varied repertoire of music.

MU:Pr4.2.H.5

a) Identify prominent melodic and harmonic characteristics in a varied repertoire of music that includes melodies, repertoire pieces, and chordal accompaniments selected for performance, including at least some based on reading standard notation.

MU:Pr6.1.2

a) Perform music for a specific purpose with expression and technical accuracy.

MU:Pr6.1.E.5

a) Demonstrate attention to technical accuracy and expressive qualities in prepared and improvised performances of a varied repertoire of music.

MU:Pr6.1.H.5

a) Perform with expression and technical accuracy in individual performances of a varied repertoire of music that includes melodies, repertoire pieces, and chordal accompaniments, demonstrating understanding of the audience and the context.

Performance Notes

The second Full Band Song can highlight a lot of the recently learned chords and comping patterns, and, like the previous song, the simple structure leaves room to experiment and approximate. Here are a few ideas to make a variety of lessons out of a three-chord progression:

Add an Introduction or Solo Section

- Once students have learned their parts, the progression can be repeated and extended in different sections to explore concepts of improvisation, such as using the Four-Note Solo in the key of E minor. This will have a particularly piquant quality due to the E major triad, giving it a blue note of a minor 3rd over major 3rd.
- Build into the song by having just the bass and drums start off, adding guitar and keys after a couple phrases, or vice-versa. Allow students the opportunity to experiment with different arrangements.

Change the feel and add dynamics

- The suggested rhythms follow the song closely, but there are lots of opportunities to change the feel of the music in parts as a whole by adding in more active rhythms. For example, playing with variations of quarter notes and eighth notes will give it more of a driving feel. Adding a syncopated rhythm will make it sound funkier.
- Have the band play quietly throughout the Verses and then loudly during the Chorus. This is a great way to show how dynamics can be used for variation and musicality. You can expand this by including a crescendo during the B chord on the Pre-Chorus.

Adding Vocals

- Begin with students learning the Chorus melody and have everyone sing along to it as they play.
- Highlight all singers by breaking up the Verses, letting each singer have a two-bar solo, and then have everyone come back in to sing the Chorus.

Suggestions for Similar Repertoire

- "The Suburbs" by Arcade Fire (Verse only)

Iconic Score

Melody Phrase 1

|B^CB G B^CB G| E |B^CB G B^CB G| E

Melody Phrase 2

||E|D C ^ED C ^E|^E B |E|D C ^ED C ^E|^E B ||

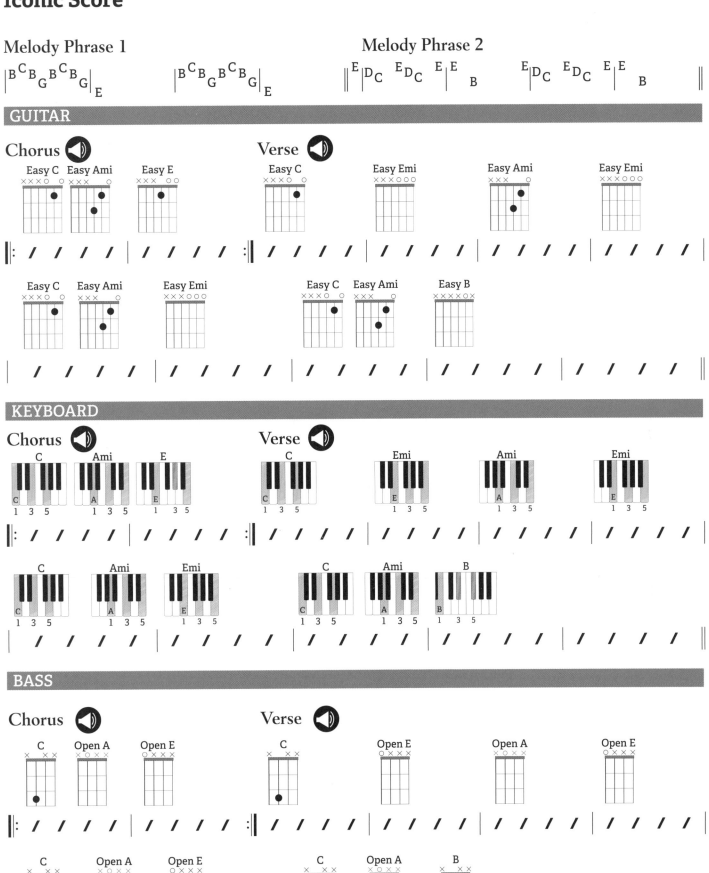

GUITAR

Chorus

Easy C   Easy Ami   Easy E

Easy C   Easy Ami   Easy Emi

Verse

Easy C   Easy Emi   Easy Ami   Easy Emi

Easy C   Easy Ami   Easy B

KEYBOARD

Chorus

C   Ami   E

C   Ami   Emi

Verse

C   Emi   Ami   Emi

C   Ami   B

BASS

Chorus

C   Open A   Open E

C   Open A   Open E

Verse

C   Open E   Open A   Open E

C   Open A   B

63

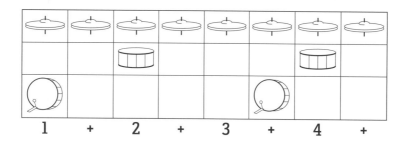

Standard Staff Score

Intro Riff/Vocal Melody

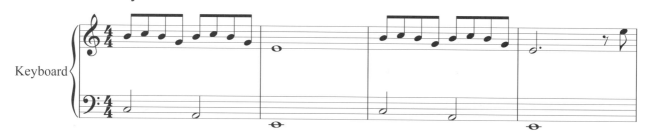

Verse/Chorus

Pre-Chorus

CHORUS
C   Ami   E C   Ami   E
All my friends are heathens, take it slow. Wait for them to ask you who you know.

        C   Ami   E   C   Ami   E
Please don't make any sudden moves. You don't know the half of the abuse.

VERSE
C
Welcome to the room of people who have rooms of people

        Emi
that they loved one day docked away.

Ami
Just because we check the guns at the door doesn't mean

       Emi
our brains will change from hand grenades.

C   Ami   Emi
You'll never know the psychopath sitting next to you.
   You'll never know the murderer sitting next to you.

C   Ami   B
You'll think, "How'd I get here, sitting next to you?"
   But after all I've said, please don't forget.

from SUICIDE SQUAD
Words and Music by Tyler Joseph
© 2016 WARNER-TAMERLANE PUBLISHING CORP. and STRYKER JOSEPH MUSIC
All Rights Administered by WARNER-TAMERLANE PUBLISHING CORP.
All Rights Reserved Used by Permission

SECTION 2—SAMPLE RUBRIC					
Skill	**4**	**3**	**2**	**1**	**Next Steps**
GUITAR/ KEYBOARD Chord Performance	Student and play Emi, C, and G chords without use of diagrams as reference	Student and play Emi, C, and G chords with use of diagrams as reference	Student and play Emi, C, and G chords with use of diagrams and photo or model	Student cannot play Emi, C, or G chords	
GUITAR/ KEYBOARD/ BASS Chord Progressions	Student can perform a chord progression based on a diagram	Student can perform a chord progression based on a diagram with one or two errors	Student can perform a chord progression based on a diagram with several errors	Student cannot perform a chord progression based on a diagram	
KEYBOARD Naming the Black Keys	Student can name any black key on the Keyboard by both enharmonic names	Student can name any black key on the Keyboard with at least one name.	Student can name some of the black keys on the Keyboard	Student cannot name the black keys on the Keyboard	
DRUMS Technique	Student can perform a three-part, two-handed backbeat at a variety of tempos	Student can perform three-part, quarter-note backbeat	Student can perform two-limb backbeat	Student can play one part of a backbeat	
DRUMS Comping	Student can play the crash cymbal on any beat of a backbeat	Student can play a crash cymbal on beat 1 of an eighth-note backbeat	Student play the crash cymbal on beat 1 of a quarter-note backbeat	Student can identify and play the crash cymbal with correct technique	
GUITAR/ KEYBOARD/ BASS Melodic Improvisation	Student can improvise a variety of four-beat phrases with the four-note solo	Student can echo a variety of four-beat phrases with the four-note solo	Student can play the four notes of the four-note solo in time	Student can play the four notes	
GUITAR/ KEYBOARD/ BASS/ DRUMS Ensemble Performance	Student can consistently play in time with ensemble	Student can mostly play in time with ensemble	Student can sometimes play in time with ensemble	Student cannot play in time with ensemble	

Instrument Technique: Guitar, keyboard, and bass players will practice playing chromatic notes with "Dazed and Confused." Drummers will apply the open hi-hat to their performances and practice switching cymbals between song sections.

New Chords: Students will play the D chord and apply it to performances of several songs that use only A and D chords. Drummers will modify the backbeat with each of these songs.

Music Theory: Students will read quarter notes, eighth notes, quarter rests, and familiar comping patterns in standard staff notation.

Improvisation: Students will expand the Four-Note Solo to six notes and use the complete major pentatonic scale.

Composition: Students will use the major pentatonic scale to write original riffs. Drummers will write a verse and chorus drumbeat with different kick drum hits and cymbals.

Instrument Techniques

MU:Pr4.2.3

a) Demonstrate understanding of the structure in music selected for performance.

MU:Pr4.2.3

b) When analyzing selected music, read and perform rhythmic patterns and melodic phrases using iconic and standard notation.

MU:Pr5.1.3

b) Rehearse to refine technical accuracy, expressive qualities, and identified performance challenges.

MU:Pr6.1.4

a) Perform music, alone or with others, with expression and technical accuracy, and appropriate interpretation.

MU:Pr4.2.H.8

a) Identify prominent melodic, harmonic, and structural characteristics and context (social, cultural, or historical) in a varied repertoire of music that includes melodies, repertoire pieces, and chordal accompaniments selected for performance, including at least some based on reading standard notation.

MU:Pr4.3.E.5

a) Identify expressive qualities in a varied repertoire of music that can be demonstrated through prepared and improvised performances.

MU:Pr6.1.E.8

a) Demonstrate attention to technical accuracy and expressive qualities in prepared and improvised performances of a varied repertoire of music representing diverse cultures and styles.

MU:Pr5.1.H.8

a) Apply teacher-provided criteria to critique individual performances of a varied repertoire of music that includes melodies, repertoire pieces, and chordal accompaniments selected for performance, and identify practice strategies to address performance challenges and refine the performances.

MU:Pr6.1.H.5

a) Perform with expression and technical accuracy in individual performances of a varied repertoire of music that includes melodies, repertoire pieces, and chordal accompaniments, demonstrating understanding of the audience and the context.

This Modern Band warm-up on the next page is from the song "Dazed and Confused" by Led Zeppelin. Using this phrase as a warm-up gives us an opportunity to work on a riff that can be used to teach on a variety of musical skills: technique, ear-training, theory, and note reading.

Scaffolding Suggestions & Performance Notes: "Dazed and Confused" Band Jam Warm-Up

ALL INSTRUMENTS:

While this song is in 12/8, you don't need to introduce this concept yet. Instead, ask students to listen to the music to find the feel, reinforcing the concept that we can play complex ideas without fully understanding them, which can come later.

GUITAR AND BASS:

This example should use all four fingers on the neck in order to work on achieving a good hand position and strengthening the fingers. Students should have their thumb perpendicular to the neck with the wrist flat, fingers curved, and use their fingertips to fret. If done properly, all four fingers should fit on the neck at the same time with little effort, and they can raise the fingers one at a time. If students have smaller hands, they may need to shift slightly.

KEYBOARD:

This example introduces how to use the left hand independently. Students should use a different finger for each note and should shift their hand between the first and second measure.

DRUMS:

This is a good opportunity to play a basic beat without eighth notes at a very nice slow pace. It is also a great way to scaffold: Students who can play the basic beat with ease can add in some of the swung eighth notes on the kick drum or ride cymbal. The student book introduces drumset staff notation here.

DAZED AND CONFUSED

Led Zeppelin

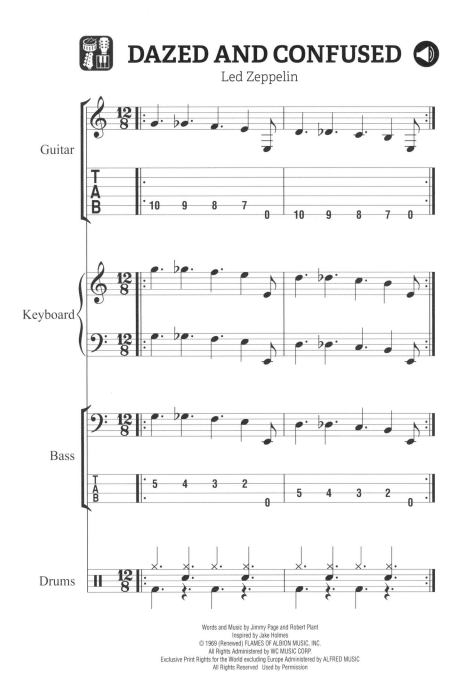

GUITAR

Instrument Technique: Chromatic Riffs

In this next tab example, use a different finger to play each different fret. When we move like this from one fret to the next in an upward or downward line, it is called **chromatic**. If you need to, you can move your hand up and down on the neck.

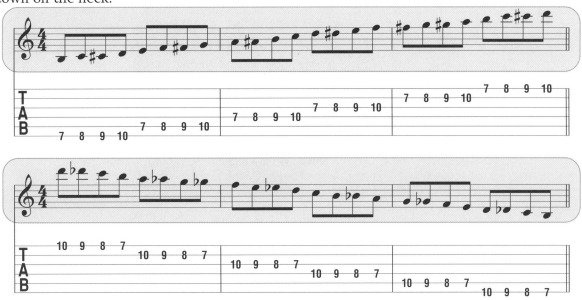

Now, check out your chromatic skills with this heavy Led Zeppelin riff. Listen to the original recording to hear the rhythms.

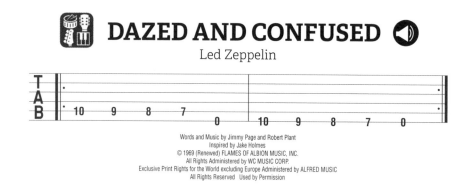

KEYBOARD

Instrument Technique: Separate Hands

To play this next riff, line up your hands in two different places on the keyboard, keeping space between them. Shift your pinky finger from the G note to D between the measures. The darkened keys below are the ones you'll need to play this riff (listen to the original recording to determine the rhythm):

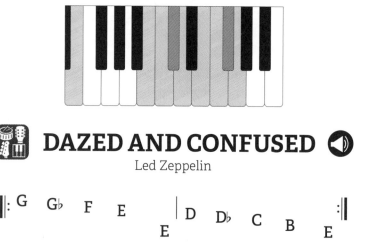

BASS

Instrument Technique: Chromatic Riffs

In this next tab example, use a different finger to play each different fret. When we move like this from one fret to the next in an upward or downward line, it is called **chromatic**. If you need to, you can move your hand up and down on the neck.

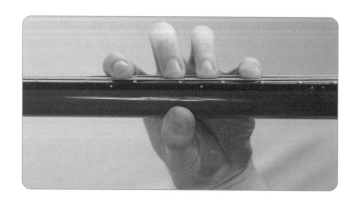

70

Now, check out your chromatic skills with this heavy Led Zeppelin riff. Listen to the original recording to hear the rhythms.

DAZED AND CONFUSED 🔊
Led Zeppelin

Or, you can play this riff like this.

DRUMS

Instrument Technique: Slow Backbeat

There are many ways to write music. One way is to use **staff notation**. The **staff** is made up of five lines and four spaces:

The drums are part of the percussion family, so the staff uses a **percussion** or **neutral clef** at the beginning of every system:

The symbols on this staff (called **noteheads**) each represent an instrument on the drumset. Since each note in the following examples lasts for one beat of music, they are all quarter notes. These notes represent the kick drum:

These represent the snare:

And these X-shaped noteheads represent the hi-hat:

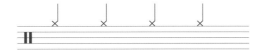

Here is a new symbol that is called a **quarter rest**; this simply means that instead of playing, you'll rest for one quarter note value: 𝄽 You can also combine two quarter rests into one **half rest**: ▬

71

Slow the quarter note backbeat down to play this '70s rock tune:

DAZED AND CONFUSED
Led Zeppelin

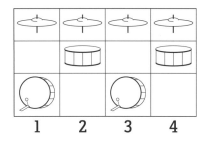

These symbols are called **repeat signs**; they're used to tell the player to repeat the music contained between the symbols:

The eighth-note backbeat that you previously played looks like this:

Playing Drumbeats: Backbeat Variation

Play a backbeat, but this time, play the ride cymbal instead of the hi-hat. The following example uses the ride cymbal, which is placed on the top line of the staff. All cymbals are written with X-shaped noteheads.

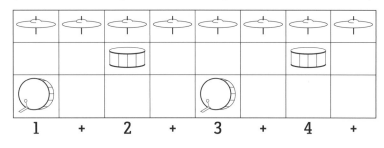

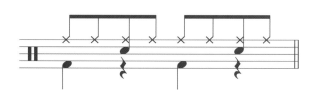

Playing Chords/Lines/Drumbeats: D

🎸 16　🎹 16　🎸 16　🥁 20

MU:Pr4.2.2

a) Demonstrate knowledge of music concepts (such as tonality and meter) in music from a variety of cultures selected for performance.

MU:Pr4.1.2

a) Demonstrate and explain personal interest in, knowledge about, and purpose of varied musical selections.

MU:Pr4.1.E.5

a) Select varied repertoire to study based on interest, music reading skills (where appropriate), an understanding of the structure of the music, context, and the technical skill of the individual or ensemble.

MU:Pr5.3.E.5

a) Use self-reflection and peer feedback to refine individual and ensemble performances of a varied repertoire of music.

MU:Pr4.2.H.5

a) Identify prominent melodic and harmonic characteristics in a varied repertoire of music that includes melodies, repertoire pieces, and chordal accompaniments selected for performance, including at least some based on reading standard notation.

> ### New Chord, New Songs
> The next chord for guitar and keyboard is D major. With D, students can now play the I–IV progression in the key of A, a common progression in popular music. Included are a few song examples to play through as a group. Ideas for scaffolding instruction include: Have half the students play A, the other half D, and then switch. Or, play the downbeat only and use the rest of the measure(s) to switch chords.

GUITAR

Playing Chords: D

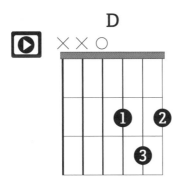

Using the D and A chords, you can play a variety of songs.

KEYBOARD

Playing Chords: The D Chord

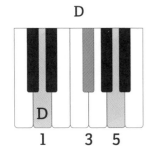

When you combine the D chord with the A chord, you can play a variety of songs. Try playing each with both your right and left hands.

Here are a couple of tunes you can play with the new chord along with chords you've already learned:

IMAGINE
John Lennon

GUITAR

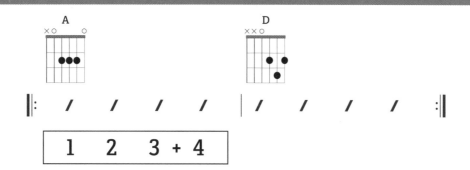

KEYBOARD

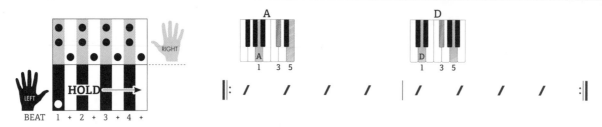

BASS

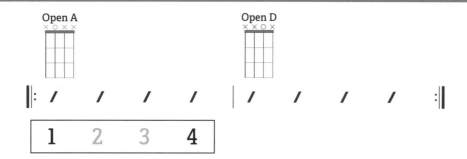

DRUMS

This example has eighth notes in the kick drum line:

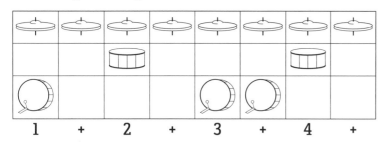

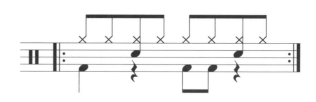

This example has eighth notes in the snare drum:

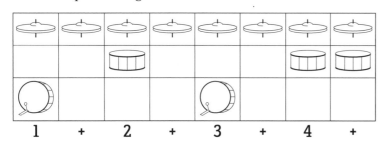

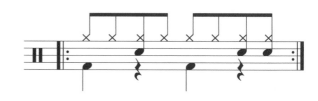

A   **D**   **A**   **D**
Imagine there's no heaven. It's easy if you try.

A   **D**   **A**   **D**
No hell below us. Above us only sky.

A   **D**   **A**   **D**
Imagine there's no countries. It isn't hard to do.

A   **D**   **A**   **D**
Nothing to kill or die for, and no religion, too.

BEST DAY OF MY LIFE

American Authors

GUITAR

A   D

| 1 | 2 | 3 | 4 | + |

KEYBOARD

A   D

1   3   5   1   3   5

BEAT   1   +   2   +   3   +   4   +

BASS

Open A   Open D

| 1 | 2 | 3 | 4 | + |

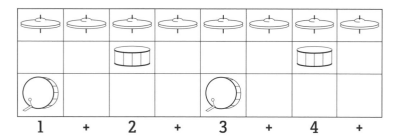

A

I had a dream so big and loud. I jumped so high I touched the clouds.

D

Whoa-o-o-o-o-oh. Whoa-o-o-o-o-oh.

A

I stretched my hands out to the sky. We danced with monsters through the night.

D

Whoa-o-o-o-o-oh. Whoa-o-o-o-o-oh.

A   **D**

Woo-o-o-o-oo! This is gonna be the best day of my life, my life.

A   **D**

Woo-o-o-o-oo! This is gonna be the best day of my life, my life.

Music Theory: Quarter and Eighth Notes

 18   17   17

MU:Pr4.2.2

  b) When analyzing selected music, read and perform rhythmic and melodic patterns using iconic or standard notation.

MU:Pr5.1.2

  b) Rehearse, identify, and apply strategies to address interpretive, performance, and technical challenges of music.

MU:Pr6.1.2

  a) Perform music for a specific purpose with expression and technical accuracy.

Half notes can be broken into two **quarter notes**. Each quarter note gets one beat.

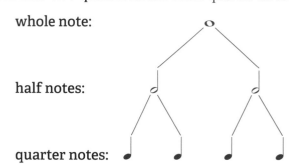

Playing and Resting ▶

You can also use a **rest** when you want to stop the strings from ringing and leave some space. Try this with the A chord. A rest means "count, but don't play." Each **quarter rest** gets one beat.

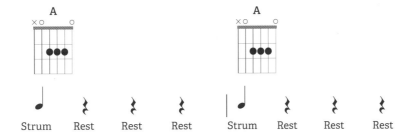

This strumming pattern is useful to practice changing chords.

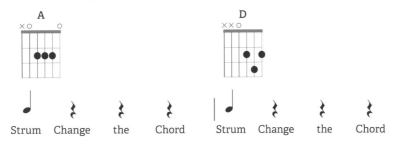

This comping pattern uses only quarter notes:

Here is the same pattern in standard rhythmic notation:

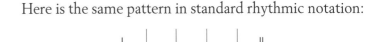

Playing and Resting a Chord ▶

You can also use a quarter rest when you want to stop the chord and leave some space. Try this on the A chord:

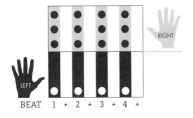

You can use a **half rest** to take the place of two quarter rests: ▬

Sometimes, you'll see a symbol called a **whole rest**; it's used to let you know when no notes or chords will be played for the entire measure: ▬

This comping pattern is useful to practice when changing chords:

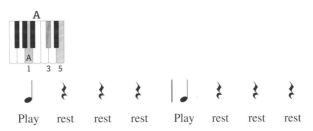

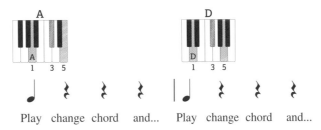

Playing and Resting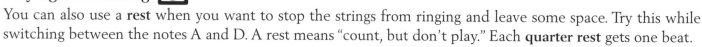

You can also use a **rest** when you want to stop the strings from ringing and leave some space. Try this while switching between the notes A and D. A rest means "count, but don't play." Each **quarter rest** gets one beat.

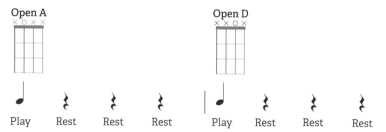

Quarter notes can be broken into **eighth notes**. Each eighth note gets a half of a beat.

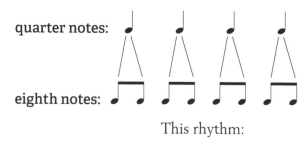

This rhythm:

GUITAR AND BASS	KEYBOARD

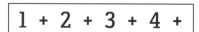

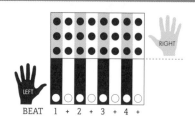

…is just eight eighth notes:

These rhythms combine quarter notes and eighth notes. Try counting and playing them.

GUITAR AND BASS

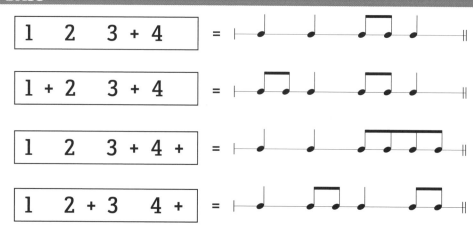

78

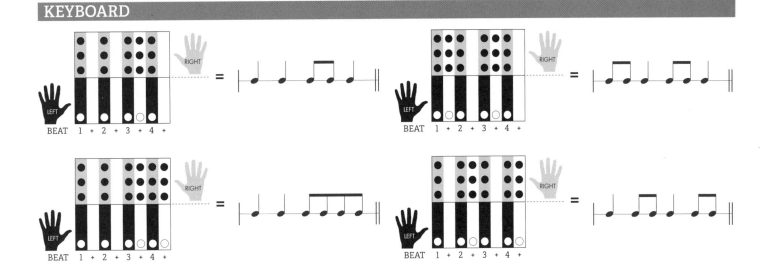

Improvisation (Guitar, Keyboard, Bass); Instrument Technique and Music Theory (Drums)

🎸 19   🎹 19   🎸 18   🥁 21

MU:Cr1.1.2

a) Improvise rhythmic and melodic patterns and musical ideas for a specific purpose.

MU:Pr6.1.4

a) Perform music, alone or with others, with expression and technical accuracy, and appropriate interpretation.

MU:Cr2.1.3

b) Use standard and/or iconic notation and/or recording technology to document personal rhythmic and melodic musical ideas.

MU:Cr3.2.3

a) Present the final version of personal created music to others, and describe connection to expressive intent.

MU:Pr5.1.3

a) Apply teacher-provided and collaboratively-developed criteria and feedback to evaluate accuracy of ensemble performances.

MU:Pr6.1.3

a) Perform music with expression and technical accuracy.

MU:Cr1.1.E.8

a) Compose and improvise ideas for melodies and rhythmic passages based on characteristic(s) of music or text(s) studied in rehearsal.

MU:Cr3.2.E.8

a) Share personally-developed melodies and rhythmic passages—individually or as an ensemble—that demonstrate understanding of characteristics of music or texts studied in rehearsal.

MU:Pr4.3.E.8

a) Demonstrate understanding and application of expressive qualities in a varied repertoire of music through prepared and improvised performances.

MU:Pr6.1.E.8

a) Demonstrate attention to technical accuracy and expressive qualities in prepared and improvised performances of a varied repertoire of music representing diverse cultures and styles.

MU:Cr1.1.H.5

a) Generate melodic, rhythmic, and harmonic ideas for simple melodies (such as two-phrase) and chordal accompaniments for given melodies.

MU:Cr2.1.H.5

a) Select, develop, and use standard notation or audio/video recording to document melodic, rhythmic, and harmonic ideas for drafts of simple melodies (such as two-phrase) and chordal accompaniments for given melodies.

MU:Pr4.2.H.5

a) Identify prominent melodic and harmonic characteristics in a varied repertoire of music that includes melodies, repertoire pieces, and chordal accompaniments selected for performance, including at least some based on reading standard notation.

MU:Pr6.1.H.5

a) Perform with expression and technical accuracy in individual performances of a varied repertoire of music that includes melodies, repertoire pieces, and chordal accompaniments, demonstrating understanding of the audience and the context.

This next improvisation exercise is best used in a group setting. Students can take the previously learned A-to-D progressions and improvise over any of those songs. Soloists can also play over the grooves that the bassists compose.

- Guitarists should focus on only six notes.
- Keyboardists can use the full pentatonic scale.
- Bassists can use the notes of the Six-Note Groove to compose their own original grooves.
- Drummers can focus on backbeat variations and playing a crash on beat 1 while the other students practice their scales.
- This is an opportunity for students to work on vocal technique and musicality with or without their instruments.
- Students can compose a short vocal line (embellishment). These short runs can be used as vocal fillers during a section of their compositions. They can use their six-note scale or just a few notes from it, similar to what they use to make a catchy riff.
- Students can use their instruments to transcribe their pitches, using either standard notation or an iconic equivalent.
- For an ear training/transcription activity, students may also want to improvise a run without notation or an instrument and have another student attempt a transcribe or replicate the run with their voice or instrument.
- Students can incorporate runs into vocal performances with the major pentatonic scale. Many pop and R&B vocalists use this scale in their riffs and runs.

GUITAR

Improvisation: Six-Note Solo 🔊 ▶

You can add two more notes to the four-note solo to make a six-note solo. In order to play along with the past two Jam Tracks, move your first finger down to fret 2. Use the previous two songs to practice this solo!

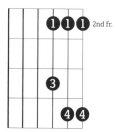

Improvisation: The Major Pentatonic Scale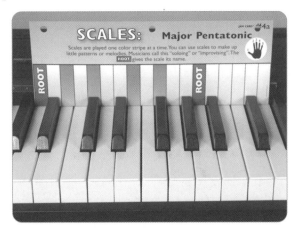

The Jam Card is a tool you can use to learn chords and scales on the keyboard. There are many Jam Cards in the Modern Band Method, but we've only included a handful of them in Book 1. Locate Jam Card #4a, which looks like a piano keyboard with different, shaded vertical bars. Then, place the card behind the keys of the keyboard, lining the root bars up with the note A.

This Jam Card shows you which notes are used in the major pentatonic scale. Use the gray notes to play the complete scale and solo. You can practice improvising over the Jam Track.

Improvisation: Creating a Groove

Bass players don't often take solos, but they almost never stop playing, even when another band member is soloing. The key to being a great bass player is to lay down a solid groove for the other bandmates to sing or play with.

Here are a few basic grooves to get you started. Feel free to create variations on these to compose your own grooves.

Instrument Technique: Playing the Hi-Hat

Depending on how much you lift your foot from the hi-hat pedal, the sound will be tighter or looser. To play a "tight" or "closed" hi-hat, keep your foot firmly planted on the hi-hat pedal. The hi-hat cymbal should look like this:

Tight (closed)

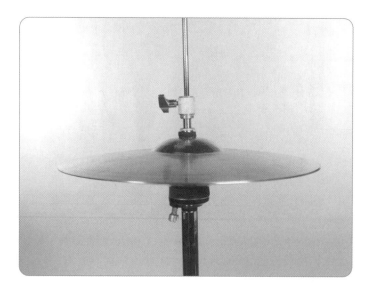

The symbol that we've used in our drumbeat diagrams so far is the one that we will now use for the closed hi-hat:

The following example shows the notehead used to notate a closed hi-hat. It simply places a "+" sign above the note:

To play a "loose" or "half-open" hi-hat, lift up your left foot from the hi-hat pedal. The picture below shows the cymbals placed slightly open, but not all the way:

Loose (half-open)

This is the symbol we will use in our drumbeat diagrams for the loose hi-hat:

This is the notehead used to notate the open hi-hat, over which a small circle is placed above the note:

If you see a measure of hi-hat noteheads with no symbols written above them, then assume that they will be played closed. If there are mixed open and closed hi-hats within the same measure, then the appropriate symbols will appear above each notehead.

Here are some songs that feature drumbeats with open and closed hi-hats in different sections. The first drumbeat features a symbol called an **eighth rest**. It functions just like the quarter rest, but for the value of one eighth note: ⁊

SAY IT AIN'T SO
Weezer

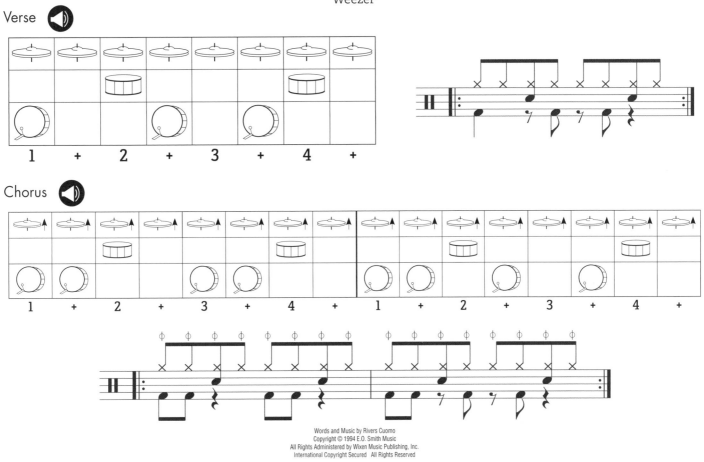

VIOLET
Hole

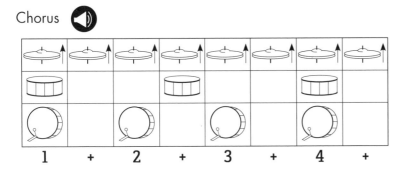

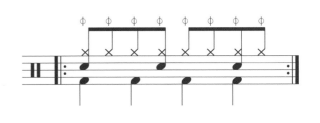

Music Theory: Form

Here is an example of a song that changes grooves between the Verse and Chorus:

SEVEN NATION ARMY

The White Stripes

The Verse looks like this:

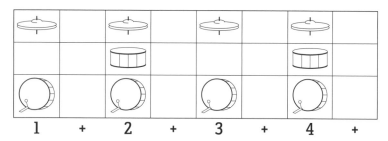

During the Chorus, play the ride cymbal instead of the hi-hat (don't be afraid to dig in!):

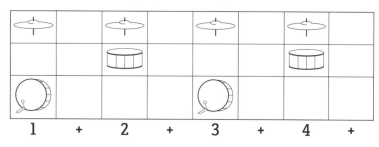

Remember when you practiced playing the crash on beat 1? You can use this to signify a new section of a song, such as a chorus or verse. Playing the crash and bass drum together on beat 1 is commonly used to introduce new song sections. The following example shows the symbol used for the crash cymbal as it appears in standard staff notation. It uses a symbol called a **ledger line**; ledger lines are used to show notes that appear above or below the standard five-line staff:

ROAR

Katy Perry

The different cymbals show up on separate lines in staff notation:

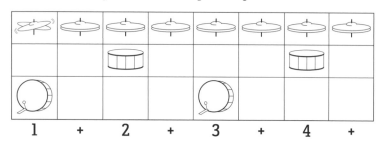

On songs like "Radioactive" by Imagine Dragons and "Come as You Are" by Nirvana, you can use a crash on beat 1 of a new section to signify the change.

Composition

MU:Cr1.1.2
a) Improvise rhythmic and melodic patterns and musical ideas for a specific purpose.

MU:Pr6.1.4
a) Perform music, alone or with others, with expression and technical accuracy, and appropriate interpretation.

MU:Cr2.1.3
b) Use standard and/or iconic notation and/or recording technology to document personal rhythmic and melodic musical ideas.

MU:Cr3.2.3
a) Present the final version of personal created music to others, and describe connection to expressive intent.

MU:Pr5.1.3
a) Apply teacher-provided and collaboratively-developed criteria and feedback to evaluate accuracy of ensemble performances.

MU:Pr6.1.3
a) Perform music with expression and technical accuracy.

MU:Cr1.1.E.8
a) Compose and improvise ideas for melodies and rhythmic passages based on characteristic(s) of music or text(s) studied in rehearsal.

MU:Cr3.2.E.8
a) Share personally-developed melodies and rhythmic passages—individually or as an ensemble—that demonstrate understanding of characteristics of music or texts studied in rehearsal.

MU:Pr4.3.E.8
a) Demonstrate understanding and application of expressive qualities in a varied repertoire of music through prepared and improvised performances.

MU:Pr6.1.E.8
a) Demonstrate attention to technical accuracy and expressive qualities in prepared and improvised performances of a varied repertoire of music representing diverse cultures and styles.

MU:Cr1.1.H.5
a) Generate melodic, rhythmic, and harmonic ideas for simple melodies (such as two-phrase) and chordal accompaniments for given melodies.

MU:Cr2.1.H.5
a) Select, develop, and use standard notation or audio/video recording to document melodic, rhythmic, and harmonic ideas for drafts of simple melodies (such as two-phrase) and chordal accompaniments for given melodies.

MU:Pr4.2.H.5
a) Identify prominent melodic and harmonic characteristics in a varied repertoire of music that includes melodies, repertoire pieces, and chordal accompaniments selected for performance, including at least some based on reading standard notation.

MU:Pr6.1.H.5
a) Perform with expression and technical accuracy in individual performances of a varied repertoire of music that includes melodies, repertoire pieces, and chordal accompaniments, demonstrating understanding of the audience and the context.

> During this next composition exercise, students can either work independently or together. The melodic instruments (guitar, keyboard, and bass) can each come up with their own riff and then take turns with harmonic accompaniment, adding drums, to put it all together. Subsequently, all instruments can also work independently.

Composition: Compose a Riff

Using the notes in the six-note solo, create your own riff. Here are a few sample riffs:

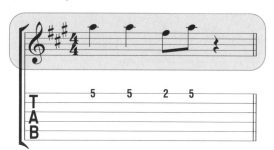

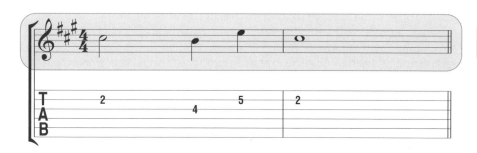

Write your original riff here:

T
A
B

You can play your composed riff over the A to D chord progression. Here are some new strumming patterns you can use:

| 1 + 2   3 + 4 | | 1   2   3 + 4 |

Composition: Composing a Riff

Here are some sample riffs, with rhythms underneath. Practice them first by playing each measure separately, and then play them all together. These use only the notes highlighted by the Jam Card.

Write your original two-bar riff here; you can use the Jam Card as a reference if you'd like:

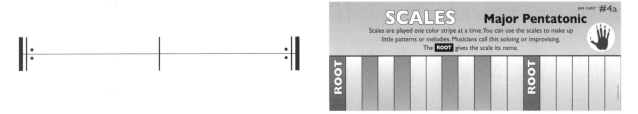

You can play your composed riff over the A-to-D chord progression. Here are some new comping patterns you can use:

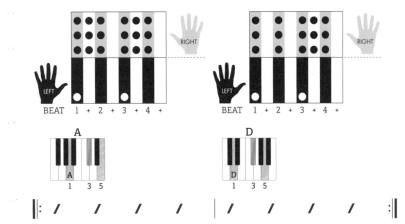

BASS

Composition: Compose a Riff

Using the notes we've already learned, try creating your own bass riff. Here is a sample two-bar riff:

Write your original riff here:

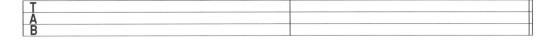

Composition: Verse and Chorus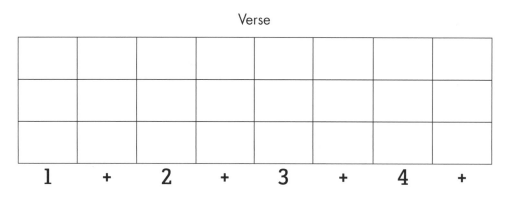

Let's practice writing grooves for our own original songs. Write a groove to be used for the verse, and then change it slightly for the chorus. Don't veer too far from the backbeat, but feel free to move a kick drum or snare drum hit to make it your own. You might also want to switch to different cymbals or drums to add variety.

Verse

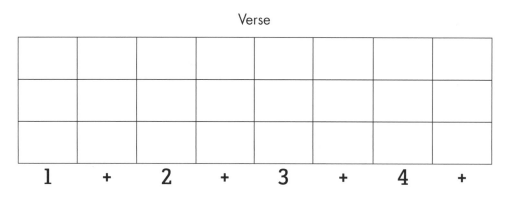

Chorus

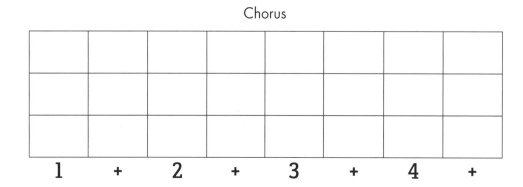

SECTION 3—SAMPLE RUBRIC					
Skill	**4**	**3**	**2**	**1**	**Next Steps**
GUITAR/ KEYBOARD Playing Chords	Student can play D chord without use of diagrams as reference	Student can play D chord with use of diagrams as reference	Student can play D chord with use of diagrams and photo or model	Student cannot play D chord	
GUITAR/ KEYBOARD/ BASS Playing Rhythms	Student can read and perform unique quarter- and eighth-note patterns	Student can read and perform rehearsed quarter- and eighth-note patterns	Student can read and perform quarter- and eighth-note patterns with some mistakes	Student identify quarter notes and eighth notes	
GUITAR/ KEYBOARD/ BASS Improvisation	Student can improvise a variety of four-beat phrases with the Six-Note Solo	Student can echo a variety of four-beat phrases with the Six-Note Solo	Student can play the notes of the Six-Note Solo in time	Student can play the notes of the Six-Note Solo	
DRUMS Technique	Student can perform open hi-hats on any beat of a backbeat	Student can perform open hi-hat on beat 1 of a backbeat	Student can play isolated open–closed hi-hat pattern	Student can open and close the hi-hat	
GUITAR/ KEYBOARD/ BASS/ DRUMS Ensemble Playing	Student can consistently play in time with ensemble	Student can mostly play in time with ensemble	Student can sometimes play in time with ensemble	Student cannot play in time with ensemble	
DRUMS Composition	Student can compose and perform unique drum patterns for a verse and chorus of a song and seamlessly transition between the two	Student can compose and perform unique drum patterns for a verse and chorus of a song	Student can composer and perform a unique drum pattern for a verse or chorus of a song	Student can compose a unique drum pattern	

SECTION 4

 20   20   19   25

Instrument Technique: Guitar, keyboard, and bass players will practice their dexterity and reading skills by learning a few riffs. Drummers will play the drumbeats for these songs.

Comping: Guitar, keyboard, and bass players will learn the full E chord. Keyboardists will apply bass notes in the left hand. Drummers will play one- and two-beat fills with eighth and 16th notes. Students will then apply these techniques to songs with D, E, and A chords.

Composition: Students will write chord progressions as before, but they can apply lyrics to their compositions using various lyric writing tips and prompts.

Full Band Song: Students will apply comping patterns and reading skills to play "Stir It Up" by Bob Marley & the Wailers.

Instrument Technique: Learning New Riffs and Patterns

 20   20   19   25

MU:Pr4.2.2

a) Demonstrate knowledge of music concepts (such as tonality and meter) in music from a variety of cultures selected for performance.

MU:Pr4.1.2

a) Demonstrate and explain personal interest in, knowledge about, and purpose of varied musical selections.

MU:Pr4.1.E.5

a) Select varied repertoire to study based on interest, music reading skills (where appropriate), an understanding of the structure of the music, context, and the technical skill of the individual or ensemble.

MU:Pr5.3.E.5

a) Use self-reflection and peer feedback to refine individual and ensemble performances of a varied repertoire of music.

MU:Pr4.2.H.5

a) Identify prominent melodic and harmonic characteristics in a varied repertoire of music that includes melodies, repertoire pieces, and chordal accompaniments selected for performance, including at least some based on reading standard notation.

Riffs are a great way to use familiar songs to learn new skills, review reading skills, and reinforce previously learned skills. Included are a couple quick play-alongs for each instrument.

GUITAR

Instrument Technique: Some New Riffs

Listen to the following songs to get a sense of the rhythms. In this first riff, focus on changing strings and alternating the pick up and down in the fast part.

UNDER PRESSURE

Queen ft. David Bowie

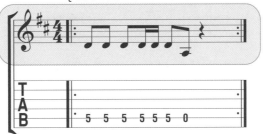

Practice this next riff using different finger combinations, or even just using your first finger the whole time.

SEVEN NATION ARMY

The White Stripes

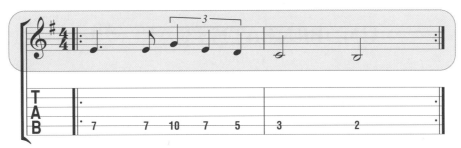

KEYBOARD

Instrument Technique: Learning New Riffs

KIDS

MGMT

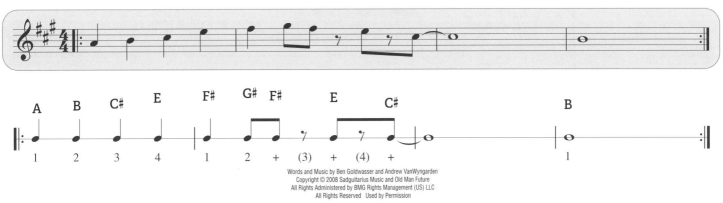

In the second measure of the example above, the melody has several notes that land on the upbeats (the "+" between the beats). This is called a **syncopated rhythm**. **Syncopation** is when there is an accent on the upbeats. "Take on Me" by aha has a melody that rises up and descends down a scale with syncopation:

TAKE ON ME 🔊

aha

Music by Pal Waaktaar and Magne Furuholmne
Words by Pal Waaktaar, Magne Furuholmne and Morton Harket
Copyright © 1984, 1985 Sony Music Publishing LLC
All Rights Administered by Sony Music Publishing LLC, 424 Church Street, Suite 1200, Nashville, TN 37219
International Copyright Secured   All Rights Reserved

BASS

Instrument Technique: Some New Riffs

Here are some bass riffs that use multiple strings. Listen to the following songs to get a sense of the rhythms.

UNDERNEATH IT ALL 🔊

No Doubt

Words and Music by David A. Stewart and Gwen Stefani
Copyright © 2001 by Universal Music Publishing MGB Ltd., Eligible Music Ltd., Universal Music Corp. and World Of The Dolphin Music
All Rights for Universal Music Publishing MGB Ltd. and Eligible Music Ltd. in the United States and Canada Administered by Universal Music - MGB Songs
All Rights for World Of The Dolphin Music Controlled and Administered by Universal Music Corp.
International Copyright Secured   All Rights Reserved

WANNABE 🔊

Spice Girls

Words and Music by Geri Halliwell, Emma Bunton, Melanie Brown, Victoria Adams, Melanie Chisholm, Matthew Rowebottom and Richard Stannard
Copyright © 1996 EMI Music Publishing Ltd., Red Girl Productions Ltd. and Universal - PolyGram International Publishing, Inc.
All Rights on behalf of EMI Music Publishing Ltd. Administered by Sony Music Publishing LLC, 424 Church Street, Suite 1200, Nashville, TN 37219
All Rights on behalf of Red Girl Productions Ltd. Administered by Peermusic (UK) Ltd.
International Copyright Secured   All Rights Reserved

For these next two riffs, focus on changing strings. If you're playing fingerstyle for "Under Pressure," alternate your right-hand index and middle fingers to play the fast part.

UNDER PRESSURE

Queen ft. David Bowie

SEVEN NATION ARMY

The White Stripes

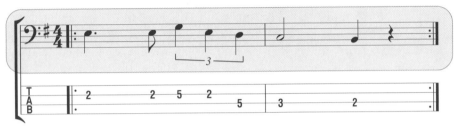

DRUMS

Instrument Technique: Different Kick Drum Patterns

Play through these few drum patterns as a warm-up:

KIDS

MGMT

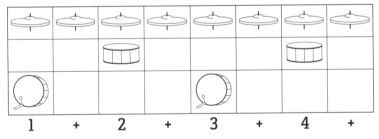

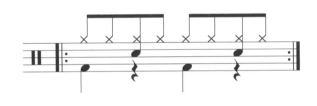

UNDER PRESSURE

Queen ft. David Bowie

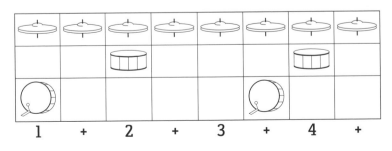

HOLD ON
Alabama Shakes

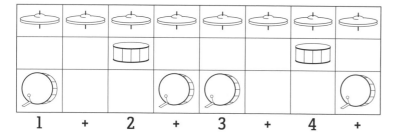

Playing Chords/Instrument Technique:
E Chord, Muting Notes, and Fills

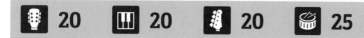

MU:Pr4.2.3

b) When analyzing selected music, read and perform rhythmic patterns and melodic phrases using iconic and standard notation.

MU:Pr4.3.3

a) Demonstrate and describe how intent is conveyed through expressive qualities (such as dynamics and tempo).

MU:Pr4.1.E.5

a) Select varied repertoire to study based on interest, music reading skills (where appropriate), an understanding of the structure of the music, context, and the technical skill of the individual or ensemble.

MU:Pr5.3.E.5

a) Use self-reflection and peer feedback to refine individual and ensemble performances of a varied repertoire of music.

MU:Pr4.2.H.5

a) Identify prominent melodic and harmonic characteristics in a varied repertoire of music that includes melodies, repertoire pieces, and chordal accompaniments selected for performance, including at least some based on reading standard notation.

> The next new chord is the E chord. In this next section, each instrument learns a new chord or technique, but then comes together to play through some new songs.

GUITAR

Playing Chords: Full E

E

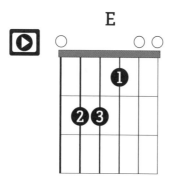

Playing Chords: Chord Review and New Songs

You played the E chord in "Heathens":

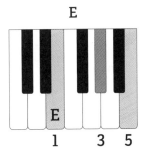

When playing the E chord on the keyboard, you can make the instrumentation sound fuller by playing the root note of the chord (E) with your left hand, lower on the left side of the keyboard, while the right hand plays the full chord.

Instrument Technique: Muting Notes ▶

As a bass player, you serve both a rhythmic (like a drummer) and harmonic (like a guitarist or keyboardist) role in a band. It's very important that you play in time. To help make your notes last only as long as you want them, you can **mute** them with either your left or right hand. To mute an open string, touch the string lightly to stop the vibration; you can do this with your left hand, right hand, or both. To mute fretted notes, lift the finger you're fretting with to stop the string from vibrating. Try muting in these examples. If you listen to the original recordings, you can hear these notes are played short.

Playing Drumbeats: Drum Fills ▶

Fills accent something that's happening in the music, usually a change in form or melody. They tend to lead up to a new section and often end on beat 1 with a crash and kick. The following examples show different kinds of fills. Keep in mind that each suggested rhythm could be played on any combination of instruments. This section also introduces a new instrument, the **rack tom**:

Here's the symbol that we'll use in our drumbeat diagrams:

95

The following fills are labeled according to where they are played within the measure:

"4 + 1" Fills

Example 1

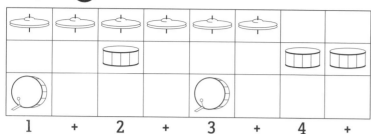

1 + 2 + 3 + 4 +

Example 2

The eighth notes here are split between three instruments:

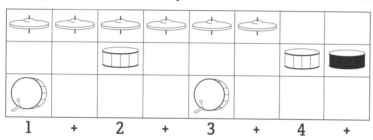

1 + 2 + 3 + 4 +

3 + 4 + 1 Fills

Example 3

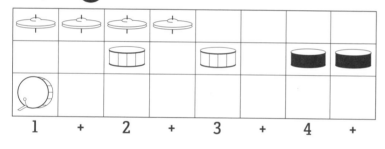

1 + 2 + 3 + 4 +

Example 4

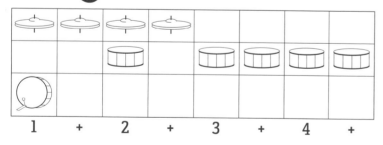

1 + 2 + 3 + 4 +

Example 5

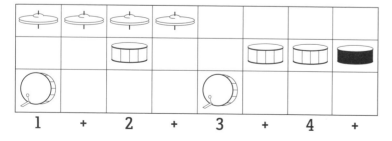

1 + 2 + 3 + 4 +

Music Theory: Sixteenth Notes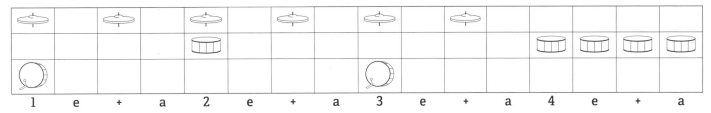

In this next example, there are four evenly played notes on the snare drum during beat 4. These are called **sixteenth notes**. They are counted "1–e–and–a, 2–e–and–a…":

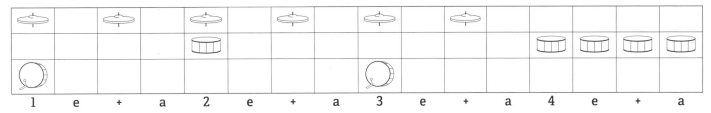

They are written like this in staff notation:

The drumbeat diagram from above looks like this in standard staff notation:

Here are a few new songs that include the E chord. Once again, scaffolding can make this easier for all. Have students split the change so they each take a different chord until they feel comfortable switching in time. With the E chord, students can now play any song with the I, IV, and V chord in the key of A (A, D, and E). Some song recommendations for expanding repertoire are listed in Appendix A.

WE WILL ROCK YOU
Queen

	CHORDS	COMPING PATTERN
GUITAR	E	1 + 2 3 + 4
KEYBOARD	E 1 3 5	BEAT 1 + 2 + 3 + 4 +
BASS	Open E	1 + 2 3 + 4
DRUMS		1 + 2 + 3 + 4 +

BACK IN BLACK

AC/DC

CHORDS **COMPING PATTERN**

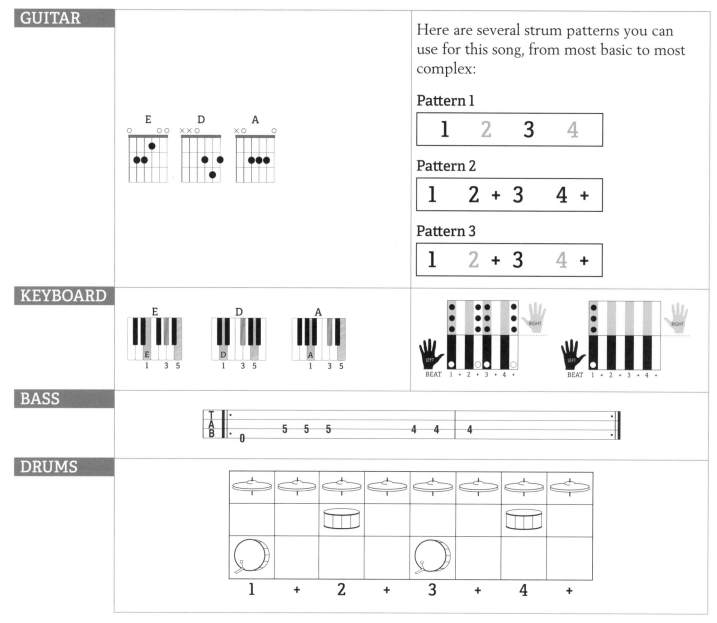

WHAT MAKES YOU BEAUTIFUL

One Direction

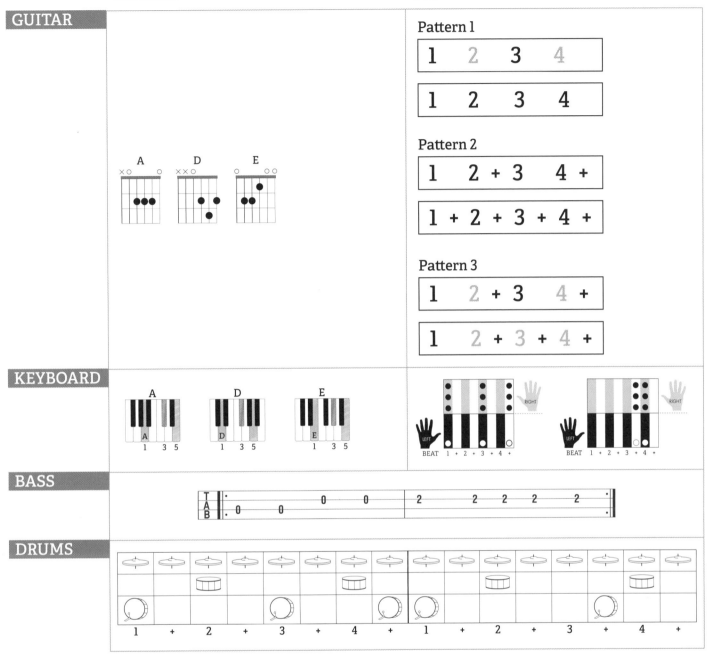

Composition: Writing Lyrics

MU:Cr1.1.4

a) Improvise rhythmic, melodic, and harmonic ideas, and explain connection to specific purpose and context (such as social and cultural).

b) Generate musical ideas (such as rhythms, melodies, and simple accompaniment patterns) within related tonalities (such as major and minor) and meters.

MU:Pr5.1.3

a) Apply teacher-provided and collaboratively-developed criteria and feedback to evaluate accuracy of ensemble performances.

MU:Pr6.1.4

a) Perform music, alone or with others, with expression and technical accuracy, and appropriate interpretation.

MU:Cr2.1.4

b) Use standard and/or iconic notation and/or recording technology to document personal rhythmic, melodic, and simple harmonic musical ideas.

MU:Pr6.1.3

a) Perform music with expression and technical accuracy.

MU:Cr1.1.E.8

a) Compose and improvise ideas for melodies and rhythmic passages based on characteristic(s) of music or text(s) studied in rehearsal.

MU:Cr3.2.E.8

a) Share personally-developed melodies and rhythmic passages—individually or as an ensemble—that demonstrate understanding of characteristics of music or texts studied in rehearsal.

MU:Pr4.3.E.8

a) Demonstrate understanding and application of expressive qualities in a varied repertoire of music through prepared and improvised performances.

MU:Pr6.1.E.8

a) Demonstrate attention to technical accuracy and expressive qualities in prepared and improvised performances of a varied repertoire of music representing diverse cultures and styles.

MU:Cr1.1.H.5

a) Generate melodic, rhythmic, and harmonic ideas for simple melodies (such as two-phrase) and chordal accompaniments for given melodies.

MU:Cr2.1.H.5

a) Select, develop, and use standard notation or audio/video recording to document melodic, rhythmic, and harmonic ideas for drafts of simple melodies (such as two-phrase) and chordal accompaniments for given melodies.

MU:Pr4.2.H.5

a) Identify prominent melodic and harmonic characteristics in a varied repertoire of music that includes melodies, repertoire pieces, and chordal accompaniments selected for performance, including at least some based on reading standard notation.

MU:Pr6.1.H.5

a) Perform with expression and technical accuracy in individual performances of a varied repertoire of music that includes melodies, repertoire pieces, and chordal accompaniments, demonstrating understanding of the audience and the context.

> This next composition section will focus on adding lyrics to a song. While this section solely focuses on getting new ideas on paper, feel free to have students speak their lyrics over a drumbeat or a chord progression, such as the one from the previous section. They can also make up a melody if they are feeling comfortable.

Composition: Writing Lyrics

Here are three steps you can take to write your own song lyrics:

1. Pick a theme. Lyrics can be easy to write when you have something you want to say. Think of something you care about and write based on that, such as friends, family, hobbies, or dreams.

2. Choose two words that rhyme, such as "great" and "late," or "thrill" and "chill." Then, choose another pair.

3. Turn your words into sentences. Try to speak the words in rhythm and sing them with the Jam Track. Here is an example of a verse for a song written about songwriting:

Writing	lyrics	is	so	fun,	can	be	done	by	any -	one.
/	/	/	/		/	/	/	/	/	

Think	of	what	to	write	a - bout;	play	some	chords,	and	sing	or	shout!
/	/	/	/		/	/	/	/	/		

Write a Drum Fill ▶

Write your own drum fills that lead to beat 1, using eighth notes or sixteenth notes:

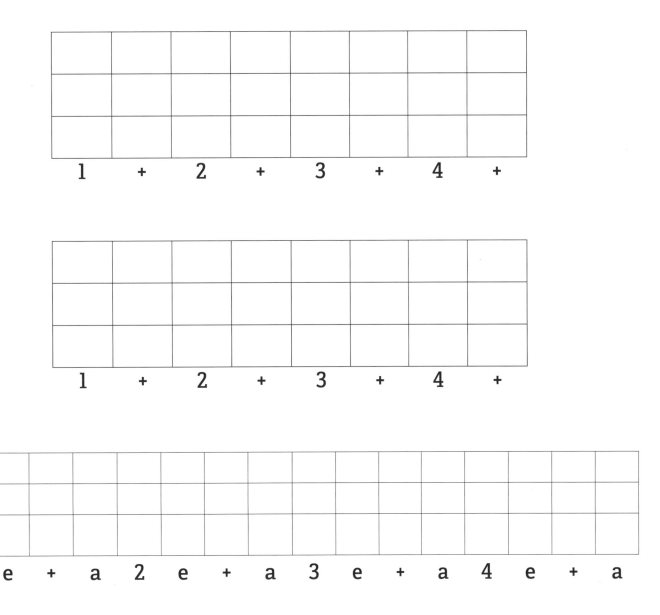

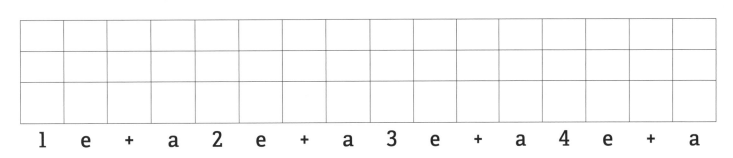

Fills are fun to play, but playing them too often can cover up what your bandmates are doing. Fills should be used only for specific reasons, such as switching to a new section of a song.

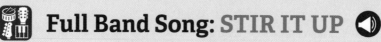 **Full Band Song:** STIR IT UP

Bob Marley & the Wailers

 22   22   21   30

MU:Cr1.1.4

a) Improvise rhythmic, melodic, and harmonic ideas, and explain connection to specific purpose and context (such as social and cultural).

b) Generate musical ideas (such as rhythms, melodies, and simple accompaniment patterns) within related tonalities (such as major and minor) and meters.

MU:Cr2.1.4

b) Use standard and/or iconic notation and/or recording technology to document personal rhythmic, melodic, and simple harmonic musical ideas.

MU:Cr3.2.4

a) Present the final version of personal created music to others, and explain connection to expressive intent.

MU:Pr4.2.2

a) Demonstrate knowledge of music concepts (such as tonality and meter) in music from a variety of cultures selected for performance.

MU:Pr4.1.2

a) Demonstrate and explain personal interest in, knowledge about, and purpose of varied musical selections.

MU:Pr4.1.E.5

a) Select varied repertoire to study based on interest, music reading skills (where appropriate), an understanding of the structure of the music, context, and the technical skill of the individual or ensemble.

MU:Pr5.3.E.5

a) Use self-reflection and peer feedback to refine individual and ensemble performances of a varied repertoire of music.

MU:Pr4.2.H.5

a) Identify prominent melodic and harmonic characteristics in a varied repertoire of music that includes melodies, repertoire pieces, and chordal accompaniments selected for performance, including at least some based on reading standard notation.

MU:Pr6.1.2

a) Perform music for a specific purpose with expression and technical accuracy.

MU:Pr6.1.E.5

a) Demonstrate attention to technical accuracy and expressive qualities in prepared and improvised performances of a varied repertoire of music.

MU:Pr6.1.H.5

a) Perform with expression and technical accuracy in individual performances of a varied repertoire of music that includes melodies, repertoire pieces, and chordal accompaniments, demonstrating understanding of the audience and the context.

MU:Cr1.1.E.8

a) Compose and improvise ideas for melodies and rhythmic passages based on characteristic(s) of music or text(s) studied in rehearsal.

MU:Cr3.2.E.8

a) Share personally-developed melodies and rhythmic passages—individually or as an ensemble—that demonstrate understanding of characteristics of music or texts studied in rehearsal.

MU:Pr4.1.E.8

a) Select a varied repertoire to study based on music reading skills (where appropriate), an understanding of formal design in the music, context, and the technical skill of the individual and ensemble.

MU:Pr4.3.E.8

a) Demonstrate understanding and application of expressive qualities in a varied repertoire of music through prepared and improvised performances.

MU:Pr5.1.E.8

a) Develop strategies to address technical challenges in a varied repertoire of music and evaluate their success using feedback from ensemble peers and other sources to refine performances.

MU:Pr6.1.E.8

a) Demonstrate attention to technical accuracy and expressive qualities in prepared and improvised performances of a varied repertoire of music representing diverse cultures and styles.

Performance Notes

The next Full Band Song is the reggae song "Stir It Up" by Bob Marley & the Wailers. This song has a progression that uses all three of the open chords that were just emphasized in the previous section. There are opportunities to combine riffs and chords in the same jam by having some students play the guitar/bass riff while some strum. Note the new drum pattern, which is an approximated version of a typical reggae beat.

- Encourage all of your singers to sing along at the Chorus section and any soloists to sing the Verse.
- This song lends itself well to vocal improvisation. In the recording, Bob Marley adds in vocal improvisations on the sound "oh." Students can use Marley's improvisations as a jumping-off point to creating their own vocal riffs.
- Vocal riffing—improvising a vocal melody over a vowel sound—is common across popular music. Marley's examples are much less complex than those of pop stars such as Ariana Grande, Stevie Wonder, and Rihanna, so it's a great place to start, as it serves as a less intimidating example. Students can take ideas they created in vocalizing the Six-Note Solo and put them into practice here.
- Have the students sing "Stir It Up" from the Chorus section. Once they feel comfortable, have students sing the same phrase but begin to add various pitches. This can be done with students taking turns improvising over the Chorus section.
- Rhythm guitarists should focus on playing short notes. The key to this is to mute the strings after playing. You can do this in the following three ways:
  1. Mute the strings by placing the picking hand gently on the strings to stop the vibration.
  2. Lift the fretting hand just enough to stop the string vibration. (The fingers should remain in contact with the strings, but be sure to release the pressure from the fretboard.)
  3. A combination of 1) and 2).
- Keyboardists can also focus on playing short notes. This is accomplished by playing the notes and releasing the key quickly. Students should be encouraged to experiment with note length. This will both open their ears up to how note length changes and then allow them to explore the techniques needed to achieve different note lengths. Keyboardists should also be encouraged to try different tones with this song. Reggae music often uses an organ instead of a piano sound, and most electric keyboards have an organ patch as an optional sound. Students can try the different organ sounds out and determine which will work best for their performance.
- Bassists should also focus on note length. This is accomplished the same way it is on the guitar.

Suggestions for Similar Repertoire

To find songs with that use these chords, you can search for any song that uses just the I, IV, and V chord of the key and transpose it to A if it's not already there. To provide instrumentalists the opportunity to practice playing reggae style music, they could perform a variety of songs in a reggae style.

- "Two to One (Hold On Riddim)" by Half Pint & Anthony B
- "Free Fallin'" by Tom Petty
- "The Lion Sleeps Tonight" by The Tokens
- "Angel" by Shaggy
- "Bidi Bidi Bom Bom" by Selena
- "Blitzkrieg Bop" by The Ramones
- "Born to Run" by Bruce Springsteen

- "Thinking Out Loud" by Ed Sheeran (Verse and Chorus only)
- "Twist and Shout" by The Beatles
- "What Makes You Beautiful" by One Direction
- "Wild Thing" by The Troggs

Iconic Score

Chord Progression (Chorus/Verse)

GUITAR

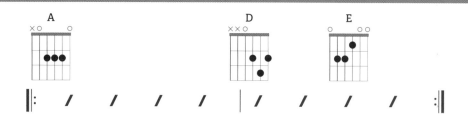

KEYBOARD

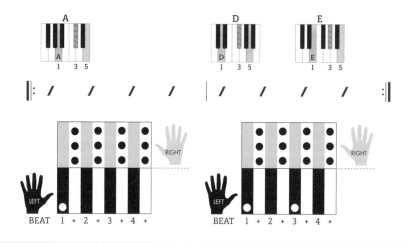

BASS

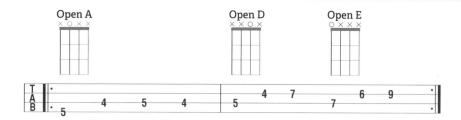

DRUMS

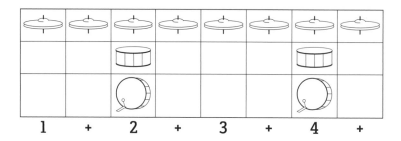

Standard Staff Score

CHORUS

A   D   E   A   D   E
Stir it up. Little darlin', stir it up. Come on, baby.

                  A   D   E A   D   E
Come on and stir it up. Little darlin', stir it up. O-oh!

VERSE

       A   D
It's been a long, long time, yeah (stir it, stir it, stir it together).

E   A   D   E
Since I got you on my mind (ooh-ooh-ooh-ooh).

A   D   E
Now you are here (stir it, stir it, stir it together). I said, it's so clear.

A   D   E
To see what we could do, baby (ooh-ooh-ooh-ooh). Just me and you.

SECTION 4—SAMPLE RUBRIC					
Skill	4	3	2	1	Next Steps
GUITAR/ KEYBOARD/ BASS Composition	Student can compose and notate a variety of original riffs using the notes in the Six-Note Solo/Groove that fit with the accompaniment	Student can compose a riff using the Six-Note Solo that fits with the accompaniment	Student can compose a riff using the Six-Note Solo that mostly fits with the accompaniment	Student cannot compose a riff	
GUITAR/ KEYBOARD Chord Performance	Student can play E and C chords without use of diagrams as reference	Student can play E and C chords with use of diagrams as reference	Student can play E and C chord with use of diagrams and photo or model as reference	Student cannot play E and C chords	
KEYBOARD Adding Bass Notes	Student can perform a chord progression in time with bass notes in the left hand	Student can perform a chord progression with bass notes in the left hand	Student can perform chords with bass notes in the left hand	Student cannot perform chords with bass notes in the left hand	
BASS Note Length	Student can perform notes with great control over note length	Student can perform notes with control over note length	Student can perform notes with some control over note length	Student has little control over the length of the notes	
DRUMS Open Hi-Hat	Student can perform open hi-hat hits on any beat of a backbeat	Student can perform open hi-hat on beat 1 of a backbeat	Student can play isolated open–closed hi-hat patterns	Student cannot play open–closed hi-hat patterns in time	
GUITAR/ KEYBOARD/ BASS/ DRUMS Ensemble Playing	Student can play in time with ensemble consistently	Student can play in time with ensemble mostly	Student can play in time with ensemble sometimes	Student cannot play in time with an ensemble	

SECTION 5 23 23 22 31

Instrument Technique: Guitar players will play hammer-ons, keyboardists will play chords as arpeggios, and bassists will focus on performing songs with various note lengths. Drummers will play the following rudiments: singles, doubles, and paradiddles.

Music Theory: Students will cover vocabulary surrounding techniques they've already learned: notes, chords, scales.

Comping: Guitar players will play alternate picking patterns, keyboardists will apply arpeggios to a variety of songs, bassists and drummers will practice allying drum and bass patterns.

Improvisation: Students will use the full minor pentatonic scale to play solos.

Instrument Technique

 23 23 22 31

MU:Cr3.1.2

a) Interpret and apply personal, peer, and teacher feedback to revise personal music.

MU:Pr4.2.2

a) Demonstrate knowledge of music concepts (such as tonality and meter) in music from a variety of cultures selected for performance.

b) When analyzing selected music, read and perform rhythmic and melodic patterns using iconic or standard notation.

MU:Pr4.3.2

a) Demonstrate understanding of expressive qualities (such as dynamics and tempo) and how creators use them to convey expressive intent.

MU:Pr5.1.2

b) Rehearse, identify, and apply strategies to address interpretive, performance, and technical challenges of music.

Here are some new warm-ups that use familiar songs to teach new instrument specific techniques. Note that because the techniques are instrument specific the songs are as well.

GUITAR

Instrument Technique: Hammer-Ons

To play a **hammer-on**, pick the first note and then hammer your fret-hand fingertip down on the next note to create the sound without picking it. Here are some examples. Try them with different finger combinations. The curved line over the hammer-ons is called a **slur**, which tells you not to pick the second note.

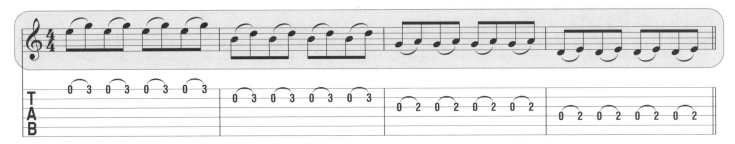

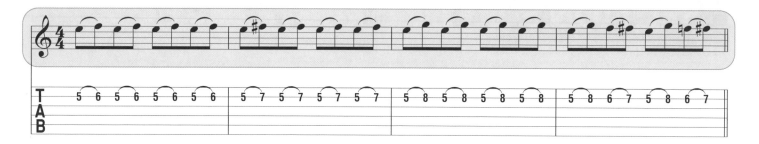

You can add hammer-ons into melodies you've already played:

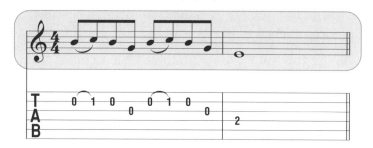

You can play that same melody on a different set of strings and frets. Is it easier to play hammer-ons with open strings or with fretted notes?

You can do multiple hammer-ons in a row as well, like in this song:

AM I EVIL?
Metallica

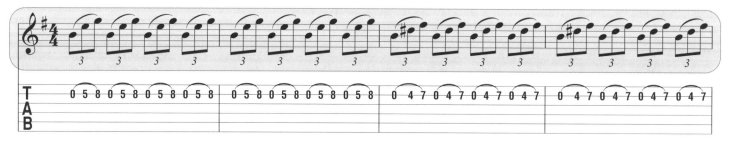

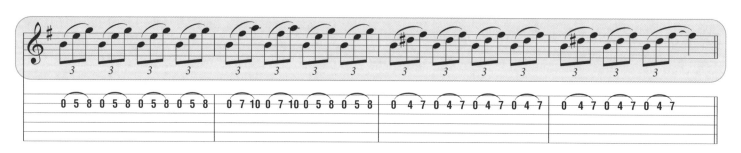

Instrument Technique: Arpeggios

Another way you can play chords is by playing **arpeggios**. Instead of playing all the notes at once, split the chord up, playing each note one at a time. Here are three ways you might arpeggiate new chords:

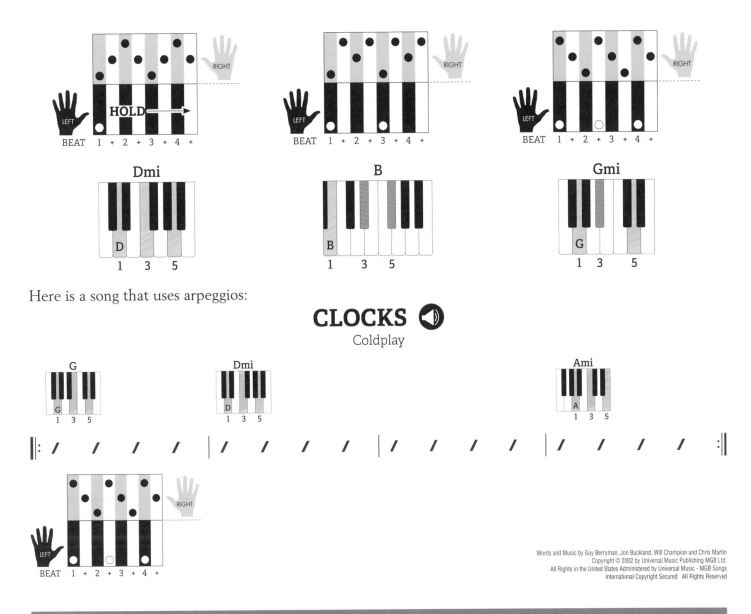

Here is a song that uses arpeggios:

CLOCKS
Coldplay

Instrument Technique: Muted Note Review & Rhythms

Play these bass lines, keeping the length of each note in mind. Having control over the length of each note is an important skill for a bass player. Also, do you notice how these songs all use almost all the same notes, but are different genres?

From this point on, standard staff notation will be included with the tabs. Use this to begin familiarizing yourself with where the notes are on the staff. If you see any symbols or rhythms you don't understand, continue listening to the original recordings to hear the rhythms. You'll learn more about music reading as you continue through the Modern Band program.

109

HYPNOTIZE

The Notorious BIG

MY OWN WORST ENEMY

Lit

DRUMS

Instrument Technique: Rudiments

Rudiments are the building blocks of drumming. They are patterns assigned to the right and left hands that can change the **articulation** (how a note is first sounded or struck) of a note along with helping you navigate the drumset as your grooves become more complex. Play this fill by alternating your right and left hands on sixteenth notes, starting on beat 3:

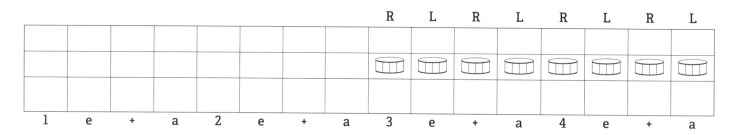

Fills like this are used in songs like "Day Tripper" by the Beatles.

Practicing rudiments is a great way to build up your musical vocabulary so that you can play more of the ideas that you hear, eventually using them to play solos or grooves. There are many rudiments, but here are three of the most common ones. Practice these on the snare drum in time with a metronome or with a Jam Track:

Singles

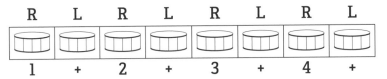

Doubles

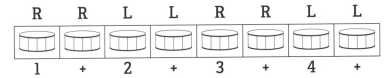

Paradiddles

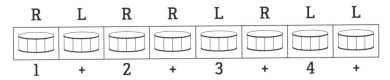

Instrument Technique: The Hi-Hat Pedal

You can also play singles, doubles, and paradiddles with your feet. Practice these with your kick drum and hi-hat pedal, in time with a metronome or a Jam Track. The hi-hat pedal is played with your left foot, so it's placed on the bottom of the staff. Since it's a cymbal, it's written with an X-shaped notehead:

Here is the symbol we'll use for the hi-hat played with the foot pedal in our drumbeat diagrams:

Singles

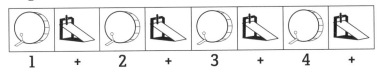
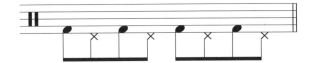

Doubles

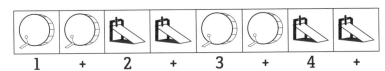
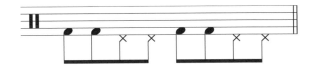

Paradiddles

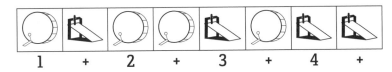

Music Theory: Notes, Chords, and Scales

GUITAR

Music Theory: Notes, Chords, and Scales

All music is made up of the notes of the musical alphabet. All the riffs and chords you have been playing are made up of these individual notes. There are seven **natural notes**: A–B–C–D–E–F–G.

Chords are a combination of notes played together. For instance, the easy E chord has three different notes in it, while the full E chord has six.

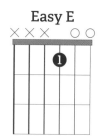
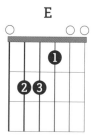

A **scale** is a series of notes. The notes we've been using for soloing are an example of a scale. Below is a sample scale that we will learn more about later in the book.

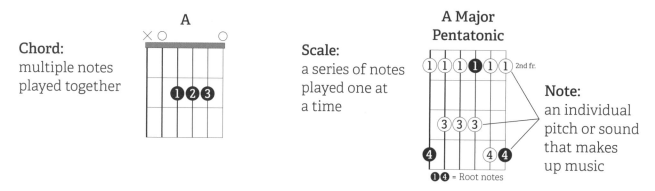

Chord: multiple notes played together

Scale: a series of notes played one at a time

Note: an individual pitch or sound that makes up music

The combination of notes, chords, and scales put to rhythm defines all the music we experience.

KEYBOARD

Music Theory: Notes, Chords, and Scales

All music is made up of the notes of the musical alphabet. All the riffs and chords you have been playing are made up these individual notes. There are seven natural notes: A–B–C–D–E–F–G.

Chords are a combination of notes played together. The chords you've played are each made of three notes.

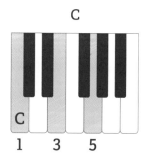

Chord: multiple notes played together

Scale: a series of notes played one at a time

Note: an individual pitch or sound that makes up music

A **scale** is a series of notes. The collection of notes we've been using to solo is an example of a scale. The combination of notes, chords, and scales put to rhythms creates all the music we experience.

Music Theory: Notes, Chords, and Scales

All music is made up of the notes of the musical alphabet. All the riffs and chords you have been playing are made up of these individual notes. There are seven **natural notes**: A–B–C–D–E–F–G.

Chords are a combination of notes played together. Bass players rarely play chords. But it is important to know that other musicians, such as guitarists and keyboardists, often do.

A **scale** is a series of notes. The notes we've been using to improvise grooves all part of one scale or another. We will learn more about this later in the book.

The combination of notes, chords, and scales put to rhythm defines all the music we experience.

Comping/Instrument Technique

 24

MU:Pr4.3.2

a) Demonstrate understanding of expressive qualities (such as dynamics and tempo) and how creators use them to convey expressive intent.

MU:Pr5.1.2

a) Apply established criteria to judge the accuracy, expressiveness, and effectiveness of performances.

b) Rehearse, identify, and apply strategies to address interpretive, performance, and technical challenges of music.

MU:Pr4.2.2

b) When analyzing selected music, read and perform rhythmic and melodic patterns using iconic or standard notation.

Instrument Technique: Alternate Picking ▶

Just as you can strum up and down, you can pick single strings up and down. Alternate up and down picking on the next two exercises.

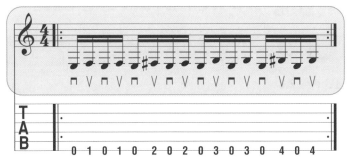

You can also use this exercise to practice hammer-ons. In this case, just use down picks:

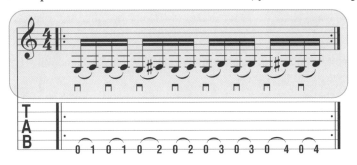

Here is a riff example that uses alternate picking:

MISERLOU
Dick Dale

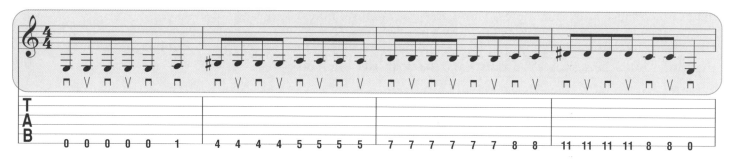

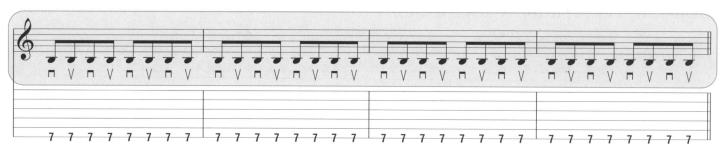

Now, try creating your own riff using alternate picking:

Playing Grooves: Drum and Bass

 23   32

MU:Pr4.2.2

a) Demonstrate knowledge of music concepts (such as tonality and meter) in music from a variety of cultures selected for performance.

b) When analyzing selected music, read and perform rhythmic and melodic patterns using iconic or standard notation.

MU:Pr4.3.4

a) Demonstrate and explain how intent is conveyed through interpretive decisions and expressive qualities (such as dynamics, tempo, and timbre).

MU:Pr5.1.2

b) Rehearse, identify, and apply strategies to address interpretive, performance, and technical challenges of music.

MU:Re8.1.2

a) Demonstrate knowledge of music concepts and how they support creators'/ performers' expressive intent.

> This section focuses on drum and bass sectional skills. All the repertoire and activities parallel and should be done as a drum and bass sectional.

CRUEL

St. Vincent

Play this next example with a drummer.

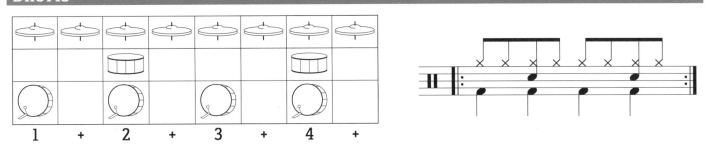

Notice how both the bass guitar and bass drum play on all four downbeats in this groove. Since it is the same rhythm, make sure your playing lines up exactly with the bass drum.

Both the bass drum and bass guitar are called "bass" because they sound low in pitch.

For this exercise, counting is included between the standard notation and the tab.

In both measures of this example from Weezer's "Say It Ain't So," the second note of each measure lands on the "and" between beats 2 and 3, rather than on the beat.

SAY IT AIN'T SO

Weezer

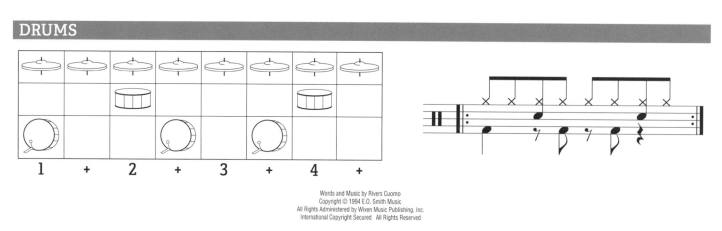

DRUMS

In this example, there is an eight-beat groove (two measures of four beats each). Count along and be sure to notice which notes are played on the "and" and which are played on the downbeats.

FREE FALLIN'

Tom Petty

BASS

DRUMS

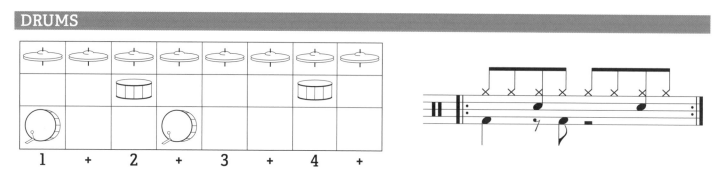

In a great band, all the musicians pay close attention to what their bandmates are playing. For bassists, listening to the drummer is especially important. Together, the bass and drums tell the rest of the band important information about tempo, rhythm, style, and note lengths. In this section, you've been encouraged to practice with a drummer, and should be starting to notice some examples of the bass-drum connection in music. With that in mind, let's try two more examples.

DOO WOP (THAT THING)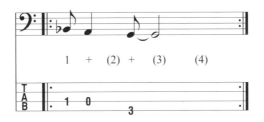
Lauryn Hill

BASS

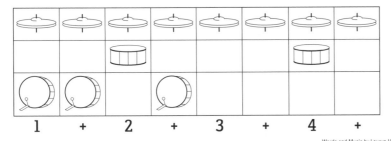

DRUMS

YOU KNOW I'M NO GOOD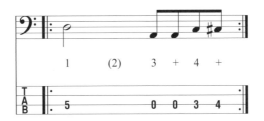
Amy Winehouse

BASS

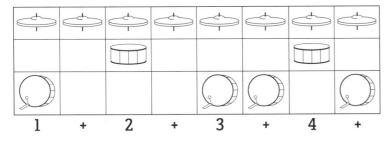

DRUMS

Composition: Mastering the Grid

 25   34

BASS

MU:Cr1.1.E.5

a) Compose and improvise melodic and rhythmic ideas or motives that reflect characteristic(s) of music or text(s) studied in rehearsal.

MU:Cr2.1.E.5

a) Select and develop draft melodic and rhythmic ideas or motives that demonstrate understanding of characteristic(s) of music or text(s) studied in rehearsal.

MU:Cr3.2.E.5

a) Share personally developed melodic and rhythmic ideas or motives—individually or as an ensemble—that demonstrate understanding of characteristics of music or texts studied in rehearsal.

MU:Cr1.1.2

a) Improvise rhythmic and melodic patterns and musical ideas for a specific purpose.
b) Generate musical patterns and ideas within the context of a given tonality (such as major and minor) and meter (such as duple and triple).

MU:Pr5.1.2

b) Rehearse, identify, and apply strategies to address interpretive, performance, and technical challenges of music.

Composition: Mastering the Grid ▶

Now that you've played several examples of grooves where the bass drum and bass guitar play the same rhythms, try writing some of your own. First, look at every eighth-note option below. Then, create riffs in the empty tab below using different rhythm patterns and any notes of your choice. If a drummer is available, practice the new rhythms together.

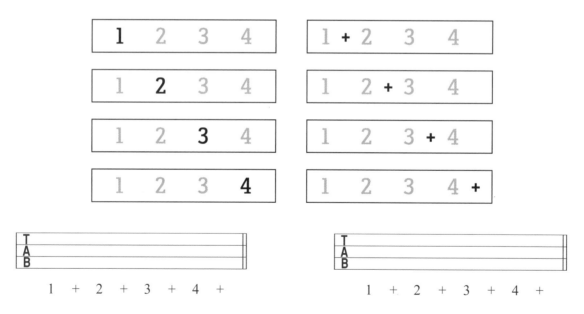

Drummers don't only use the bass drum to line up with the bassist. Work with your drummer to find drum sounds that work best with the notes and rhythms that you're playing. For example, you may want the lower notes you play to be matched with a bass drum or other lower-pitched drum, and the higher notes with a higher-pitched drum (like a snare drum). Try creating a few more riffs together with that in mind.

As you listen to more music—with the drum-bass relationship in mind—you'll notice that a lot of the rhythms won't line up *exactly*, but rather, the bass and drums work together to emphasize, or **accent**, certain notes.

Composition: Mastering the Grid ▶

Now that you've played several examples of grooves where the bass drum and bass guitar play the same rhythms, try writing some of your own. First, see what all the options are on this eighth-note grid. When you first start this, play eighth notes on your hi-hat as you play the bass drum hits with your right foot. Then, add in the snare drum backbeat as well. When writing these in staff notation, you can see where the noteheads line up vertically, just like in the drumbeat diagram. You can practice these grooves together with a bass player:

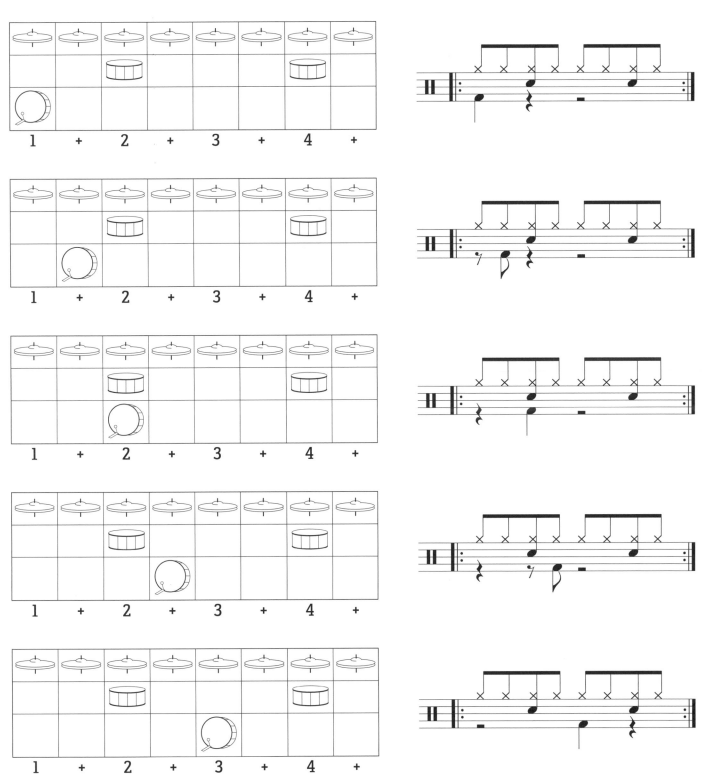

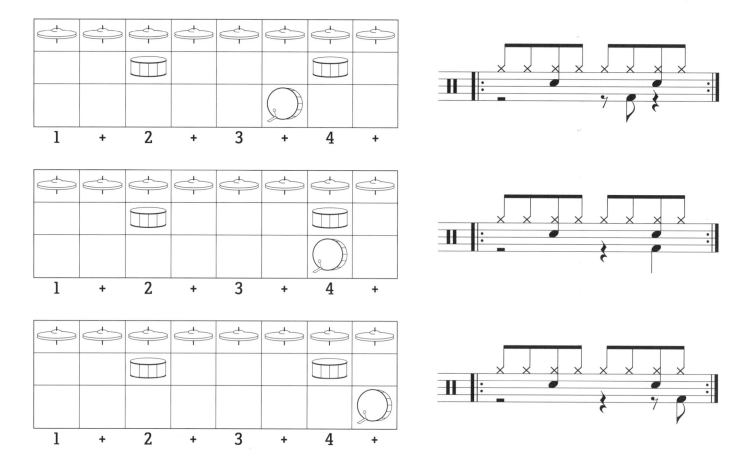

Use the grids below to come up with a rhythm that you and the bass player can play together:

1	+	2	+	3	+	4	+

It doesn't have to be the bass drum that lines up with the bass guitar. You could mix up the bass drum with the snare drum to play rhythms that fit in with the bass line. Try that with another drumbeat, and write your ideas in this diagram below:

1	+	2	+	3	+	4	+

Closing Thought

As you listen to more music with this bass guitar-kick drum relationship in mind, you'll notice that many of the rhythms don't line up together exactly, but they **accent** (emphasize) certain notes together (more on accents later in the book).

Improvisation

25   **24**   **25**

MU:Cr1.1.E.5

a) Compose and improvise melodic and rhythmic ideas or motives that reflect characteristic(s) of music or text(s) studied in rehearsal.

MU:Cr2.1.E.5

a) Select and develop draft melodic and rhythmic ideas or motives that demonstrate understanding of characteristic(s) of music or text(s) studied in rehearsal.

MU:Cr3.2.E.5

a) Share personally-developed melodic and rhythmic ideas or motives—individually or as an ensemble—that demonstrate understanding of characteristics of music or texts studied in rehearsal.

MU:Pr5.3.E.5

a) Use self-reflection and peer feedback to refine individual and ensemble performances of a varied repertoire of music.

MU:Cr1.1.2

a) Improvise rhythmic and melodic patterns and musical ideas for a specific purpose.

b) Generate musical patterns and ideas within the context of a given tonality (such as major and minor) and meter (such as duple and triple).

MU:Cr3.1.2

a) Interpret and apply personal, peer, and teacher feedback to revise personal music.

MU:Pr5.1.2

b) Rehearse, identify, and apply strategies to address interpretive, performance, and technical challenges of music.

The Full Minor Pentatonic

The next improvisation activity includes the full minor pentatonic scale for all melodic instruments. There are many practical ways to work on this as an entire class and also, some challenges, since each instrument has a different number of notes in its scale; the guitar scale is a full two octaves while the piano and bass are one. Here are some ideas:

- Students run through the scale individually while you walk around the room, checking for understanding.
- Play an A minor jam track while each instrument group plays through the scale together, first with each note as a whole note, then two half notes, and then four quarter notes. Ascend, repeat the top note, and then descend.
- Have the entire class play an A jam progression, such as "Born in the USA" or "Best Day of My Life" from Section 3. Then, while three of the groups continue playing the jam, the other group solos. Using a minor solo scale over a major chord progression will give the solo a bluesy sound.
- To work on vocal technique and musicality, students can practice without their instruments.
- Students can compose a short vocal line (embellishment). These short runs can be used as vocal fillers during a section of their compositions. They can use their Six-Note Scale or just a few notes from it, similar to what they use to make a catchy riff.
- Students can use their instruments to transcribe their pitches using either standard notation or an iconic equivalent.
- For an ear training/transcription activity, students may also want to improvise a run without notation or an instrument and have another student attempt a transcribe or replicate the run with their voice or instrument.
- Students can incorporate runs into vocal performances with the major pentatonic scale. Many pop and R&B vocalists use this scale in their riffs and runs.

For each instrument throughout, the scale is introduced, an instrument specific skill is used to reinforce the scale, and some sample riffs are given.

Improvisation: Minor Pentatonic Scale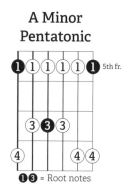

The first scale you'll learn is the **minor pentatonic scale**. The six-note solo from earlier can be expanded to cover all the strings.

A Minor Pentatonic

●●= Root notes

The **tonic**, or **root**, is the note a scale or chord is named after. For this scale, starting at the 5th fret on string 6, the tonic is A. All the darkened notes in the diagram are A notes.

This scale sounds good with songs that have a bluesy or funky sound, like "Low Rider" by War.

One way to practice this scale is to play it using hammer-ons:

Here are a few riffs that use the pentatonic scale. Note the use of hammer-ons in a few measures.

Try to make some of your own riffs with the minor pentatonic scale:

Improvisation: The Full Minor Pentatonic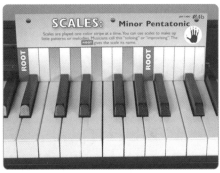

The next scale is the **minor pentatonic scale**. If you place the root bar of Jam Card #4b on A, then you can play an A minor pentatonic scale with the notes A, C, D, E, and G.

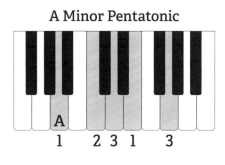

How is this different from the **major pentatonic scale**? What are the different notes? How does it sound different?

This scale can be played with songs that are in the **key** (a collection of notes that form the basis of a song) of A minor or have a bluesy or funky sound, such as "Low Rider" by War. Since this scale spans a lot of space on the keyboard, you'll need to shift your hand. Here are a few different melodic ideas that show you how to shift your fingers:

Stepwise and Skipping Motion

Stepwise motion: Skipping motion:

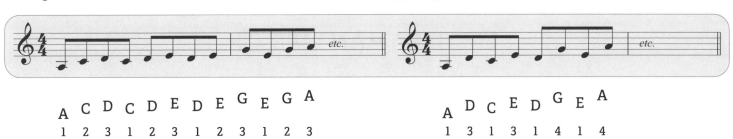

Here are some riffs that use the pentatonic scale:

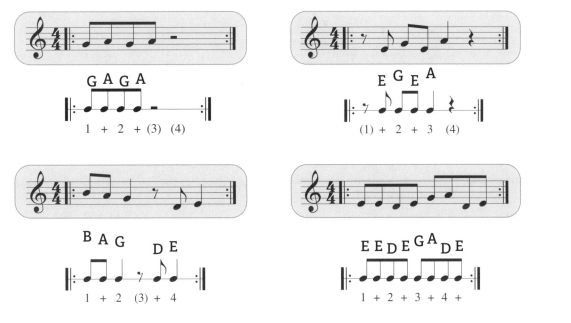

Now, try composing your own riff:

Improvisation: Full Minor Pentatonic Scale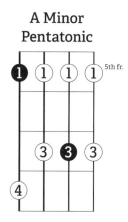

The first scale you'll learn is the **minor pentatonic scale**.

A Minor
Pentatonic

The **tonic**, or **root**, is the note a scale or chord is named after. For this scale, starting at the 5th fret on string 4, the tonic is A. Both darkened notes in the diagram are A notes.

This scale sounds good with songs that have a bluesy or funky sound, like "Low Rider" by War.

A fun way to practice this scale is to create bass lines using notes from the scale. Practice playing up and down the scale, using different rhythms. Next, try skipping different notes of the scale. Finally, try playing some notes long and some notes short. Many bass lines are based on the pentatonic scale.

Here are a few riffs that use the pentatonic scale.

LARGER THAN LIFE
Backstreet Boys

BILLIE JEAN
Michael Jackson

THRILLER
Michael Jackson

Try to make some of your own riffs with the minor pentatonic scale:

In this section, drummers should be focusing on the new drum and bass skills they've just learned, locking in with the bassist to play a strong, foundational groove together.

SECTION 5—SAMPLE RUBRIC					
Skill	**4**	**3**	**2**	**1**	**Next Steps**
GUITAR Hammer-Ons	Student can perform multiple hammer-on examples in time and at tempo and achieve even tone and dynamic	Student can perform hammer-on examples in time or achieve mostly consistent tone and dynamic	Student can perform a hammer-on example out of time or achieves inconsistent tone and dynamic	Student can perform a single hammer-on	
GUITAR Alternate Picking	Student can perform multiple alternate picking examples in time and at tempo	Student can perform alternate picking examples in time	Student can perform an alternate picking example out of time	Student can perform alternate picking	
KEYBOARD Arpeggios, Notes, Chords, and Scales	Student can perform written arpeggios time and at a variety of tempos	Student can perform written arpeggios in time	Student can perform written arpeggios out of time	Student cannot perform written arpeggios	
GUITAR/ KEYBOARD/BASS Minor Pentatonic Scale	Student can perform unique solos using all the notes of the minor pentatonic scale	Student can perform short phrases using the notes of the minor pentatonic scale	Student can play the notes of the minor pentatonic scale	Student cannot play or identify the notes of the minor pentatonic scale	
BASS Muted Notes	Student can mute notes to perform notes at a variety of note lengths in time	Student can mute notes in time	Student can mute notes	Student cannot mute notes	
DRUMS Fills 16th-Note Patterns	Student can perform a variety of drum fills in time and at multiple tempos	Student can perform multiple drum fills in time	Student can perform a drum fill	Student cannot perform a drum fill	

SECTION 6

 26   25   27   36

Comping: Student will focus on playing as an ensemble with one-chord songs, playing rhythmically in sync and playing hits together.

Instrument Technique: Guitar players will play pull-offs, keyboardists will play legato and staccato phrases, and bassists will focus on playing and reading various rhythms and note lengths. Drummers will focus on note length and timbre by playing various drums and cymbals.

Improvisation: Guitar players will apply hammer-ons and pull-offs to solos with the pentatonic scale. Keyboard players will apply legato and staccato technique. Drummers will play double-stroke rolls in the context of solos and fills.

Music Theory: Guitar, bass, and keyboard players will read notes on the staff to learn various songs.

Full Band Song: "Someone Like You" by Adele

Playing Chords/Lines/Drumbeats

 26   25   27   36

MU:Pr5.1.2

b) Rehearse, identify, and apply strategies to address interpretive, performance, and technical challenges of music.

MU:Pr6.1.2

a) Perform music for a specific purpose with expression and technical accuracy.

MU:Re7.2.2

a) Describe how specific music concepts are used to support a specific purpose in music.

MU:Pr5.3.E.5

a) Use self-reflection and peer feedback to refine individual and ensemble performances of a varied repertoire of music.

MU:Pr6.1.E.5

a) Demonstrate attention to technical accuracy and expressive qualities in prepared and improvised performances of a varied repertoire of music.

Here is a song that uses just one chord. You can practice with either a recording of the song or with your whole band.

 # LAND OF A THOUSAND DANCES

Wilson Pickett

GUITAR

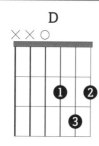

KEYBOARD

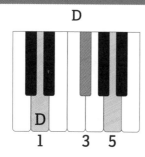

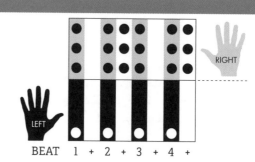

126

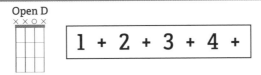

Open D

1 + 2 + 3 + 4 +

DRUMS

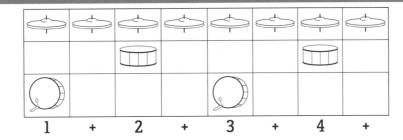

1 + 2 + 3 + 4 +

Staff notation is especially helpful for showing longer examples of music. Where is the crash cymbal played in the example below? Play this with your bandmates in "Land of a Thousand Dances":

Instrument Technique

26   25   27   36

MU:Pr5.1.2

a) Apply established criteria to judge the accuracy, expressiveness, and effectiveness of performances.

b) Rehearse, identify, and apply strategies to address interpretive, performance, and technical challenges of music.

MU:Pr6.1.3

a) Perform music with expression and technical accuracy.

GUITAR

Instrument Technique: Pull-Offs

A **pull-off** is the opposite of a hammer-on. Instead of creating sound by hammering a finger down on the fretboard, create it by pulling a finger off. To get a full sound, you need to pull the finger downward off of the string, as opposed to just lifting it off.

Here are some riffs with pull-offs to open strings.

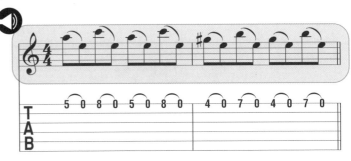

127

When pulling off to another fretted finger, be sure to keep the fretted finger held in place. Practice with the A minor pentatonic scale.

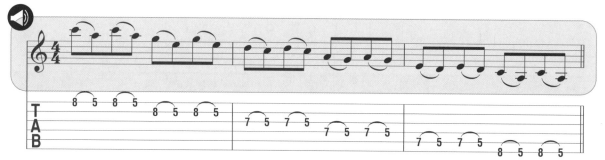

KEYBOARD

Instrument Technique: Phrasing—Legato and Staccato

One of the best ways to create interest with very few notes is with **phrasing** and **articulation**, particularly how long and connected (**legato**) or separated and short (**staccato**) you play a note.

In music, when there is a **slur** or **tenuto** marking over or under a series of notes, play them smoothly:

When there is a dot included with one or multiple notes, play them staccato:

Here are a few riffs that demonstrate this; listen to each and play them with the appropriate phrasing:

FUNKYTOWN
Lipps Inc.

MOVES LIKE JAGGER
Maroon 5

Here is a riff that alternates between long and short articulations:

BASS

MU:Pr4.1.2

a) Demonstrate and explain personal interest in, knowledge about, and purpose of varied musical selections.

MU:Pr5.1.2

a) Apply established criteria to judge the accuracy, expressiveness, and effectiveness of performances.

b) Rehearse, identify, and apply strategies to address interpretive, performance, and technical challenges of music.

MU:Pr6.1.3

a) Perform music with expression and technical accuracy.

MU:Re8.1.2

a) Demonstrate knowledge of music concepts and how they support creators'/performers' expressive intent.

Instrument Technique: Changing the Rhythm

A bass player can change the feel of a song by playing different rhythms, just as a drummer can change the feel of a song by changing up their drumbeat.

Play these different rhythms on the note A (as written), or any other single note of your choice.

MU:Pr5.1.2

   a) Apply established criteria to judge the accuracy, expressiveness, and effectiveness of performances.

   b) Rehearse, identify, and apply strategies to address interpretive, performance, and technical challenges of music.

MU:Re8.1.2

   a) Demonstrate knowledge of music concepts and how they support creators'/performers' expressive intent.

Instrument Technique: Dynamics ▶

The beat of this song doesn't change much throughout, so how do you keep the music interesting? This is where we can use **dynamics** to add variety within the song. Dynamics are how loud or soft you play. Using a variety of dynamics is a great way to make different sections of the form stand out from each other. For "Life Is a Highway," you can play at a softer dynamic on the Verses and a louder dynamic on the Chorus. You can generally control the volume of your playing with the height of your drumstick:

For softer sounds, position the tip of your stick closer to the drumhead.

For louder sounds, position the tip of your stick higher above the drumhead.

Here is a drumbeat that is used in songs like "Life Is a Highway" as recorded by the country band Rascal Flatts; you can vary your dynamics in the different sections of the song.

LIFE IS A HIGHWAY 🔊
Rascal Flatts

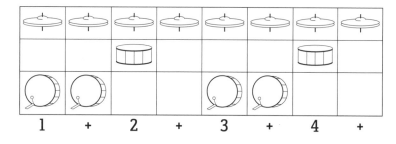

Long Sounds vs. Short Sounds ▶

Each piece in the drumset is made to be played just about anywhere regarding the different surfaces of the drumheads and areas of the cymbals. Experiment with your drumset and find which drums, cymbals, rims, etc., make the shortest sounds and which ones ring out for longer sounds. Each of these sounds has a marking in staff notation.

Examples of Longer Sounds:

Ride cymbal near the edge

Un-muffled floor tom

Loose hi-hat

Examples of Shorter Sounds:

Ride cymbal bell

Snare drum (especially in the middle)

Closed hi-hat

Changing Instrumentation

Because you have access to all these different sounds on your instrument, you can often change a drumbeat slightly by switching out one or more sounds with something similar. Here are some examples that switch out the hi-hat for the floor tom:

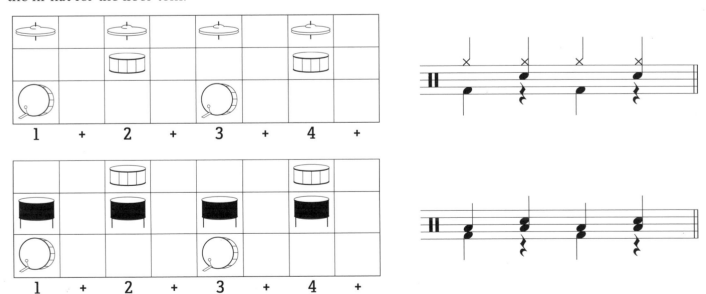

These drumbeats are used in songs such as "Holiday" by Green Day:

HOLIDAY

Green Day

Intro/Interlude

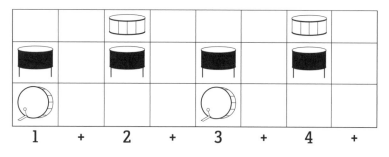

Verse

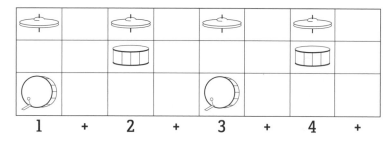

Chorus

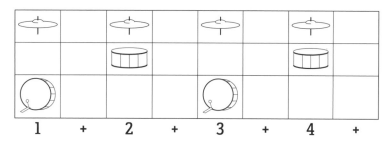

The next sound we'll discuss is the **rim click**. Rim clicks are shown by replacing the regular notehead with an X. We'll use this symbol in our drumbeat diagrams to show rim clicks:

Here is a song that uses rim clicks:

AIN'T IT FUN

Paramore

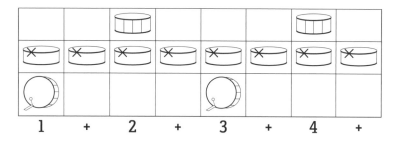

Improvisation

 26   26

MU:Cr1.1.E.5

a) Compose and improvise melodic and rhythmic ideas or motives that reflect characteristic(s) of music or text(s) studied in rehearsal.

MU:Cr2.1.E.5

a) Select and develop draft melodic and rhythmic ideas or motives that demonstrate understanding of characteristic(s) of music or text(s) studied in rehearsal.

MU:Cr3.2.E.5

a) Share personally-developed melodic and rhythmic ideas or motives—individually or as an ensemble—that demonstrate understanding of characteristics of music or texts studied in rehearsal.

MU:Pr5.3.E.5

a) Use self-reflection and peer feedback to refine individual and ensemble performances of a varied repertoire of music.

MU:Cr1.1.2

a) Improvise rhythmic and melodic patterns and musical ideas for a specific purpose.

b) Generate musical patterns and ideas within the context of a given tonality (such as major and minor) and meter (such as duple and triple).

MU:Cr3.1.2

a) Interpret and apply personal, peer, and teacher feedback to revise personal music.

MU:Pr5.1.2

b) Rehearse, identify, and apply strategies to address interpretive, performance, and technical challenges of music.

GUITAR

Improvisation: Applying Hammer-Ons and Pull-Offs

Try including hammer-ons and pull-offs in your improvisation. When using these techniques, make sure that the second note is as loud as the first. Here are some sample riffs.

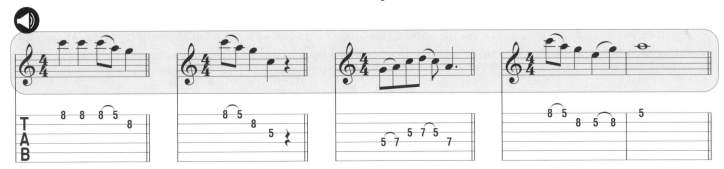

KEYBOARD

Improvisation: Applying Legato and Staccato

When improvising during the jams, be sure to mix in legato and staccato phrasing. Here are some riffs to try out with legato and staccato articulations:

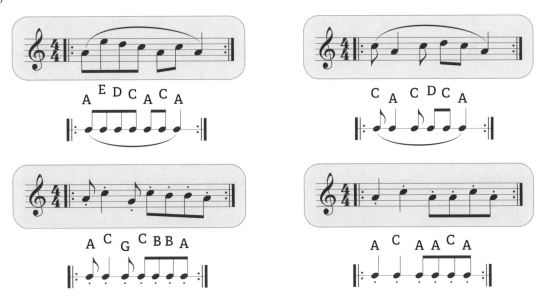

133

Music Theory: The Music Staff

MU:Cr2.1.2

b) Use iconic or standard notation and/or recording technology to combine, sequence, and document personal musical ideas.

> The following section discusses how to read notes on the staff, using familiar melodies. Note that the lesson for each instrument is a bit different, since each is currently reading music differently and work on notes in different ranges. All of the lessons are included throughout in separate sections. While some of the songs connect from instrument to instrument, others differ.

Music Theory: The Music Staff

Look at this melody from a song you have already learned, "Heathens" by Twenty One Pilots. This is the vocal melody written in tablature:

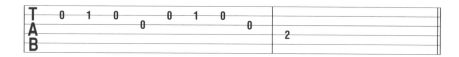

Every note on the guitar has a place on the **music staff**. To start, look at a music staff, which is similar to a tab staff but with a few differences—there are five lines instead of six, and the lines *do not* refer to strings.

The next important feature on a staff is the **treble clef**. It assigns specific note names to the lines and spaces on the staff.

You have already seen note heads used with rhythms. Here they are placed on the staff in the lines and spaces to let the musician know which notes to play. The vertical placement of each note determines what note it is. Here is the same vocal melody in both tab and staff notation.

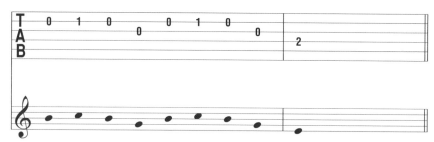

Finally, add the rhythms you learned earlier to the note heads on the staff. In the case of this song, there is a full measure of eighth notes followed by a whole note. Here, the eighth notes are beamed in groups of four instead of two.

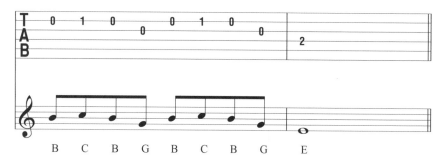

134

Each note is named by one of the seven (natural) letters of the musical alphabet. For now, look at the notes on the first three frets of the guitar and on the first four strings. Notice that the staves are switched this time. In guitar music, the tab staff is usually shown on the bottom.

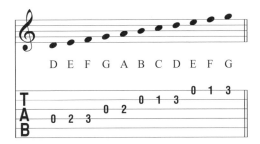

For the song below, write the notes of the tab numbers in the bottom staff for the first two measures. Then, write the tab numbers in the top staff for the notes shown in measures 3–5. We have slightly changed the rhythm so it uses only the note values we have discussed so far.

BAD ROMANCE

Lady Gaga

Now, try playing your example, reading the staff notation and then the tab.

From this point on, standard staff notation will be included with the tabs. Use this to begin familiarizing yourself with where the notes are on the staff. If you see any symbols or rhythms you don't understand, continue listening to the original recordings to hear the rhythms. You'll learn more about music reading as you continue through the Modern Band program.

To play the next melody from "Bad Romance," we'll need to know the **eighth rest**: ♪. This rest takes the place of one eighth note. Combined with another eighth note or eighth rest, it makes up a full beat. Find a recording of this song and listen to the melody to hear how the rhythm works with the notation. This melody happens at the 0:29 mark on the original recording.

KEYBOARD

Music Theory: Notes on the Staff

You've learned how to play several melodies so far using letter name notation. But this notation is sometimes not perfectly clear. For instance, which A should you use when there are seven different ones to choose from? This is where **standard staff notation** can be helpful.

To start, look at a familiar melody from a song you have already learned, "Heathens" by Twenty One Pilots. The song begins with the notes B, C, and G, but where do we find them on the piano? Here is where these pitches are located on the keyboard:

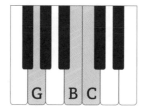

Each note on the keyboard has an exact place it appears on a **music staff**. A music staff has five lines and four spaces, and it looks like this:

The next important feature on a staff is the **clef**. There are quite a few of these in the music world, but for now, we will just use the **treble clef.** Here is what the treble clef looks like on the staff:

You have already seen noteheads in standard staff rhythms. Here, they are placed on the staff in the lines and spaces to let the musician know which notes to play. The notehead's vertical placement determines which specific pitch it is. Here is the vocal melody in staff notation:

Finally, add in the rhythms you learned earlier to show the rhythm in the same place as the notes. In the case of this song, there is a full measure of eighth notes followed by a measure filled entirely by one whole note:

B C B G B C B G   E

Each note corresponds to one of the seven letters of the musical alphabet. While every note name can be found in multiple places, each specific name for the note is only in one place on the staff. Look at the notes on the staff that take us from the bottom line to the top line and their location on the keyboard:

E F G A B C D E

Write the melody in the staff below for the first two measures and the last part of the fourth measure. Then, write the note names over the single-line notes for the third and fourth measures. We have slightly changed the rhythm so it only uses the note values we have discussed so far.

BAD ROMANCE
Lady Gaga

Now, try playing your example by reading the staff notation.

To play the next melody from the song, you'll need to know the **eighth rest:** ♭

This rest is the same value as one eighth note. When combined with another eighth note or eighth rest, it makes up a full beat. Listen to a recording of the song to hear the original rhythms. This melody happens at the 0:29 mark:

BASS

Music Theory: The Music Staff

While tablature is useful for guitarists and bass guitarists, it doesn't translate to most other instruments. However, **standard staff notation** can be shared between different instruments.

Look at this bass line in tablature from a song you have already learned, "Heathens" by Twenty One Pilots.

Every note on the bass has a place on the **music staff**. To start, look at a music staff, which is similar to a tab staff but with a few differences—there are five lines instead of four, and the lines *do not* refer to strings.

Bass Tablature		Standard Music Staff

vs.

The next important feature on a staff is the **bass clef**. It assigns specific note names to the lines and spaces on the staff.

You have already seen note heads used with rhythms. Here they are placed on the staff in the lines and spaces to let the musician know which notes to play. The vertical placement of each note determines what note it is. Every number in the tab staff corresponds to *exactly* one place on a music staff.

Using the tab and rhythms from "Heathens," we can now write the bass line in standard staff notation.

Play a few bass lines using traditional staff notation. The rhythms of some have been simplified to use only the rhythms covered so far. (The dot after the half note in measure 1 means to hold that note for three beats instead of two—and of course, the quarter note lasts for one beat.) Once you play them, write the tab showing how you played it.

BABA O'RILEY
The Who

UNDER PRESSURE
Queen ft. David Bowie

LIVIN' ON A PRAYER

Bon Jovi

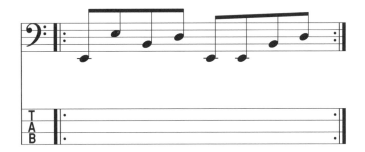

To play the next melody from "I Can't Help Myself (Sugar Pie, Honey Bunch)," we'll need to know the **eighth rest**: ꜆. This rest takes the place of one eighth note. Combined with another eighth note or eighth rest, it makes up a full beat. Find a recording of the following song and listen to the intro to hear how the rhythm works with the notation.

I CAN'T HELP MYSELF (SUGAR PIE, HONEY BUNCH)

The Four Tops

DRUMS

MU:Pr5.1.2

b) Rehearse, identify, and apply strategies to address interpretive, performance, and technical challenges of music.

Instrument Technique: Double-Stroke Rolls ▶

A **double-stroke roll** combines several short sounds to make an overall longer sound. This technique takes practice, so start slow and have fun with it. On each snare drum hit, let the stick bounce and hit the drumhead one more time. So in one motion, the stick will hit the head of the drum twice.

Improvisation: Using Rudiments in Solos ▶

Using the rudiments (singles, doubles, and paradiddles) you learned in Section 5, play some of these rhythms. First, use only your hands. The later exercises combine hands and feet. Later, you can practice adding in your double-stroke rolls. Standard staff notation can be especially helpful when there are multiple instruments.

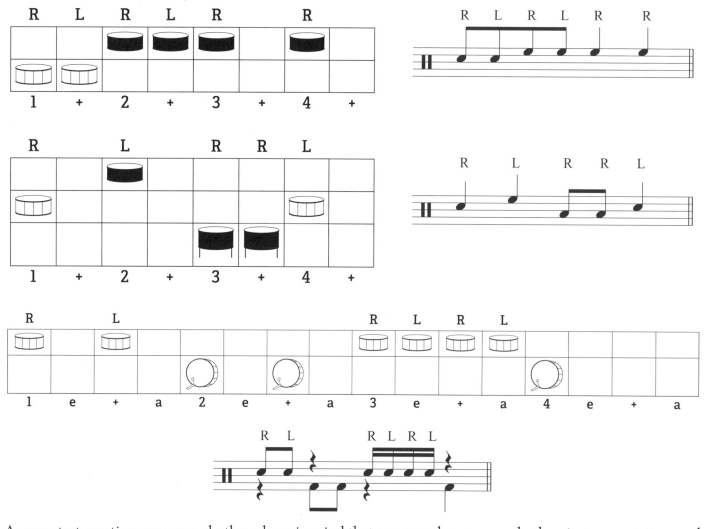

As you start creating your own rhythms, keep in mind that you can change your rhythm, instrumentation, and dynamics as much as you want. Put on any Jam Track and try soloing along.

Full Band Song: SOMEONE LIKE YOU 🔊
Adele

🎸 28   🎹 28   🎸 30   🥁 39

MU:Pr5.1.3
a) Apply teacher-provided and collaboratively-developed criteria and feedback to evaluate accuracy of ensemble performances.
b) Rehearse to refine technical accuracy, expressive qualities, and identified performance challenges.

MU:Pr6.1.3
a) Perform music with expression and technical accuracy.

MU:Re7.2.2
a) Describe how specific music concepts are used to support a specific purpose in music.

MU:Re8.1.3
a) Demonstrate and describe how the expressive qualities (such as dynamics and tempo) are used in performers' interpretations to reflect expressive intent.

MU:Pr5.3.E.5
a) Use self-reflection and peer feedback to refine individual and ensemble performances of a varied repertoire of music.

MU:Pr6.1.E.5
a) Demonstrate attention to technical accuracy and expressive qualities in prepared and improvised performances of a varied repertoire of music.
b) Demonstrate an awareness of the context of the music through prepared and improvised performances.

MU:Re7.1.E.5

a) Identify reasons for selecting music based on characteristics found in the music, connection to interest, and purpose or context.

MU:Re8.1.E.5

a) Identify interpretations of the expressive intent and meaning of musical works, referring to the elements of music, contexts, and (when appropriate) the setting of the text.

MU:Re9.1.E.5

a) Identify and describe the effect of interest, experience, analysis, and context on the evaluation of music.

MU:Cr1.1.E.5

a) Compose and improvise melodic and rhythmic ideas or motives that reflect characteristic(s) of music or text(s) studied in rehearsal.

MU:Cr2.1.E.5

a) Select and develop draft melodic and rhythmic ideas or motives that demonstrate understanding of characteristic(s) of music or text(s) studied in rehearsal.

b) Preserve draft compositions and improvisations through standard notation and audio recording.

MU:Cr3.1.E.5

a) Evaluate and refine draft compositions and improvisations based on knowledge, skill, and teacher-provided criteria.

MU:Cr3.2.E.5

a) Share personally developed melodic and rhythmic ideas or motives—individually or as an ensemble—that demonstrate understanding of characteristics of music or texts studied in rehearsal.

MU:Pr5.3.E.5

a) Use self-reflection and peer feedback to refine individual and ensemble performances of a varied repertoire of music.

MU:Pr6.1.E.5

a) Demonstrate attention to technical accuracy and expressive qualities in prepared and improvised performances of a varied repertoire of music.

b) Demonstrate an awareness of the context of the music through prepared and improvised performances.

MU:Re8.1.E.5

a) Identify interpretations of the expressive intent and meaning of musical works, referring to the elements of music, contexts, and (when appropriate) the setting of the text.

MU:Re8.1.E.8

a) Identify and support interpretations of the expressive intent and meaning of musical works, citing as evidence the treatment of the elements of music, contexts, and (when appropriate) the setting of the text.

Performance Notes

This ballad affords students a couple opportunities for growth. The original song's instrumentation is just piano and voice, but approximation can lend to new and inventive ways of expressing the music. Here are some thoughts on interpretation:

- This song's chord progression is used in a wide variety of popular songs (See Appendix A). Learning this one song can open the doors to learning many songs.
- Guitarists can play along to the entire song, or they can come in at key moments to bring more excitement and raise the energy. Also, like any melodic instrument, the guitar can be used to improvise short riffs in the spaces between vocal lines.
- The pianists can focus on the arpeggiated keyboard comping pattern, either with two different players on the same piano or one person doing the pattern with both hands. Focus on long legato phrasing. Advanced keyboardists can begin learning about chord inversions (page [x]) and applying those to this song to give a more authentic performance. Less-advanced keyboardists can play the chords in root position.
- The bass can mimic the left hand of the piano, but can also introduce inversions to chords here for a more interesting line. For example, the bassist can play an F♯ under the D chord to play the notes G–F♯–E for the G, D, and Emi chords to create a descending bassline. Like the guitar, think about

having the bassist keep tacet during the Verse and Pre-Chorus but joining at the Chorus to bring up the energy.

- The original recording of this song has no drums, so it is important to be sensitive with the dynamics. If available, have the drummer use brushes. The drum book also has a composition activity leading into this song, so drummers should be encouraged to use their compositions and adjust them as they workshop the song.
- Vocalists should be mindful not to belt this song in a way that may harm their voices. Adele herself suffered from vocal nodes. Allowing students to sing with a microphone will be important, as it will allow the microphone do the projecting so the student doesn't have to push their voice to a point of causing damage.
- Remember, there is no reason to keep this song as wistful yet stoic as the original. Ask students to read the lyrics and think of other musical ways to display the emotions of the songs. Change the rhythm patterns to more driving quarter notes to create an anthemic feel, or pick up the tempo and use distortion to give it more of an edgy rock feel.

Suggestions for Further Repertoire
- Appendix A has a list of songs with the song I–V–vi–IV chord progression. Any of those songs could be transposed to the key of G and be played with the chords G, D, Emi, and C.
- As with the suggestions for other reggae songs, any of those songs could be turned into a ballad by changing the comping patterns on various instruments. It's an opportunity for your students to challenge themselves to think of and produce the musical characteristics that make a ballad.

Iconic Score

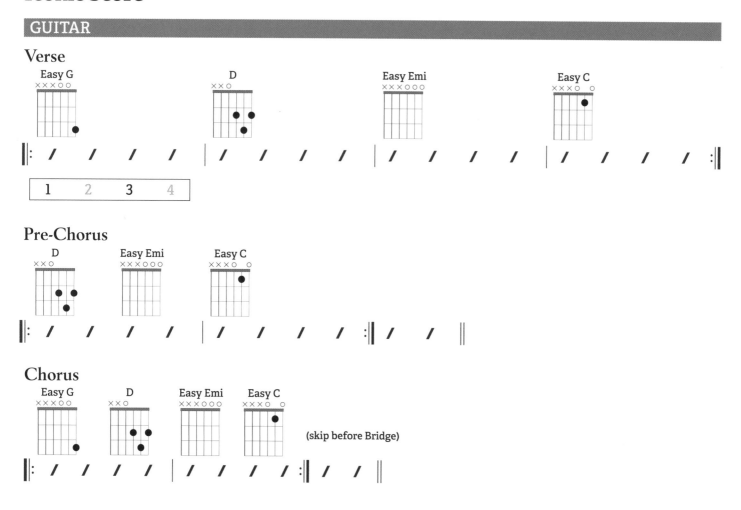

Bridge

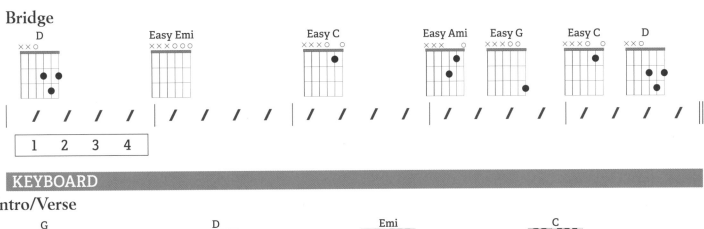

KEYBOARD

Intro/Verse

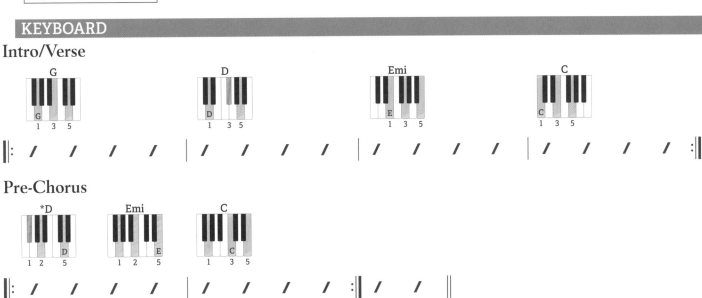

Pre-Chorus

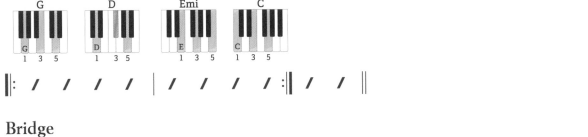

*These chords are spelled differently than you've seen so far, but you'll learn more about them in Chapter 9.

Chorus

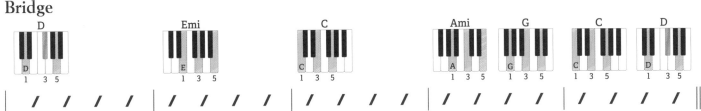

Bridge

You can use this comping pattern over each section of the song:

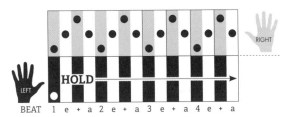

You can also use this scale to solo over the song:

G Major Pentatonic

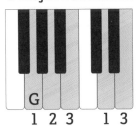

143

BASS

Verse

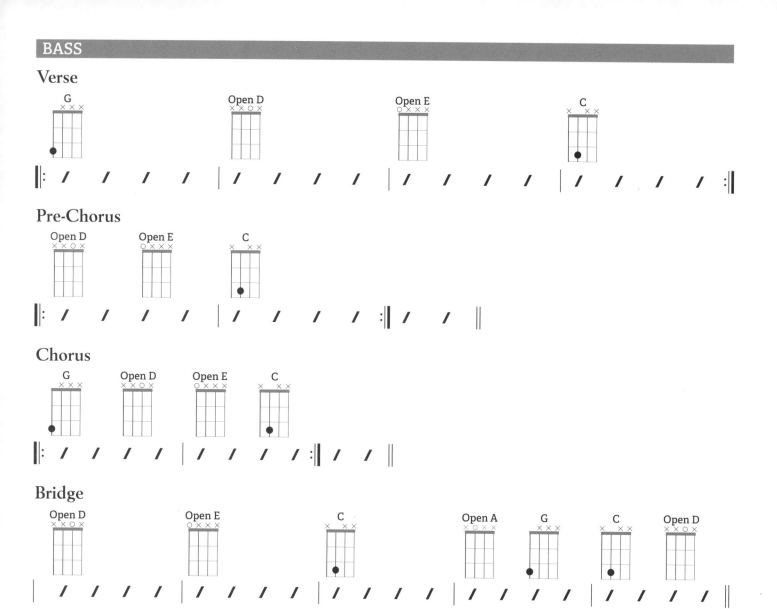

Pre-Chorus

Chorus

Bridge

Verse/Bridge Rhythm Pattern

| **1** | 2 | **3** | 4 |

Chorus Rhythm Pattern

| **1** | 2 | 3 | 4 |

DRUMS

Suggested Grooves

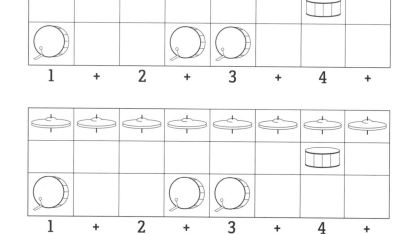

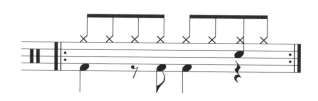

Standard Staff Score

Verse

Pre-Chorus

Chorus

Bridge

VERSE

G   D   Emi   C
I heard that you're settled down, that you found a girl and you're married now.

G   D   Emi   C
I heard that your dreams came true. Guess she gave you things I didn't give to you.

G   D   Emi   C
Old friend, why are you so shy? Ain't like you to hold back or hide from the light.

PRE-CHORUS

D   Emi   C
I hate to turn up out of the blue uninvited, but I couldn't stay away, I couldn't fight it.

D   Emi   C
I had hoped you'd see my face and that you'd be reminded that for me it isn't over.

CHORUS

G   D   Emi   C
Never mind, I'll find someone like you.

        G   D   Emi   C
I wish nothing but the best for you two.

G   D   Emi   C
Don't forget me, I beg. I'll remember you said,

        G   D   Emi   C
"Sometimes it lasts in love, but sometimes it hurts instead,

        G   D   Emi   C
Sometimes it lasts in love, but sometimes it hurts instead."

BRIDGE

D
Nothing compares, no worries or cares,

     Emi
Regrets and mistakes, they're memories made.

C   Ami   G   C   D
Who would have known how bittersweet this would taste?

Words and Music by Adele Adkins and Dan Wilson
Copyright © 2011 MELTED STONE PUBLISHING LTD., BMG MONARCH and SUGAR LAKE MUSIC
All Rights for MELTED STONE PUBLISHING LTD. in the U.S. and Canada Controlled and
Administered by UNIVERSAL - SONGS OF POLYGRAM INTERNATIONAL, INC.
All Rights for BMG MONARCH and SUGAR LAKE MUSIC
Administered by BMG RIGHTS MANAGEMENT (US) LLC
All Rights Reserved Used by Permission

SECTION 6—SAMPLE RUBRIC

Skill	4	3	2	1	Next Steps
GUITAR Pull-Offs	Student can perform multiple pull-off examples in time and at tempo and achieve consistent tone and dynamic	Student can perform pull-off examples in time and/or achieve mostly consistent tone and dynamic	Student can perform a pull-off example out of time and/or achieve inconsistent tone and dynamic	Student can perform a single pull-off	
KEYBOARD Staccato and Legato Phrasing	Student can perform multiple staccato and legato examples in time and at tempo	Student can perform staccato and legato examples in time	Student can perform a staccato and legato example out of time	Student can perform staccato and legato	
BASS Changing Rhythm	Student can accurately read and perform new rhythms with half, quarter, and eighth notes/rests	Student can perform rehearsed rhythms with half, quarter, and eighth notes/rests	Student can perform rehearsed rhythms with half, quarter, and eighth notes/rests with some mistakes	Student can perform rehearsed rhythms, but with frequent mistakes	
GUITAR/ KEYBOARD/ BASS/DRUMS Notes on Staff	Student can read and perform new music with few mistakes	Student can read and perform rehearsed music from the staff	Student can identify notes on the staff	Student can identify some of the notes on the staff	
DRUMS Dynamics	Student can perform drum patterns with a variety of dynamics in time and at varying tempos	Student can play drum patterns at a variety of dynamics in time	Student can play drum patterns at variety of dynamics	Student plays drum patterns with minimal dynamic range	
DRUMS Long/Short Sounds	Student can compose and perform unique patterns and substitute various long and short sounds on the Drumset	Student can identify and perform long and short sounds on the Drumset	Student can identify long and short sounds on the Drumset	Student struggles to identify long and short sounds on the Drumset	
DRUMS Double-Stroke Rolls	Student can perform double-stroke rolls at a variety of tempos	Student can perform a double-stroke roll in time	Student can perform a double-stroke roll	Student struggles to perform a double-stroke roll	

SECTION 7

 30   30   32   🥁 41

Comping: Musicians will play various comping patterns together, reading them as iconic and standard staff notation. Students will review Ami, A, and E chords and listen for tonality differences between Ami–E and A–E chord progressions. Keyboardists will use jam cards to practice transposition.

Composition: On top of the other composition skills students have learned, students will compose riffs using the minor pentatonic scale and apply them to their songs

Full Band Song: Students will practice reading single-line staff notation to learn the different sections of "Oye Como Va." Drummers will apply 2-3 clave, 3-2 clave, guiro, and flam patterns to their performances.

MU:Pr5.1.3

a) Apply teacher-provided and collaboratively-developed criteria and feedback to evaluate accuracy of ensemble performances.

b) Rehearse to refine technical accuracy, expressive qualities, and identified performance challenges.

Playing Chords/Lines/Drumbeats:
Playing Through Strumming, Comping, and Rhythmic Patterns

 30   30   32   41

The following patterns can be used for each instrument independently or as a group. While there are no particular chords given, any previously learned chord can be used, or students can switch chords once the patterns are more familiar to them.

Practice playing through these patterns while staying on the same chord of your choice.

GUITAR

| 1 | 2 | 3 | 4 |

| 1 | 2 | 3 | 4 |

| 1 + 2 + 3 + 4 + |

| 1 | 2 + 3 + 4 + |

| 1 | 2 + 3 + 4 |

| 1 + 2 + 3 + 4 + |

KEYBOARD

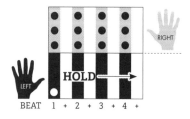

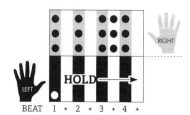

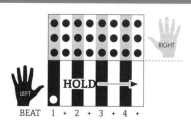

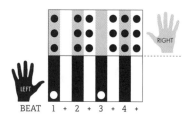

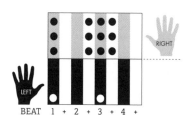

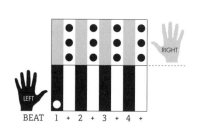

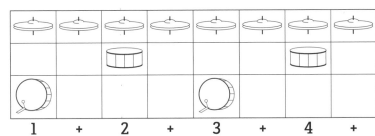

DRUMS

Warm-Up

Try reading these examples in both drumbeat diagrams and staff notation:

 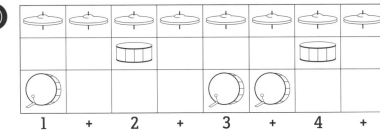

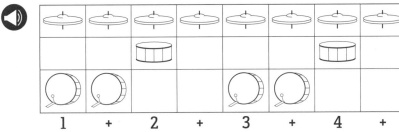
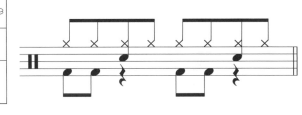

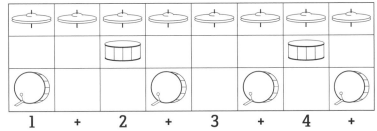

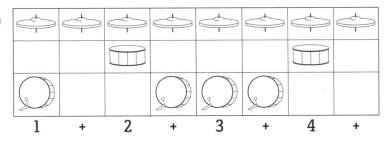

151

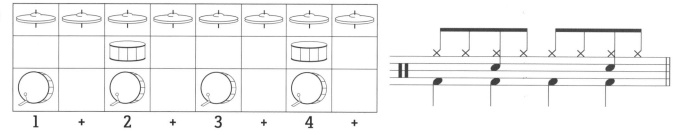

Composition: Introduction (Form)

MU:Cr1.1.2

b) Generate musical patterns and ideas within the context of a given tonality (such as major and minor) and meter (such as duple and triple).

MU:Cr2.1.2

a) Demonstrate and explain personal reasons for selecting patterns and ideas for music that represent expressive intent.

b) Use iconic or standard notation and/or recording technology to combine, sequence, and document personal musical ideas.

MU:Cr3.1.2

a) Interpret and apply personal, peer, and teacher feedback to revise personal music.

MU:Pr5.1.3

a) Apply teacher-provided and collaboratively-developed criteria and feedback to evaluate accuracy of ensemble performances.

MU:Pr6.1.3

a) Perform music with expression and technical accuracy.

MU:Cn10.0.3

a) Demonstrate how interests, knowledge, and skills relate to personal choices and intent when creating, performing, and responding to music.

MU:Cr2.1.3

a) Demonstrate selected musical ideas for a simple improvisation or composition to express intent, and describe connection to a specific purpose and context.

MU:Cr3.2.3

a) Present the final version of created music for others, and describe connection to expressive intent.

Composition: Introduction 🔊 ▶️

A lot of songs have an **introduction** (or intro). An introduction is often the instrumental section that happens before the vocalist begins. To compose an introduction, write four bars using the chords you know, and be sure to use at least one minor chord. Use the Jam Track to try out your ideas.

Chords:

Rhythm/Comping Patterns

GUITAR/BASS

Strumming Pattern:

KEYBOARD

Comping Pattern:

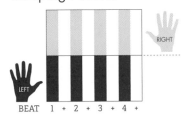

Now add a riff to your introduction using this scale:

GUITAR

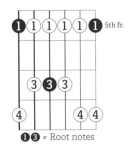

A Minor
Pentatonic

❶❸ = Root notes

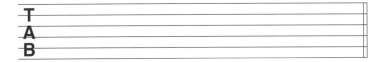

KEYBOARD

A Minor Pentatonic

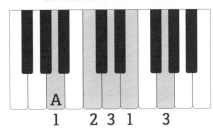

BASS

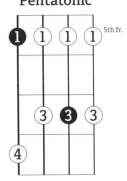

A Minor
Pentatonic

153

Your bandmates on guitar, keyboard, and bass are writing riffs and bass lines in this composition activity. When writing drumbeats here, be mindful of the rhythms that they are using and how your drumbeat compliments those rhythms. The drum sounds you choose to use will also affect the compositions. Explore the different tones you can use and pick the ones that you think will sound best:

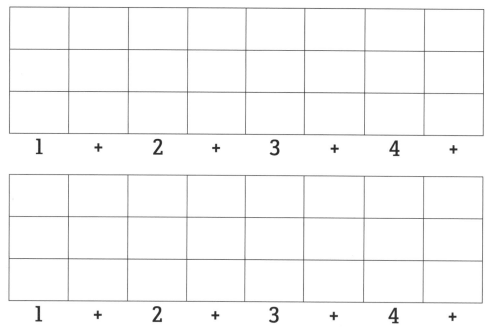

Playing Chords/Music Theory: Ami, Emi, and Transposition

 30   31

MU:Pr5.3.E.5

  a) Use self-reflection and peer feedback to refine individual and ensemble performances of a varied repertoire of music.

MU:Pr6.1.E.5

  a) Demonstrate attention to technical accuracy and expressive qualities in prepared and improvised performances of a varied repertoire of music.

MU:Pr6.1.E.5

  b) Demonstrate an awareness of the context of the music through prepared and improvised performances.

MU:Re9.1.E.5

  a) Identify and describe the effect of interest, experience, analysis, and context on the evaluation of music.

> ### Ami and Emi
> The following section contains new chords and concepts for each instrument separately. While guitar focuses on the open chords, the keyboard can now learn all the major and minor triads by using Jam Cards.

Below are the full versions of the easy Ami and Emi chords you previously learned. Now compare the sound of the A and Ami, or the E and the Emi. They center on the same pitch, but sound different.

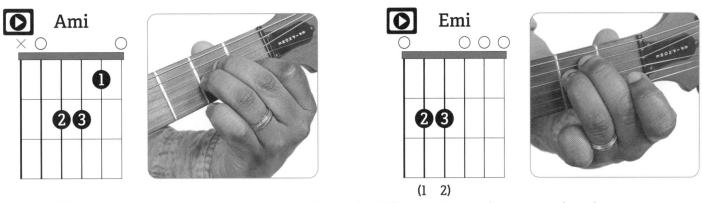

Play the following two progressions and pay attention to the difference in sound. You can select the strum pattern:

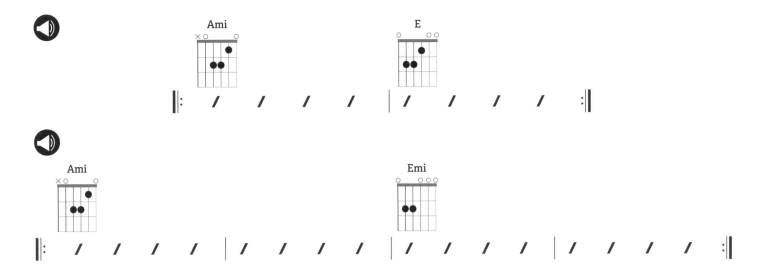

Music Theory: Transposition

Now that you are familiar with a variety of chords, you can play songs in any key through a process of **transposition**, moving the entire song up or down in pitch. To play songs in new keys, you'll need to learn more chords. Below are two Jam Cards you can use to learn new chords:

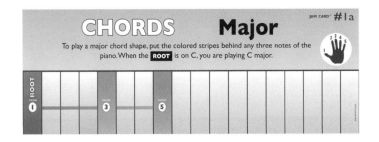

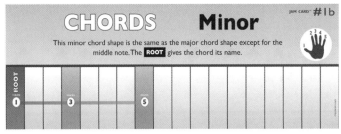

Place the root bar behind the root note of your chord, and the other shaded bars will show you which notes to use to play that chord:

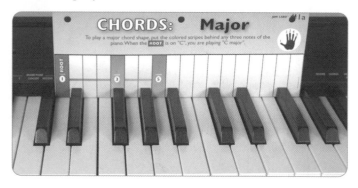 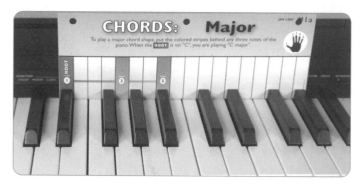

Guitarists typically like to play in keys such as G, D, and A, whereas brass players often favor keys such as F, B♭, and E♭. By using your Jam Cards on the piano, all chords are easily accessible.

Here is the same chord progression in three different keys. Use the Jam Card to learn any chords you don't already know.

BEST DAY OF MY LIFE
American Authors

Here's the original key:

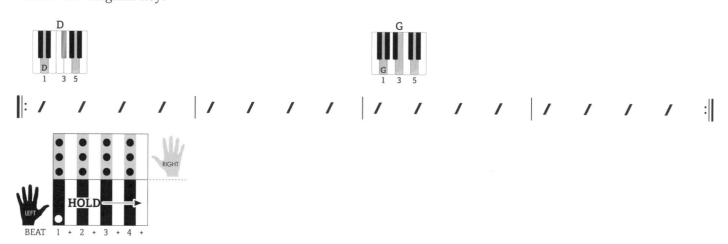

Here's the same song, transposed to a key that brass players might prefer:

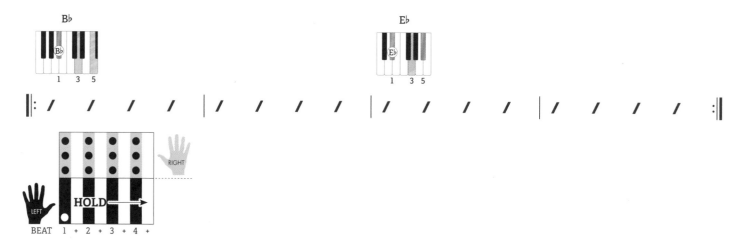

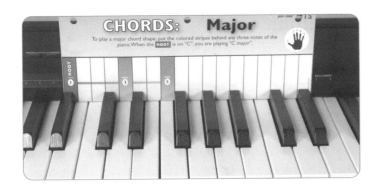

And here's a key for singers who may want to transpose it down, making it more comfortable to sing:

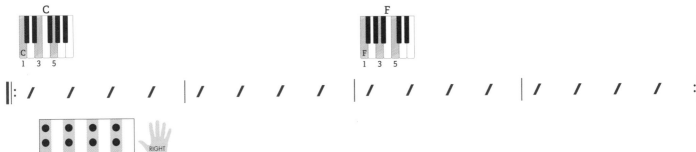

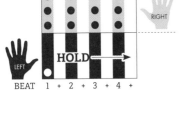

Playing Drumbeats and Instrument Technique

MU:Pr5.3.E.5

a) Use self-reflection and peer feedback to refine individual and ensemble performances of a varied repertoire of music

MU:Pr6.1.E.5

a) Demonstrate attention to technical accuracy and expressive qualities in prepared and improvised performances of a varied repertoire of music.

MU:Pr6.1.E.5

b) Demonstrate an awareness of the context of the music through prepared and improvised performances.

MU:Re9.1.E.5

a) Identify and describe the effect of interest, experience, analysis, and context on the evaluation of music.

DRUMS

Playing Drumbeats: Latin Grooves

Son Clave

The **son clave** is a common rhythm in Latin and popular music. Its two most common forms are the **2-3** clave and the **3-2** clave. This means that in every two measures of music, there are two groupings of accented beats and upbeats. In 2-3 clave, there is a group of two accented beats within the first measure and three accented points within the next measure. The same goes for 3-2 clave, except the group of three comes before the group of two. You can play the clave rhythms with **claves**, the instruments for which this groove is named:

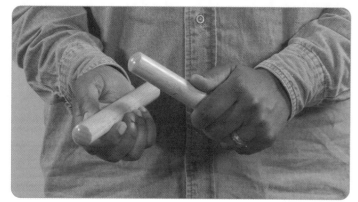
Claves in front

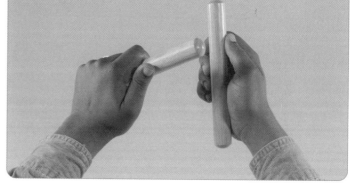
Claves from a player's perspective

Here is the symbol we'll use in our drumbeat diagrams:

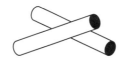

You can play clave rhythms on another instrument such as a cymbal or the rim of one of your drums.

2-3 Clave

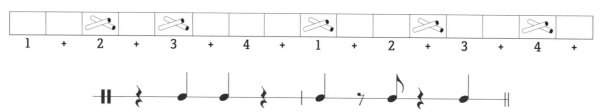

158

3-2 Clave

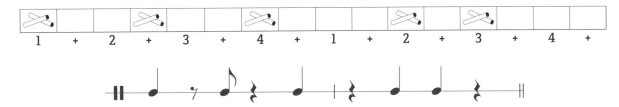

Now, listen to a song like "I Need to Know" by Marc Anthony, find the clave pattern, and try to clap along.

Here are a few other songs that use the clave rhythm in a variety of instruments:
- "Carry Out" by Timbaland ft. Justin Timberlake
- "Pa' la Paloma" by La Sonora Matancera & Celia Cruz
- "Cali Aji" by Grupo Niche

The Guiro

As a drummer, you must often approximate the auxiliary instruments used in Latin music. One such instrument is the **guiro**:

This instrument is played by striking the outer edge with a stick (called a **pua**) and then raking it across the ribbed portion of the outer shell. A typical pattern played on the guiro looks like this:

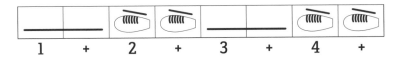 

The guiro isn't featured as a standard piece in the drumset, so drummers will often transfer its rhythms to different parts of the drumset. It's common to play guiro rhythms on the hi-hat in styles such as **salsa** and **conga**:

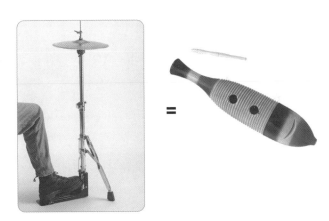

Guiro Rhythms on the Hi-Hat

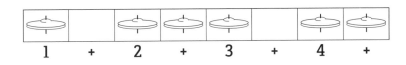 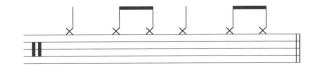

Cumbia Rhythms

Another popular groove is the **cumbia** rhythm, which is featured in songs made famous by artists such as Selena, Juanes, and the Kumbia Kings.

The hi-hat rhythm is similar to the salsa hi-hat rhythm, just twice as fast. The bass drum is also played on all the strong beats, which is called "four on the floor." The cumbia groove is typically played fast, but the overall feeling doesn't venture far from what we have encountered so far. In the next example, play the rhythms twice as fast to give the groove a **double time** feel.

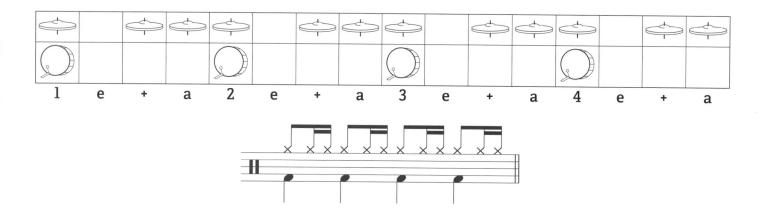

Try playing this groove along with a recording of the song "Bidi Bidi Bom Bom" by Selena.

Instrument Technique: Flams

A **flam** is a rudiment that has a big, full sound, and it is used often in Latin music. Flams can be used to accent something happening in the music and are a fun addition to solos. Flams sound like the word itself: "f-lam." A flam is played by using both sticks—one stick hits the head quietly just before the other hits at a normal volume.

Full Band Song: OYE COMO VA

Santana

31   33   33   44

MU:Pr5.1.2

a) Apply established criteria to judge the accuracy, expressiveness, and effectiveness of performances.

MU:Pr5.1.3

b) Rehearse to refine technical accuracy, expressive qualities, and identified performance challenges.

MU:Pr6.1.3

a) Perform music with expression and technical accuracy.

b) Demonstrate performance decorum and audience etiquette appropriate for the context and venue.

MU:Re7.1.3

a) Demonstrate and describe how selected music connects to and is influenced by specific interests, experiences, or purposes.

MU:Re7.2.3

a) Demonstrate and describe how a response to music can be informed by the structure, the use of the elements of music, and context (such as personal and social).

MU:Re8.1.3

a) Demonstrate and describe how the expressive qualities (such as dynamics and tempo) are used in performers' interpretations to reflect expressive intent.

MU:Pr6.1.E.5

a) Demonstrate attention to technical accuracy and expressive qualities in prepared and improvised performances of a varied repertoire of music.

MU:Re8.1.E.5

a) Identify interpretations of the expressive intent and meaning of musical works, referring to the elements of music, contexts, and (when appropriate) the setting of the text.

Performance Notes

This song sums up many of the concepts your students have previously learned, including switching chords, syncopated rhythms, and improvisation. While the song form can be replicated exactly, it can also be approximated and played in whatever form works best for the class. It is a great opportunity to work on cueing sections and keeping the band flexible on repeated sections. After all, the song was approximated by Santana from the original by Tito Puente. Here are some ideas for rehearsal:

- Once the group has learned their parts well enough to play together, have them play the Main Riff together and call instruments in and out to hear each group at different times, changing the texture of the ensemble. For instance, have only the drums and bass play, or just acoustic guitars and drums.
- Many of the rhythms here are very complicated for beginning students to read, but they can hear and replicate them. Identify some key rhythms and have them clap them allowed in a "Repeat-After-Me" exercise.
- The E chord vamp at the end is a big signal in the song that it is about to come back to the main riff again for the last time. This can be repeated for two bars, four bars, or as long as you want, and it should be a great place to work on dynamics.
- Assign each section to a hand signal: e.g., the Main Riff is a raised fist, the Breakdown is a pat on the head, E chord is both hands waving in the air. Repeat each section until you feel time is right to move on and introduce solos throughout. This really reinforces the concept that they need to listen and watch to perform well as an ensemble.
- Vocally, this song only has a one line of lyrics, but it can be tricky to sing while playing due to the various rhythms and potentially unfamiliar language. Try speaking the lyrics rhythmically over a drumbeat, and then try to add in pitches. When students are familiar enough with the material, instrumentally and vocally, they can try to add them both together.

Iconic Score—Chord and Groove Bank

This Full Band Song appears in the student books similar to other standard song charts. Here, we've included the elements that appear throughout the song.

GUITAR

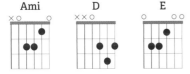

KEYBOARD

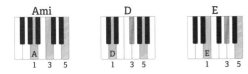

BASS

DRUMS

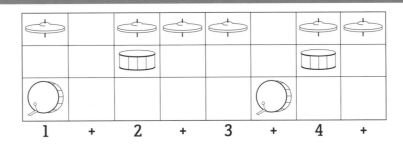

Standard Staff Score

Main Riff

Here's the breakdown that happens periodically throughout the song. It happens first at the 0:30 mark:

Here's the last section, which is played over an E chord. This shows up twice in the in the song.

The first time at the 2:04 mark. The second time, it's played twice:

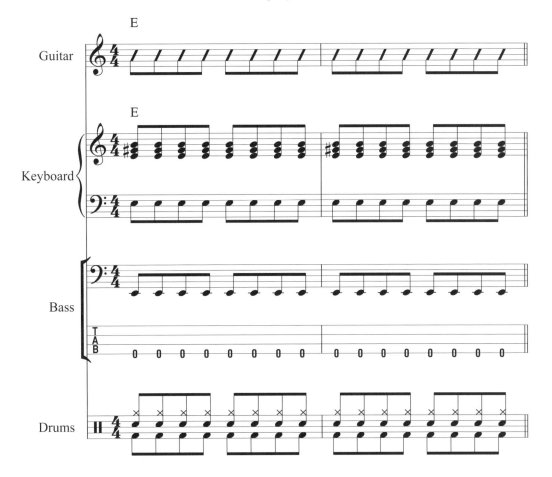

VERSE

Ami   **D**
Oye como va, mi ritmo.

Ami   **D**
Bueno pa gozar, mulata.

Ami   **D**
Oye como va, mi ritmo.

Ami   **D**
Bueno pa gozar, mulata.

Skill	4	3	2	1	Next Steps
GUITAR Ami and E Composing Riffs, Chords, and Vocals	Student can play Ami and E accurately and in time / Student can compose a unique riff and perform it in the context of a musical performance / Student can sing with accurate pitch and in time while playing the Guitar	Student can play Ami and E accurately and mostly in time / Student can compose a unique riff and play it in time / Student can sing while playing the Guitar	Student can play Ami and E / Student can compose a unique riff / Student can speak lyrics while playing the Guitar	Student struggles to play Ami and E / Student struggles to compose a unique riff / Student cannot sing or speak lyrics while playing the Guitar	
KEYBOARD Composing Riffs, Chords, and Vocals Transposition	Student can perform any major or minor triad / Student can compose a unqiue riff and perform it in the context of a musical performance / Student can sing with accurate pitch and time while playing the Keyboard	Student can perform any major or minor triad using Jam Cards / Student can compose a unique riff and play it in time / Student can sing while playing the Keyboard	Student struggles to use Jam Cards to identify new chords / Student can compose a unique riff / Student can speak lyrics while playing the Keyboard	Student struggles to use Jam Cards to identify new chords / Student struggles to compose a unique riff / Student cannot sing or speak lyrics while playing the Keyboard	
BASS Composing Riffs, Chords, and Vocals Creating a Bass Part	Student can compose a unique riff and perform it in the context of a musical performance / Student can sing with accurate pitch and in time while playing the Bass / Student can compose a bass part using appropriate passing tones	Student can compose a unique riff and play it in time / Student can sing while playing the Bass / Student can compose a bass part using root notes	Student can compose a unique riff / Student can speak lyrics while playing the Bass / Student can play root notes in time	Student struggles to compose a unique riff / Student cannot sing or speak lyrics while playing the Bass / Student struggles to compose a unique bass line	
DRUMS Latin Grooves Clave Guiro Flam	Student can play 3-2 and 2-3 clave and guiro patterns in time at a variety of tempos and switch smoothly between them / Student can play flams accurately and add them to their performance in stylistically appropriate places	Student can play 3-2 and 2-3 clave and guiro patterns in time at a variety of tempos / Student can play flams accurately and add them to their performance	Student can play 3-2 and 2-3 clave and guiro patterns in time and at least one tempo / Student can play flams accurately	Student struggles to play 3-2 and 2-3 clave and guiro patterns in time / Student cannot play flams accurately	

> **Music Theory:** Guitar, keyboard, and bass players will practice reading various patterns and playing syncopated patterns. Guitarists will apply muted strumming technique. Drummers will read a new pattern in preparation for the reggaeton pattern they will learn this section and will practice playing accented hi-hat notes on upbeats.
>
> **Instrument Technique:** Guitarists will play bends, keyboardists will read parts with separate hands, bassists will focus on straight eighth-note patterns, and drummers will play cross-stick patterns.
>
> **Music Theory:** Guitar, keyboard, and bass players will play syncopated patterns.
>
> **Full Band Song:** "Waka Waka (This Time for Africa)" by Shakira

Instrument Technique/Music Theory

 33 34 34

MU:Pr5.1.3

b) Rehearse to refine technical accuracy, expressive qualities, and identified performance challenges.

MU:Pr6.1.4

a) Perform music, alone or with others, with expression and technical accuracy, and appropriate interpretation.

GUITAR

Instrument Technique: Riffs on 5th and 6th Strings

One way to keep your fingers nimble is to learn more riffs. Here are a few more that focus on strings 5 and 6.

COME AS YOU ARE
Nirvana

U CAN'T TOUCH THIS
MC Hammer

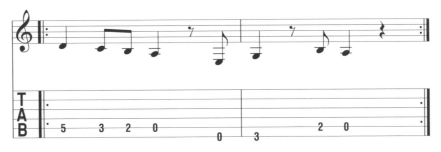

UPTOWN FUNK
Mark Ronson ft. Bruno Mars

KEYBOARD

Music Theory: Melodic Note Reading

One way to keep practicing your reading is to learn more riffs. With these riffs, you can focus on some new rhythmic concepts. This song has rhythms we haven't yet read in this book. However, you can use your ear to listen to the song to learn the rhythms.

BURN
Ellie Goulding

This example has many notes played on the upbeats. We've added counting underneath the notes:

PUSH IT
Salt-N-Pepa

BASS

Instrument Technique: Two-String Riffs

One way to keep your fingers nimble is to learn more riffs. On the next page are a few more that focus on two strings.

COME AS YOU ARE

Nirvana

U CAN'T TOUCH THIS

MC Hammer

UPTOWN FUNK

Mark Ronson ft. Bruno Mars

Instrument Technique

🎸 33	🎹 34	🎸 34	🥁 46

MU:Pr5.1.H.5

a) Apply teacher-provided criteria to critique individual performances of a varied repertoire of music that includes melodies, repertoire pieces, and chordal accompaniments selected for performance, and apply practice strategies to address performance challenges and refine the performances.

MU:Pr5.1.3

b) Rehearse to refine technical accuracy, expressive qualities, and identified performance challenges.

Instrument Technique: The Bend ▶

To **bend** a note, play the fret shown in the tab and then pull the string down toward the floor or push up toward the ceiling. The pitch will go up as you bend. Bending to the exact pitch takes some practice, so play along with the Jam Track or the original recording to work on it.

THE MAN WHO SOLD THE WORLD 🔊
David Bowie

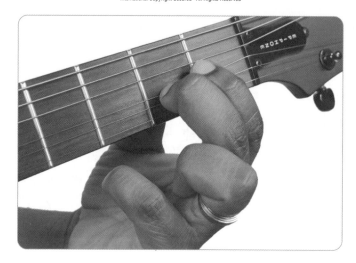

The fraction ("1/2") above the note means the bent note should sound one **half step** (or one fret) higher. So bending the 2nd fret one half step should sound like the 3rd fret on the same string.

In this next example, the "1/4" bend means to bend the string just a little bit. This will create a note that is "between the frets," which is more of an expressive effect than a specific pitch. Again, use the Jam Track or original recording as a guide and practice along with it to match the bend.

SUPERMASSIVE BLACK HOLE 🔊
Muse

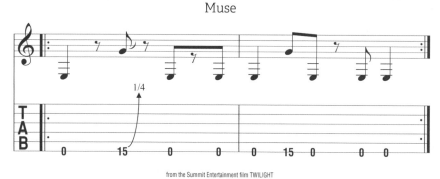

Instrument Technique: Steady Eighth Notes ▶

A bassist is just as important as a drummer when it comes to keeping time. When playing steady eighth notes, bassists often alternate between their index and middle finger. If you're using a pick, alternate between upstrokes and downstrokes.

Here are a few bass lines that have steady eighth notes:

WITH OR WITHOUT YOU 🔊
U2

SUPERMASSIVE BLACK HOLE 🔊
Muse

 # ZOMBIE 🔊
The Cranberries

Always practice these bass lines with the Jam Tracks or a metronome to make sure you're playing steady and in time.

MU:Pr5.1.3

b) Rehearse to refine technical accuracy, expressive qualities, and identified performance challenges.

MU:Re7.1.3

a) Demonstrate and describe how selected music connects to and is influenced by specific interests, experiences, or purposes.

Music Theory: Calypso

The **calypso** drumbeat has slightly different rhythms and note placements than many of the previous drumbeats, but it will help lead into the next patterns:

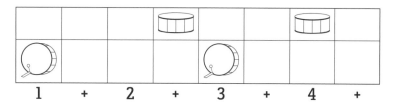 

This drumbeat, though rooted in Caribbean styles of music, has had a major influence on popular music and is used in songs such as "Cheap Thrills" by Sia ft. Sean Paul and "One Dance" by Drake ft. Wizkid & Kyla:

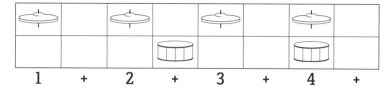 

You can add the kick drum on beats 1 and 3:

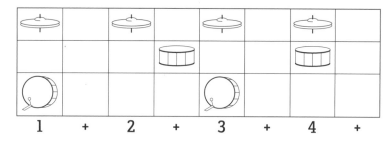 

Think of these drumbeats as being played in double time (counting it twice as fast).

New Techniques: Expanding on Calypso

You can also play this same pattern with open hi-hats on beats 1 and 3 as you play the kick drum:

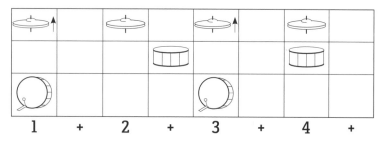 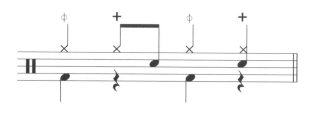

Instrument Technique: Cross-Stick

Another commonly used technique pertaining to the drums is the cross-stick. Here is the symbol we'll use in our drumbeat diagrams and in standard staff notation:

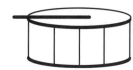

To play a cross-stick, lay your drumstick across the snare drum with about one-third of the stick hanging over the edge. Keeping the tip of the stick on the head of drum, lift it and bring it down against the rim.

Try your favorite drumbeats with a cross-stick instead of a typical snare hit

.

Music Theory/Instrument Technique: Syncopation

🎸 35   🎹 34   🎸 35   🥁 47

MU:Pr5.1.4

a) Apply teacher-provided and collaboratively-developed criteria and feedback to evaluate accuracy and expressiveness of ensemble and personal performances.
b) Rehearse to refine technical accuracy and expressive qualities, and address performance challenges.

MU:Re7.2.2

a) Describe how specific music concepts are used to support a specific purpose in music.

GUITAR

Instrument Technique: Syncopation and Muted Strums

Earlier, you played various syncopated strumming patterns. A common technique to add to these strumming patterns is the percussive muted string strum.

To get this sound, first lay the palm of your picking hand across all the strings near the bridge:

Then, without lifting your hand off the strings, strum through these muted strings. The strings should click, rather than ring out.

Muted strings are often notated with an "X." Mute the strings on beat 2 with this next song. Then, lift your palm off the strings before you play the upstroke on the "and" of beat 2. Practice this slowly until you can play the muted strum in one continuous motion. Try it out first with just the Emi chord:

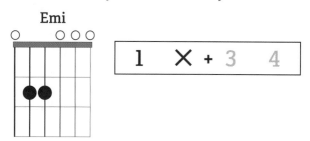

Now, try it with a song:

HELLO
Adele

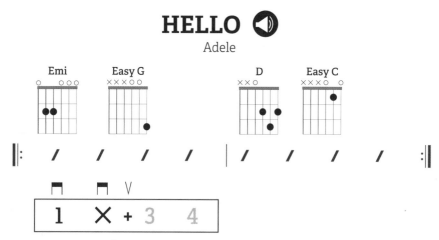

Use the same strumming pattern on this next song:

SEE YOU AGAIN
Wiz Khalifa ft. Charlie Puth

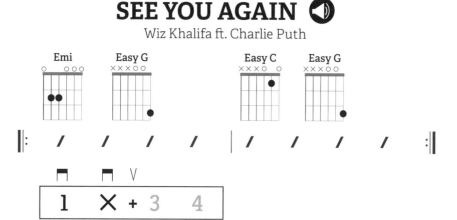

Try applying muted strumming to a song you played earlier using this syncopated reggae pattern:

STIR IT UP
Bob Marley & the Wailers

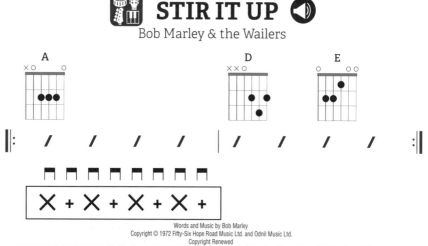

Music Theory: Syncopated Patterns

Here is a new comping pattern with syncopation; the Jam Track features only a drumbeat:

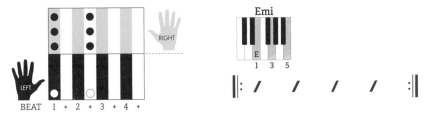

If you take that same comping pattern but change the chords (two chords per bar), then you can play some other songs:

HELLO
Adele

SEE YOU AGAIN
Wiz Khalifa ft. Charlie Puth

This last song features a **reggae** pattern; the Jam Track includes only drums for you to play with:

WAITING IN VAIN
Bob Marley & the Wailers

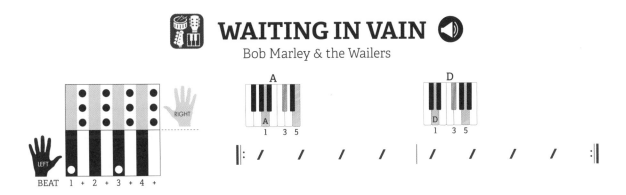

Notice that the left hand always plays on beats 1 and 3 while the right hand plays on the upbeats.

Music Theory: Syncopated Patterns

These next patterns, in which upbeats are played after skipping downbeats, are called **syncopated** rhythms. To practice with the Jam Track, follow the rhythm of the bass drum and play an open E on beats 1 and the "and" of beat 2.

If you take that same pattern but change the notes (two per bar), you can play a few other songs:

HELLO
Adele

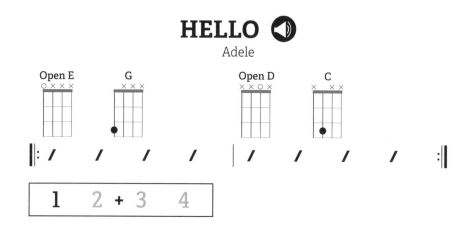

SEE YOU AGAIN
Wiz Khalifa ft. Charlie Puth

MU:Pr4.2.4

a) Demonstrate understanding of the structure and the elements of music (such as rhythm, pitch, and form) in music selected for performance.

MU:Pr4.3.3

a) Demonstrate and describe how intent is conveyed through expressive qualities (such as dynamics and tempo).

MU:Pr5.1.4

a) Apply teacher-provided and collaboratively-developed criteria and feedback to evaluate accuracy and expressiveness of ensemble and personal performances.

b) Rehearse to refine technical accuracy and expressive qualities, and address performance challenges.

MU:Pr6.1.4

a) Perform music, alone or with others, with expression and technical accuracy, and appropriate interpretation.

MU:Re7.2.2

a) Describe how specific music concepts are used to support a specific purpose in music.

Playing Bass Lines: Reggae Bass

Keeping note length and stylistically appropriate rhythms in mind, you can play this reggae song by Bob Marley & the Wailers. Keeping the bass notes short is iconic of much reggae music.

STIR IT UP
Bob Marley & the Wailers

WORLD-A-MUSIC
Ini Kamoze

54-46, THAT'S MY NUMBER
The Maytals

DRUMS

MU:Pr4.1.4

a) Demonstrate and explain how the selection of music to perform is influenced by personal interest, knowledge, context, and technical skill.

MU:Pr4.2.4

a) Demonstrate understanding of the structure and the elements of music (such as rhythm, pitch, and form) in music selected for performance.

MU:Pr4.3.3

a) Demonstrate and describe how intent is conveyed through expressive qualities (such as dynamics and tempo).

MU:Pr5.1.4

a) Apply teacher-provided and collaboratively-developed criteria and feedback to evaluate accuracy and expressiveness of ensemble and personal performances.

b) Rehearse to refine technical accuracy and expressive qualities, and address performance challenges.

Reggaeton/Ska/Rock Steady

A common pattern in **reggaeton** (another name for **reggae**), **ska**, and other Jamaican influenced music is the **one-drop** beat (previously mentioned briefly in Section 4).

This beat has the kick drum and snare playing together on beats 2 and 4:

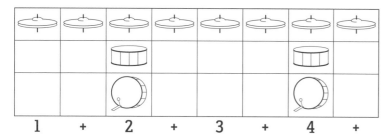 

Try playing the one-drop beat on "Waiting in Vain" by Bob Marley & the Wailers:

WAITING IN VAIN 🔊
Bob Marley & the Wailers

Music Theory: Accents ▶

To make this beat sound more authentic, you can play **accents** on the upbeats. An accent is when you play slightly louder on a note, making it "pop" within the texture. In standard notation, an accent is represented by this symbol above the note: >

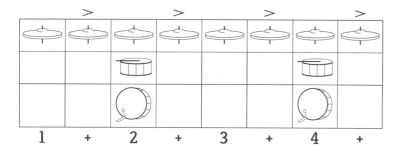 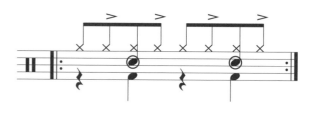

This drumbeat works for other reggae and pop songs too, such as:

- "Is This Love" by Bob Marley & the Wailers
- "With My Own Two Hands" by Ben Harper (You can try this one with cross-stick variations.)
- "One Way Ticket" by Carrie Underwood
- "Do You Really Want to Hurt Me" by Culture Club

Full Band Song: WAKA WAKA
(THIS TIME FOR AFRICA)
Shakira

 37   35   37   48

MU:Pr4.2.3

a) Demonstrate understanding of the structure in music selected for performance.

b) When analyzing selected music, read and perform rhythmic patterns and melodic phrases using iconic and standard notation.

c) Describe how context (such as personal and social) can inform a performance.

MU:Pr4.3.2

a) Demonstrate understanding of expressive qualities (such as dynamics and tempo) and how creators use them to convey expressive intent.

MU:Pr5.1.3

a) Apply teacher-provided and collaboratively-developed criteria and feedback to evaluate accuracy of ensemble performances.

b) Rehearse to refine technical accuracy, expressive qualities, and identified performance challenges.

MU:Pr6.1.2

a) Perform music for a specific purpose with expression and technical accuracy.

b) Perform appropriately for the audience and purpose.

MU:Re7.2.3

a) Demonstrate and describe how a response to music can be informed by the structure, the use of the elements of music, and context (such as personal and social).

MU:Pr4.2.E.5

a) Demonstrate, using music reading skills where appropriate, how knowledge of formal aspects in musical works inform prepared or improvised performances.

MU:Pr4.3.E.5

a) Identify expressive qualities in a varied repertoire of music that can be demonstrated through prepared and improvised performances.

MU:Pr6.1.E.5

a) Demonstrate attention to technical accuracy and expressive qualities in prepared and improvised performances of a varied repertoire of music.

MU:Pr6.1.E.5

b) Demonstrate an awareness of the context of the music through prepared and improvised performances.

MU:Re8.1.E.5

a) Identify interpretations of the expressive intent and meaning of musical works, referring to the elements of music, contexts, and (when appropriate) the setting of the text.

MU:Pr4.2.H.5

a) Identify prominent melodic and harmonic characteristics in a varied repertoire of music that includes melodies, repertoire pieces, and chordal accompaniments selected for performance, including at least some based on reading standard notation.

MU:Pr5.1.H.5

a) Apply teacher-provided criteria to critique individual performances of a varied repertoire of music that includes melodies, repertoire pieces, and chordal accompaniments selected for performance, and apply practice strategies to address performance challenges and refine the performances.

MU:Pr6.1.H.5

a) Perform with expression and technical accuracy in individual performances of a varied repertoire of music that includes melodies, repertoire pieces, and chordal accompaniments, demonstrating understanding of the audience and the context.

Performance Notes

The chord progression of this song never changes, so Modern Bands can make arrangement decisions. Students can recite the recording exactly, or they can come up with their own arrangements by using different musical elements, timbres, and dynamics during each section. For example, there are short solo sections in the recording, which is an opportunity for students to improvise their own solo. Perhaps a dance break would bring the audience to their feet? The possibilities are virtually endless!

Guitar: The rhythm the guitar plays in the verse should match the snare drum rhythm. Even though students haven't learned to read 16th-note comping patterns, they should be encouraged to listen and match the rhythm of the snare drum. In the Chorus, students can match the syncopated rhythm by playing the bass note of each chord before strumming the whole chord.

Keyboard: The keyboard part is mostly held chords. Keyboard players can use inversions to make playing the chord progression easier. They should also explore the sounds on their keyboards based on what they heard in the recording and what ideas they bring to the arrangement.

Bass: This bass line includes 5ths and octaves in the tablature, which we haven't learned as a concept yet, so it is a good first introduction. They can also explore the register by finding higher or lower octaves of the roots to change the texture.

Drums: There are really three different drum parts to this song, and each part is arranged by layering one of more of those drum parts. There are the four on the floor kick drum, the snare hits, and the hi-hat part. The textures in the recording are created by layering these in various ways. However, there are also several parts to add in hand and other auxiliary percussion parts. Feel free to throw in other instruments as well.

Vocals: There are many layers to the vocals in this song, which is a great opportunity to feature many singers. The Verses and Bridge can be sung by individual singers, while the Chorus has a large group part.

Suggestions for Further Repertoire

- The drum part for this song uses a common reggaeton drum pattern, which, due to reggaeton's influence on popular music, has become a common drum pattern in many pop songs, such as "Cheap Thrills," "One Dance," "Shape of You," and "Despacito."

Iconic Score

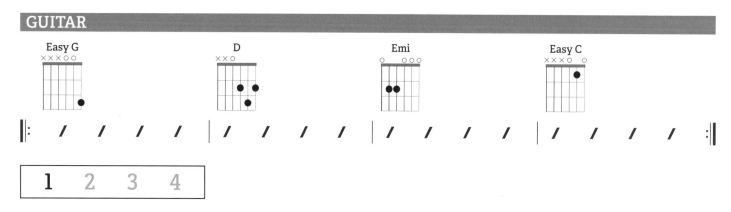

KEYBOARD

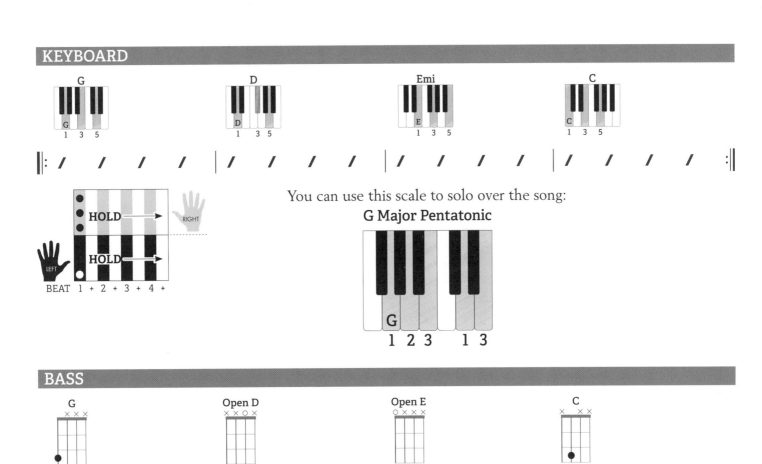

You can use this scale to solo over the song:

G Major Pentatonic

BASS

DRUMS

Rhythm Figure 1

1	e	+	a	2	e	+	a	3	e	+	a	4	e	+	a

Rhythm Figure 2

1	e	+	a	2	e	+	a	3	e	+	a	4	e	+	a

Rhythm Figure 3

1	e	+	a	2	e	+	a	3	e	+	a	4	e	+	a

Rhythm Figure 4

1	e	+	a	2	e	+	a	3	e	+	a	4	e	+	a

Standard Staff Score

Intro/Verse

Pre-Chorus/Bridge

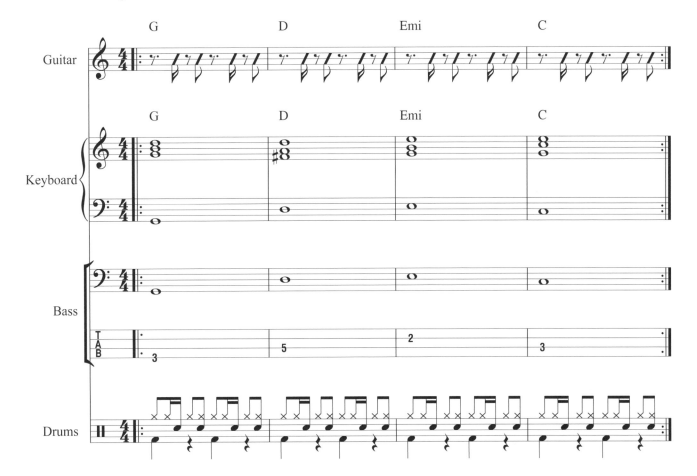

Chorus

VERSE

G   D
You're a good soldier, choosing your battles.

      Emi   C
Pick yourself up and dust yourself off and get back in the saddle.

G   D
You're on the front line, everyone's watching.

      Emi   C
You know it's serious, we're getting closer, this isn't over.

G   D   Emi   C
The pressure's on, you feel it. But you got it all, believe it.

PRE-CHORUS

G   D
When you fall get up, oh, oh. And if you fall get up, eh, eh.

      Emi   C
Tsamina mina zangalewa, 'cause this is Africa.

CHORUS

G   D   Emi   C
Tsamina mina, eh, eh. Waka waka, eh, eh. Tsamina mina zangalewa, this time for Africa.

VERSE

G   D   Emi
Listen to your God. This is our motto. Your time to shine,

                    C
don't wait in line, y vamos por todo.

G   D   Emi
People are raising their expectations. Go on and feed them,

                    C
this is your moment, no hesitation.

G   D   Emi   C
Today's your day, I feel it. You paved the way, believe it.

PRE-CHORUS

G   D
If you get down get up, oh, oh. When you get down get up, eh, eh.

      Emi   C
Tsamina mina zangalewa, this time for Africa.

BRIDGE

G
Awabuye lamajoni, ipikipiki mama wa A to Z.

Bathi susa lamajoni, ipikipiki mama from East to West.

Bathi waka waka ma eh eh,

Waka waka ma eh eh,

Zonk' izizwe mazibuye, 'cause this is Africa.

The Official 2010 FIFA World Cup Song
Words and Music by Shakira, Zolani Mahola, John Hill, Eugene Victor Doo Belley, Jean Ze Bella and Emile Kojidie
Copyright © 2010 Sony Music Publishing LLC, MyMPM Music, Freshly Ground, EMI April Music Inc., RodeoMan Music and Sony Music Publishing (Germany) Gmbh
All Rights Administered by Sony Music Publishing LLC, 424 Church Street, Suite 1200, Nashville, TN 37219
International Copyright Secured All Rights Reserved

SECTION 8—SAMPLE RUBRIC

Skill	4	3	2	1	Next Steps
GUITAR Syncopation	Student can perform bends with accurate pitch and time	Student can perform bends in time	Student can perform bends out of time	Student cannot perform bends	
KEYBOARD Two-Part Readings Syncopation	Student and learn and perform two-hand part in time	Student can learn and perform two-hand parts out of time	Student can perform individual hands of two-part music	Student can play only one of the hands of two-part music	
BASS Steady Eighth-Note Patterns Syncopated Comping Patterns	Student can perform eighth-note patterns in time with even note length and at a variety of tempos	Student can perform eighth-note patterns in time and at a variety of tempos	Student can perform eighth-note patterns	Student cannot perform eighth-note patterns	
DRUMS Island Grooves Reggaeton Beats Cross-Stick Flam	Student can play a full reggaeton pattern at a variety of tempos	Student can play a full reggaeton pattern	Student can play at least two parts of a reggaeton pattern	Student can perform one part of a reggaeton drum pattern	

SECTION 9 39 🎹 37 🎸 39 🥁 50

Music Theory: Students will read and transcribe patterns that use dotted half notes. Bassists will focus on note lengths. Drummers will practice playing snare hits on every beat or upbeat in the measure.

Comping: Full C and G chords. Guitarists will practice these chords in the context of various songs. Keyboard players will apply inversions to comping. Bassists will practice playing grooves they can use for accompaniment. Drummers will listen to songs to determine various grooves they can use to accompany different songs.

Composition: Students will write songs with verses and choruses using new chords they learned in this section.

Improvisation: Students will practice the full major and minor pentatonic scale over various songs.

Full Band Song: "Best Day of My Life" by American Authors

Music Theory: Reading Comprehension and Transcribing

 39   37   39   50

This warm-up section reinforces note reading with familiar material for the guitar and piano, while the bass re-examines the role of note length, giving value to not just when to play the note, but how the silence surrounding the note can affect feel. Drums will focus on practicing left-hand independence, working on playing the snare drum on any beat while keeping all other elements of a drumbeat consistent.

After the students have played through the riff, they can reinforce their understanding of the note names by singing the letter names first. They can say it in their speaking voices first *a cappella*. Once they feel comfortable, they can begin to play the riff on their instrument while saying and/or singing the letter names.

GUITAR

MU:Pr5.3.E.5

a) Use self-reflection and peer feedback to refine individual and ensemble performances of a varied repertoire of music.

MU:Pr5.1.C.I

c) Identify and implement strategies for improving the technical and expressive aspects of multiple works.

MU:Pr5.1.6

a) Identify and apply teacher-provided criteria (such as correct interpretation of notation, technical accuracy, originality, and interest) to rehearse, refine, and determine when a piece is ready to perform.

Music Theory: Transcribing Notation

Play through the melody of this song. The first four measures are written in tab. Then, write in the correct pitches on the traditional staff. The first note is provided for you.

LITTLE TALKS
Of Monsters and Men

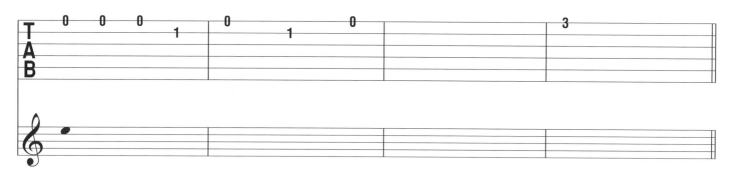

The last four measures are written below in staff notation. Write in the tab numbers. Don't worry about the rhythmic notation for now.

This last example has two new types of rhythmic symbols: the **dot** and the **tie**. When you see a dotted note, the dot adds half the value of the note to itself. So a **dotted quarter note** is one and a half beats.

Ties connect the notes. For example, the tied quarter and whole notes equal a total of five beats. You only pick the first note and then let it ring for five beats.

KEYBOARD

MU:Pr5.3.E.5

a) Use self-reflection and peer feedback to refine individual and ensemble performances of a varied repertoire of music.

MU:Pr5.1.C.I

c) Identify and implement strategies for improving the technical and expressive aspects of multiple works.

MU:Pr5.1.6

a) Identify and apply teacher-provided criteria (such as correct interpretation of notation, technical accuracy, originality, and interest) to rehearse, refine, and determine when a piece is ready to perform.

Music Theory: Notating Riffs

Play through this melody of "Little Talks" by Of Monsters and Men. The first four measures are written in notation. Write in the correct letter name above the rhythms:

LITTLE TALKS
Of Monsters and Men

In that last example, we added a new type of rhythm: the **dotted note**. The dot adds half the value of the note back to itself. In this case, the dotted quarter notes equal one and a half beats. The last four measures of this melody are written using note names and rhythms. Rewrite the melody in the staff below:

BASS

MU:Pr5.1.H.5

a) Apply teacher-provided criteria to critique individual performances of a varied repertoire of music that includes melodies, repertoire pieces, and chordal accompaniments selected for performance, and apply practice strategies to address performance challenges and refine the performances.

MU:Re7.2.2

a) Describe how specific music concepts are used to support a specific purpose in music.

MU:Re7.2.E.5

a) Identify how knowledge of context and the use of repetition, similarities, and contrasts inform the response to music.

Music Theory: A Focus on Note Length

The length of a note makes a big difference in the feel of a groove. A bass player can play the same notes and rhythms but change the feel of a song by changing whether they play short or long notes.

*Note—The next examples contain **half rests**. This is a mark that tells the performer to stop playing for two beats. One half rest is the same as two quarter rests.

Play through this exercise, making sure to mute the note at the right time by gently touching the string with your left and/or right hand.

Here's that same exercise on a different note. To mute a note that you're fretting, simply release the pressure used to play that note in the left hand. (Don't take your finger completely off the string.)

As you listen to and learn new music, be sure to listen to the length of the notes the bass player is playing. Accurately controlling note length will make a big difference in how you fill your role and sound as a bass player.

Below is a song that has changing note lengths. The first time through the pattern, the bass plays quarter notes, each lasting one beat. The second time through, the bass plays whole notes, each lasting four beats. Then, the entire sequence repeats.

Listen carefully to the recording and match the note length.

SAIL
AWOLNATION

Take another look at these bass lines you've played before, but this time, pay careful attention to note lengths. For example, in both riffs the note played on the 5th fret is held down longer than most of the other notes. Performing these bass lines with careful attention to note length will push you forward to sounding like an accomplished bass player.

> Though these examples use 16th notes, students can learn them by ear instead of focusing on reading those rhythms. This emphasis on aural skills will help students to listen carefully for note length.

Try playing these few bass lines:

HYPNOTIZE
The Notorious BIG

MY OWN WORST ENEMY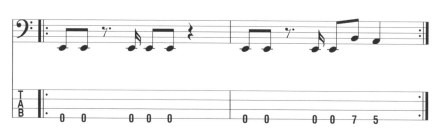
Lit

Note lengths are not always notated on the tab staff, which is one of the benefits of staff notation... and a reminder that it's important to use your ear to play these songs accurately.

MU:Pr4.1.E.5

a) Select varied repertoire to study based on interest, music reading skills (where appropriate), an understanding of the structure of the music, context, and the technical skill of the individual or ensemble.

MU:Pr4.2.1

b) When analyzing selected music, read and perform rhythmic patterns using iconic or standard notation.

MU:Pr4.3.1

a) Demonstrate and describe music's expressive qualities (such as dynamics and tempo).

MU:Pr5.1.2

a) Apply established criteria to judge the accuracy, expressiveness, and effectiveness of performances.

MU:Pr5.3.E.5

a) Use self-reflection and peer feedback to refine individual and ensemble performances of a varied repertoire of music.

Playing Drumbeats: Funk Drumming

Funk drumming is **syncopated**, or has lots of accented notes that happen between the downbeats. It also uses several types of different sounds. As you'll see in the next section, some of the most popular beats sampled in rap, R&B, and hip-hop music are from funk and soul records made in the 1960s–1980s. In funk music, having a solid grasp of hi-hat technique is crucial to getting a good sound. These types of drumbeats have a mixture of open and closed hi-hat figures.

Warm-Up: Left Hand Freedom ▶

You've practiced being independent with your right foot, now try the same idea with your left hand. To start, play with just your hands, and then add your bass drum on beats 1 and 3. Each drumbeat here is written in either staff notation or in a drumbeat diagram. After playing each drumbeat, rewrite it in standard notation and vice versa:

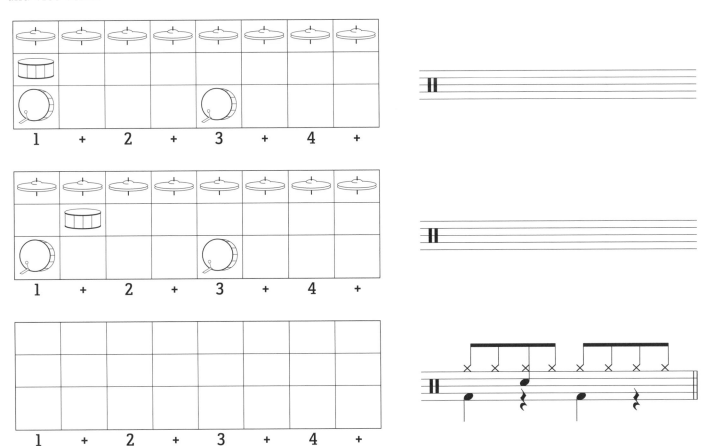

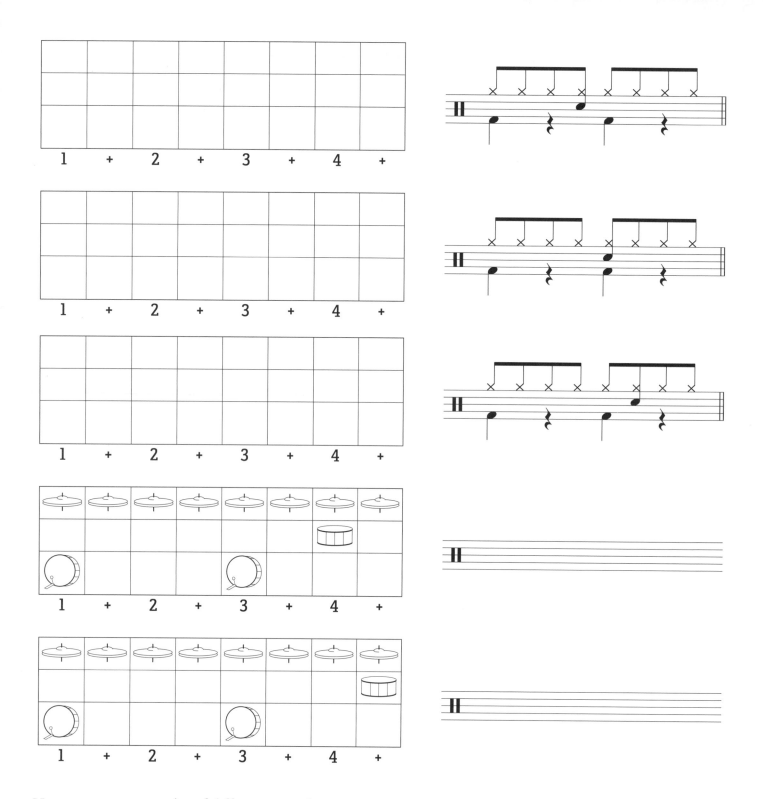

Here are some examples of different snare hits in songs:

TWIST AND SHOUT

The Beatles

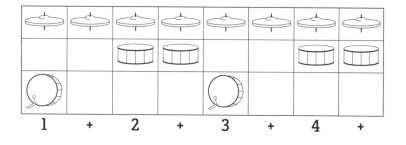

REACH OUT I'LL BE THERE

The Four Tops

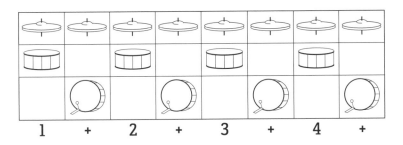

Instrument Skills: Funk Hi-Hat ▶

This beat is used in songs like "Get Up Offa That Thing" by James Brown:

GET UP OFFA THAT THING 🔊

James Brown

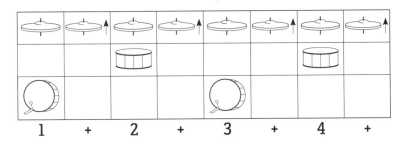

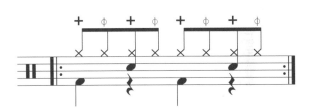

At first glance, it looks like a typical backbeat. However, the hi-hat is going to be what makes this beat sound funkier. Practice it just on its own. Your right hand will still play the same rhythm on each eighth note, but your left foot will lift up on the upbeats and close down on the beats.

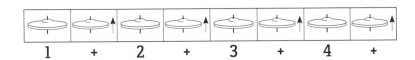

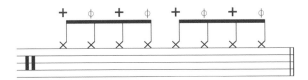

Now, try it all together:

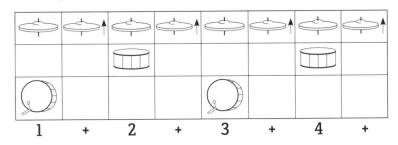

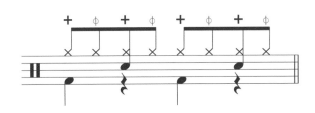

The next example has opened hi-hat only after beats 1 and 3. Notice that the second lift happens at the same time as a bass drum hit. It may help to first learn the groove without the opened hi-hat parts and then add them in later. This beat is used in songs like "Thank You (Falettin Me Be Mice Elf Again)" by Sly and the Family Stone:

THANK YOU (FALETTIN ME BE MICE ELF AGAIN)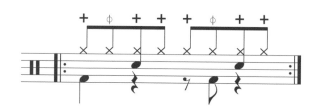
Sly and the Family Stone

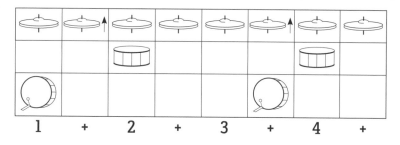

Composition: Verse and Chorus

Now that you know additional drum sounds and grooves, it's time to write more of your own verse and chorus drumbeats. Keep in mind everything you've learned about groove, beat placement, and instrument choices as you write your verse and chorus drumbeats.

Verse

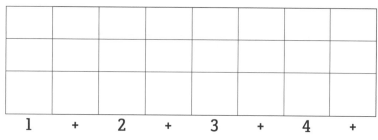

Chorus

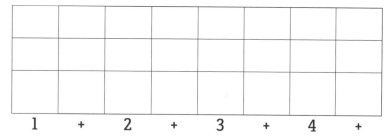

Improvisation

MU:Cr1.1.E.5

a) Compose and improvise melodic and rhythmic ideas or motives that reflect characteristic(s) of music or text(s) studied in rehearsal.

MU:Cr1.1.2

a) Improvise rhythmic and melodic patterns and musical ideas for a specific purpose.

MU:Cr2.1.2

a) Demonstrate and explain personal reasons for selecting patterns and ideas for music that represent expressive intent.

MU:Cr2.1.E.5

a) Select and develop draft melodic and rhythmic ideas or motives that demonstrate understanding of characteristic(s) of music or text(s) studied in rehearsal.

MU:Cr3.1.E.5

a) Evaluate and refine draft compositions and improvisations based on knowledge, skill, and teacher-provided criteria.

MU:Cr3.2.2

a) Convey expressive intent for a specific purpose by presenting a final version of personal musical ideas to peers or informal audience.

MU:Pr5.1.2

b) Rehearse, identify, and apply strategies to address interpretive, performance, and technical challenges of music.

This beat is used in songs like "Brown Eyed Girl" by Van Morrison:

BROWN EYED GIRL
Van Morrison

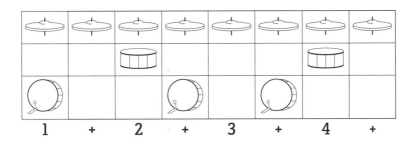

So far, you've mostly accompanied solos for other instruments, meaning the drums have kept the beat while others improvised. Now it's time for your bandmates to accompany you. Take some of the rhythmic soloing ideas from the previous sections, and play them either with the recording or with your bandmates. Here are a few solo ideas for you to try. You can combine them, switch the instrumentation, and extend them to your liking:

Here is an opportunity for your drummers to get a chance to work on soloing. To facilitate this activity in a full band setting, have the rest of the band play a chord progression, riff, or other groove. Instead of the drummer playing the beat to the song, they can play some of these solo ideas or improvise their own rhythms. It is important to not limit musicians to playing only what they are able to read, so provide students with space to improvise both freely and without limitations. Some ideas for expanding this activity are:

- Have students who aren't soloing only play on specific beats of music, such as beat one. This will help them to build their counting skills.
- Have students drop out altogether, challenging the drummer to play in time in their improvisation.
- Ask drummers to play a solo of a specific length, such as one bar, four bars, eight bars, etc. to challenge them to play freely, but while keeping track of the larger form.
- Restrict a drummer to soloing on specific instruments. Limitations can expand creativity.

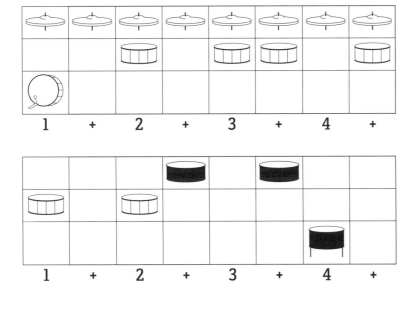

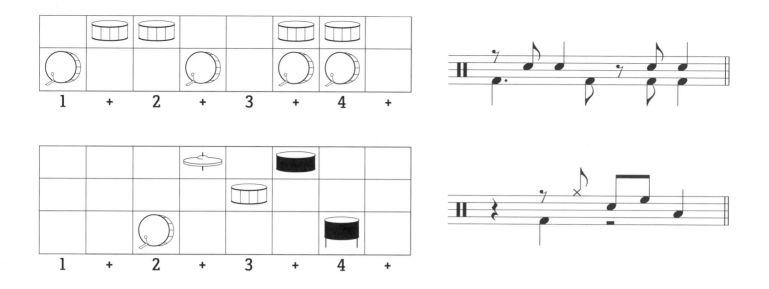

Playing Chords: C and G

 39

MU:Cr1.1.H.5

a) Generate melodic, rhythmic, and harmonic ideas for simple melodies (such as two-phrase) and chordal accompaniments for given melodies.

MU:Pr5.3.E.5

a) Use self-reflection and peer feedback to refine individual and ensemble performances of a varied repertoire of music.

MU:Cr3.2.H.5

a) Share final versions of simple melodies (such as two-phrase) and chordal accompaniments for given melodies, demonstrating an understanding of how to develop and organize personal musical ideas.

MU:Pr5.1.2

b) Rehearse, identify, and apply strategies to address interpretive, performance, and technical challenges of music.

This next instrumental section focuses on a few new chords for guitar, inversions on piano, and grooving with the band for bass and drums. Each instrument learns their technique using the same repertoire, so you can jam with each chord progression together.

Playing Chords: Full C and G

Here is the full version of the easy C chord that you learned earlier. Practice it with the next song.

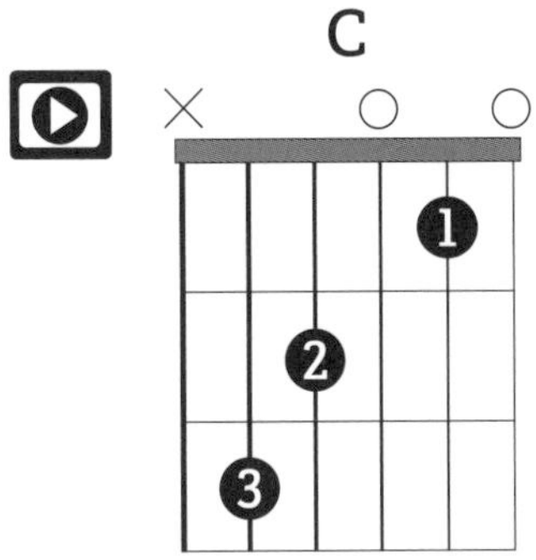

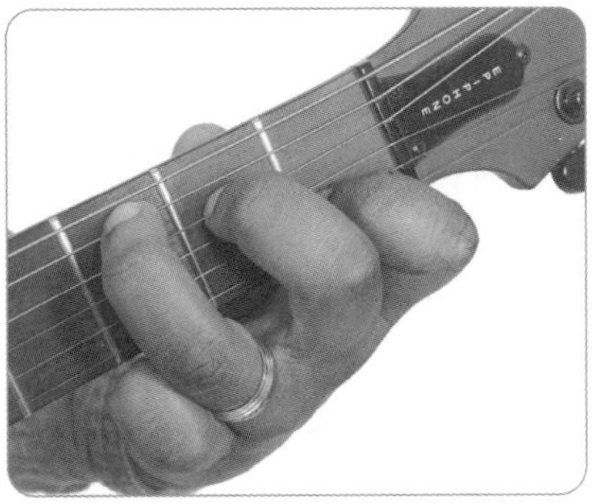

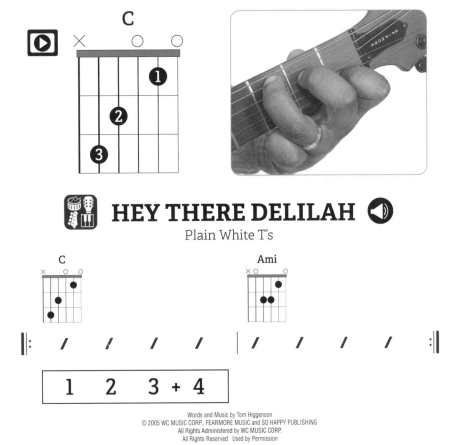

HEY THERE DELILAH

Plain White T's

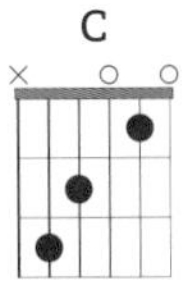

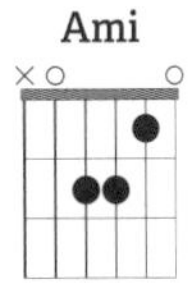

1	2	3 + 4

Rather than lifting your first and second finger between these two chords, you can leave them on the strings and just move your third finger. The fingers that stay put are called **anchor fingers**.

Here is the full version of the easy G chord that you learned earlier. Try it out in the song that follows.

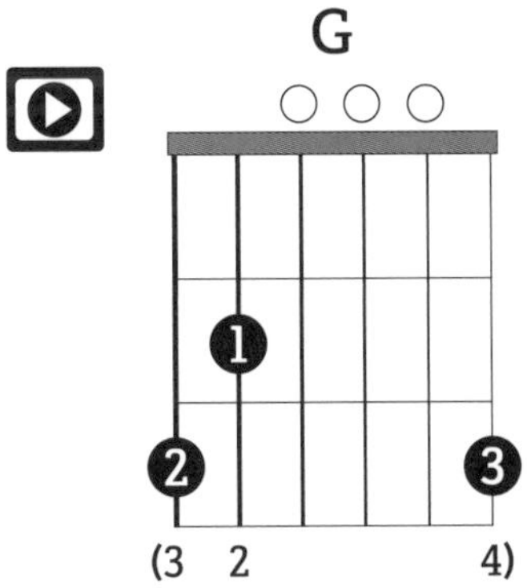

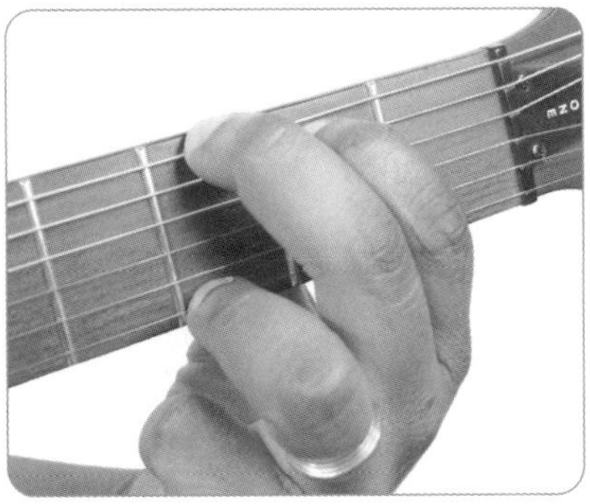

HAITI

Arcade Fire

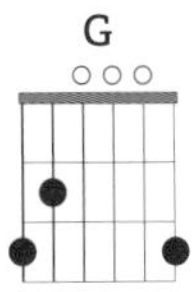

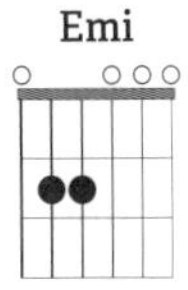

1	2 + 3 + 4

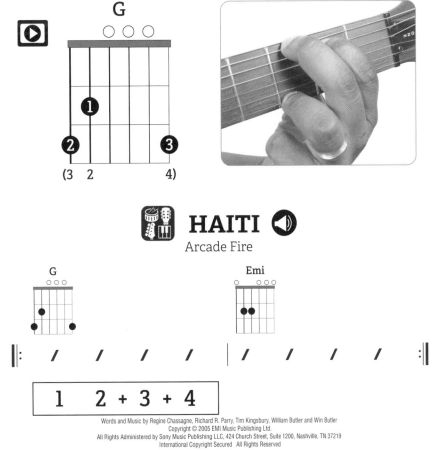

This next song uses both G and C. Play G on beats 1 and 2, then switch to C and play it on the "and" of beat 3, and again on beat 4. In the second measure, play the same pattern but this time with the D and C chords.

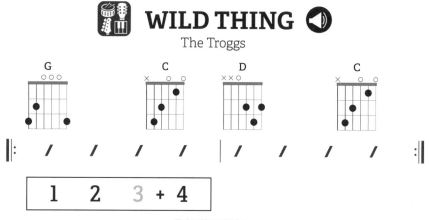

Words and Music by Chip Taylor
Copyright © 1965 EMI Blackwood Music Inc.
Copyright Renewed
All Rights Administered by Sony Music Publishing LLC, 424 Church Street, Suite 1200, Nashville, TN 37219
International Copyright Secured All Rights Reserved

Below is one of the most popular chord progressions in all of popular music:

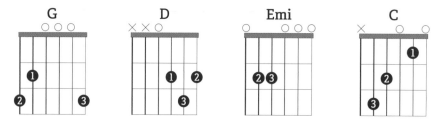

This progression can be found in many songs from the last 60 years, including "Where Is the Love," "Bored to Death," "Demons," "Apologize," "The Edge of Glory," "Someone Like You," and hundreds of others. Try it with the Chorus of the pop song "The Edge of Glory" by Lady Gaga.

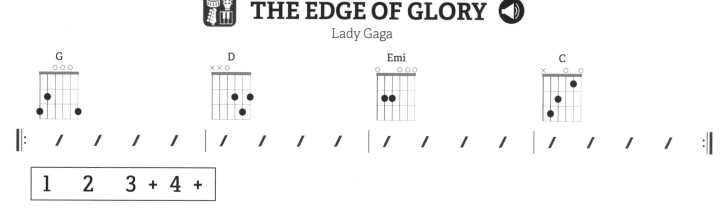

        G   **D**   **Emi**   **C**
I'm on the edge of glory, and I'm hanging on a moment of truth.

        G   **D**   **Emi**   **C**
Out on the edge of glory, and I'm hanging on a moment with you.

        G   **D**   **Emi**   **C**
I'm on the edge, the edge, the edge, the edge, the edge, the edge, the edge.

        G   **D**   **Emi**   **C**
I'm on the edge of glory, and I'm hanging on a moment with you.

        G
I'm on the edge with you.

Words and Music by Stefani Germanotta, Paul Blair and Fernando Garibay
Copyright © 2011 Sony Music Publishing LLC, House Of Gaga Publishing Inc., Universal Music Corp., PW Arrangements, Maxwell And Carter Publishing LLC, Warner-Tamerlane Publishing Corp. and Garibay Music Publishing
All Rights on behalf of Sony Music Publishing LLC and House Of Gaga Publishing Inc. Administered by Sony Music Publishing LLC, 424 Church Street, Suite 1200, Nashville, TN 37219
All Rights on behalf of PW Arrangements and Maxwell And Carter Publishing LLC Administered by Universal Music Corp.
All Rights on behalf of Garibay Music Publishing Administered by Warner-Tamerlane Publishing Corp.
International Copyright Secured All Rights Reserved

MU:Pr5.3.E.5

a) Use self-reflection and peer feedback to refine individual and ensemble performances of a varied repertoire of music.

MU:Cr3.2.H.5

a) Share final versions of simple melodies (such as two-phrase) and chordal accompaniments for given melodies, demonstrating an understanding of how to develop and organize personal musical ideas.

MU:Pr5.1.2

b) Rehearse, identify, and apply strategies to address interpretive, performance, and technical challenges of music.

Music Theory: Inversions

 37

KEYBOARD

So far, when you've played chords on the piano, you have used three notes, and the lowest note has always been the note the chord is named after (the **root**). However, you can play those same three notes in a different order, and it would still be the same chord. Here is the C chord with C as its lowest note:

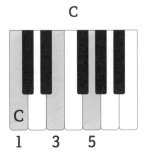

You can **invert** the C chord by taking the C note up an **octave** (same note name in a different spot on the keyboard). This shape is called **1st inversion**, reading E–G–C, from left to right:

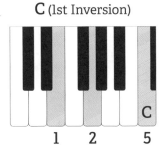

You can do this one more time by moving the E up an octave, ending up with the **2nd inversion** shape, reading G–C–E, from left to right:

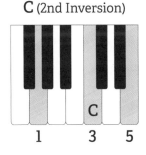

Typically, the left hand will stay on the same root note, or the note the chord is named after, while the right hand plays an inversion. Apply inversions to the progression below. Here is a progression with the chords in root position:

Words and Music by Tom Higgenson
© 2005 WC MUSIC CORP., FEARMORE MUSIC and SO HAPPY PUBLISHING
All Rights Administered by WC MUSIC CORP.
All Rights Reserved Used by Permission

Try moving from a C chord to an Ami in 1st inversion. Note how two of the notes stay in the same place between chords:

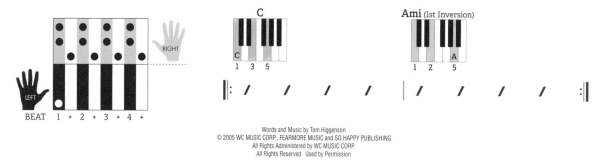

In this next example, do the same thing with a G to Emi progression, starting with the G chord in root position:

Next, try moving from a G to an Emi in 1st inversion. Note how two of the notes stay in the same place between chords:

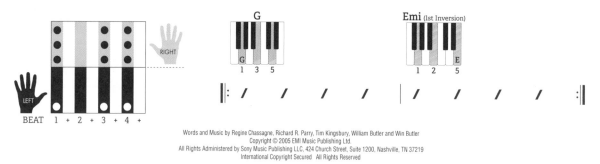

You can use different combinations of inversions and comping patterns for any song. Many professional keyboard players will use different inversions all the time, improvising which ones they want to use on the spot.

The following examples feature a common progression in popular music, giving you an opportunity to move around the keyboard with inversions.

Play the G chord on beats one and two, and then by beat 3, move to C and play "+ 4." Try it first in root position, and then play it with some inversions. Here are all the chords in root position:

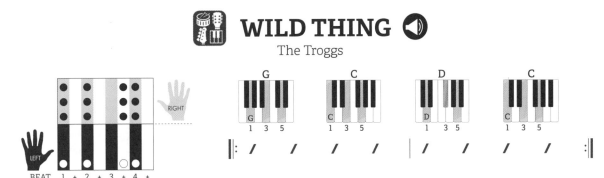

WILD THING
The Troggs

Here's a slightly easier way to play it, starting with G in 1st inversion:

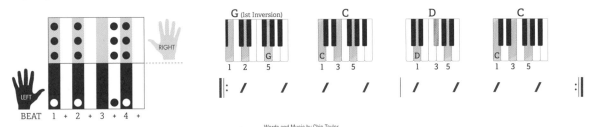

Below is one of the most common chord progressions in all of popular music:

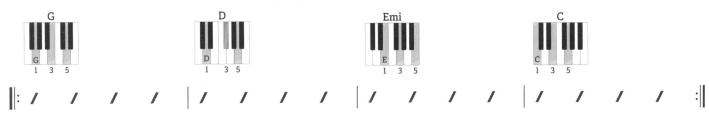

This progression can be found in many songs from the last 60 years, including: "Where Is the Love?" "Bored to Death," "Demons," "Apologize," "The Edge of Glory," "Trouble," "Someone Like You," "Poker Face," and hundreds of others. Try it with the Chorus of the pop song "The Edge of Glory" by Lady Gaga:

THE EDGE OF GLORY
Lady Gaga

Playing Bass Lines: Grooving with the Rest of the Band

 39

BASS

MU:Pr5.3.E.5

a) Use self-reflection and peer feedback to refine individual and ensemble performances of a varied repertoire of music.

MU:Cr3.2.H.5

a) Share final versions of simple melodies (such as two-phrase) and chordal accompaniments for given melodies, demonstrating an understanding of how to develop and organize personal musical ideas.

MU:Pr5.1.2

b) Rehearse, identify, and apply strategies to address interpretive, performance, and technical challenges of music.

MU:Pr6.1.1

a) With limited guidance, perform music for a specific purpose with expression.

MU:Re7.2.1

a) With limited guidance, demonstrate and identify how specific music concepts (such as beat or pitch) are used in various styles of music for a purpose.

Your bandmates who are learning full chords may not yet know just how important your bass playing is in making these songs sound stylistically appropriate. For this tune, keeping the notes long and smooth will match the ballad style of the tune.

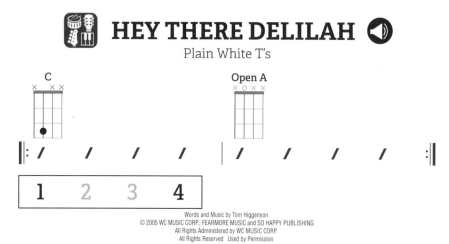

This song is much more rhythmically dynamic than the last. Keeping the notes short helps to drive that rhythm.

This song features a harsh attack on the drums and guitar; try to match that on the bass by plucking or picking the strings with a bit more force.

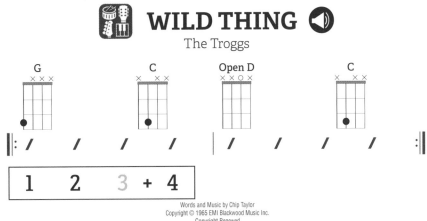

WILD THING

The Troggs

Your bandmates are focusing on the chord progression below. The way you choose to play the root notes G, D, E, and C will make a big difference in how the song sounds.

This progression can be found in many songs from the last 60 years, including "Where Is the Love?" "Bored to Death," "Demons," "Apologize," "The Edge of Glory," "Someone Like You," and hundreds of others. Try it with the Chorus of the pop song "The Edge of Glory" by Lady Gaga.

For a pop dance track, playing on every beat is typical. This reinforces the kick drum and helps drive the music.

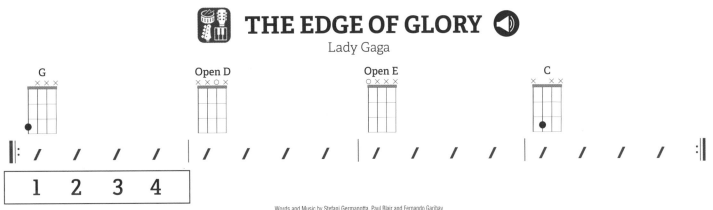

THE EDGE OF GLORY

Lady Gaga

Choosing the Right Groove

 54

DRUMS

MU:Pr4.1.2

a) Demonstrate and explain personal interest in, knowledge about, and purpose of varied musical selections.

MU:Pr4.2.2

a) Demonstrate knowledge of music concepts (such as tonality and meter) in music from a variety of cultures selected for performance.

MU:Pr4.2.2

b) When analyzing selected music, read and perform rhythmic and melodic patterns using iconic or standard notation.

MU:Pr4.3.1

a) Demonstrate and describe music's expressive qualities (such as dynamics and tempo).

MU:Pr5.1.1

a) With limited guidance, apply personal, teacher, and peer feedback to refine performances.

b) With limited guidance, use suggested strategies in rehearsal to address interpretive challenges of music.

MU:Pr6.1.1

a) With limited guidance, perform music for a specific purpose with expression.

MU:Re7.2.K

a) With guidance, demonstrate how a specific music concept (such as beat or melodic direction) is used in music.

MU:Re8.1.2

a) Demonstrate knowledge of music concepts and how they support creators'/performers' expressive intent.

Drums: Choosing the Right Groove

When learning a new tune, you may ask yourself, "What should I play for this song?" Here are some guiding questions to ask when figuring out a drum groove:

- What kinds of instruments do I hear? Which cymbals and drums are playing? Are there other percussion instruments that I might want to emphasize?
- What is the pulse? Clap along to the beat.
- What rhythms are the instruments playing? Play them one at a time, and then write them down to remember for later.
- What is the form of the song?
- What are the dynamics of the song?

Work through the following songs and fill out the blank drumbeat diagrams with new icons if you want to change the instrumentation:

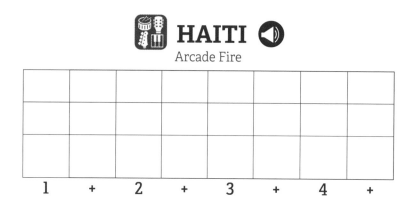

Options

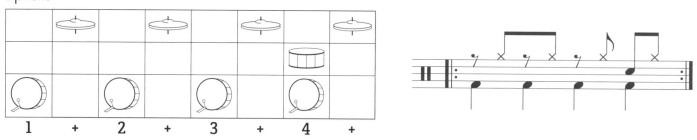

WILD THING

The Troggs

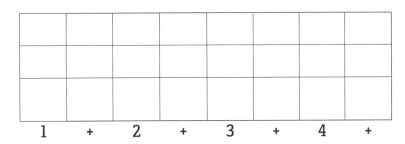

Options

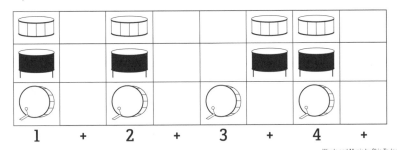

THE EDGE OF GLORY

Lady Gaga

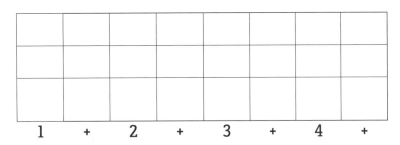

Options

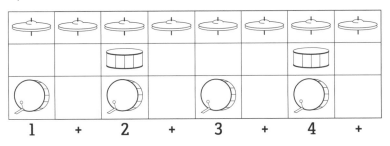

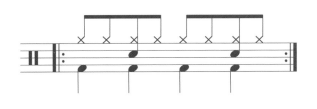

Composition: Verse and Chorus

 42   40   42

MU:Cr1.1.2

a) Improvise rhythmic and melodic patterns and musical ideas for a specific purpose.

b) Generate musical patterns and ideas within the context of a given tonality (such as major and minor) and meter (such as duple and triple).

MU:Cr2.1.2

b) Use iconic or standard notation and/or recording technology to combine, sequence, and document personal musical ideas.

MU:Cr3.1.2

a) Interpret and apply personal, peer, and teacher feedback to revise personal music.

MU:Cr3.2.2

a) Convey expressive intent for a specific purpose by presenting a final version of personal musical ideas to peers or informal audience.

MU:Cr3.2.H.5

a) Share final versions of simple melodies (such as two-phrase) and chordal accompaniments for given melodies, demonstrating an understanding of how to develop and organize personal musical ideas.

MU:Cr1.1.E.5

a) Compose and improvise melodic and rhythmic ideas or motives that reflect characteristic(s) of music or text(s) studied in rehearsal.

MU:Cr2.1.E.5

b) Preserve draft compositions and improvisations through standard notation and audio recording.

MU:Cr3.1.E.5

a) Evaluate and refine draft compositions and improvisations based on knowledge, skill, and teacher-provided criteria.

MU:Cr3.2.E.5

a) Share personally-developed melodic and rhythmic ideas or motives—individually or as an ensemble—that demonstrate understanding of characteristics of music or texts studied in rehearsal.

In order to begin the students' path towards lyric writing, they must begin with short phrases to gain confidence. Once students have created their original chord progression, they can add a one- or two-word vocal phrase on top. If they don't feel comfortable singing just yet, they can simply speak the words. The goal is to be able to repeat the phrase in time while playing the chord progression. If it is too difficult to play and vocalize the phrase, take turns as instrumentalist and singer.

Composition: Verse and Chorus ▶

Now that you know more chords, you can use them to compose songs. Create a new four-chord verse and chorus, using any of the seven open chords you have already learned (A, Ami, C, D, E, Emi, and G). Try using a syncopated rhythm for either your verse or chorus.

Verse Chords:

‖: ╱ ╱ ╱ ╱ | ╱ ╱ ╱ ╱ | ╱ ╱ ╱ ╱ | ╱ ╱ ╱ ╱ :‖

Rhythm/Comping Patterns

GUITAR/BASS

KEYBOARD

BEAT   1   +   2   +   3   +   4

Chorus Chords:

‖: ╱ ╱ ╱ ╱ | ╱ ╱ ╱ ╱ | ╱ ╱ ╱ ╱ | ╱ ╱ ╱ ╱ :‖

Rhythm/Comping Patterns

GUITAR/BASS

KEYBOARD

BEAT   1   +   2   +   3   +   4

Improvisation: Major Pentatonic Scale

 42   🎹 41   🎸 42

MU:Cr1.1.2

a) Improvise rhythmic and melodic patterns and musical ideas for a specific purpose.

b) Generate musical patterns and ideas within the context of a given tonality (such as major and minor) and meter (such as duple and triple).

MU:Cr2.1.2

a) Demonstrate and explain personal reasons for selecting patterns and ideas for music that represent expressive intent.

MU:Cr3.1.2

a) Interpret and apply personal, peer, and teacher feedback to revise personal music.

MU:Pr5.1.2

b) Rehearse, identify, and apply strategies to address interpretive, performance, and technical challenges of music.

MU:Pr6.1.2

a) Perform music for a specific purpose with expression and technical accuracy.

MU:Cr2.1.3

a) Demonstrate selected musical ideas for a simple improvisation or composition to express intent, and describe connection to a specific purpose and context.

GUITAR

Improvisation: Major Pentatonic Scale 🔊 ▶️

The **major pentatonic scale** looks a lot like the minor pentatonic scale. The only difference between the two scales is which note feels like home, or the **tonic**. Here are a couple sample riffs you can play over the Jam Track.

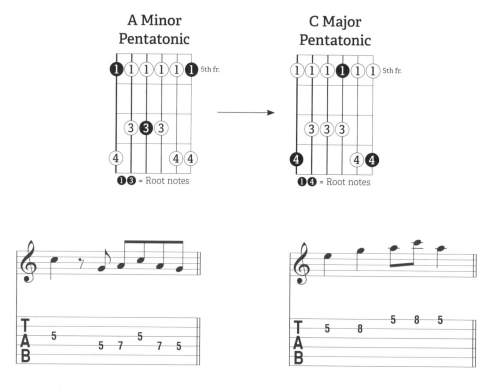

Try the scale over a few familiar progressions.

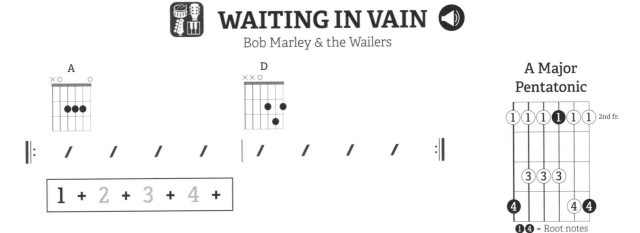

WAITING IN VAIN
Bob Marley & the Wailers

The scale pattern for this next song uses open strings and different fingerings than the previous pattern, but it has the same shape.

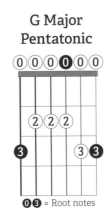

G Major
Pentatonic

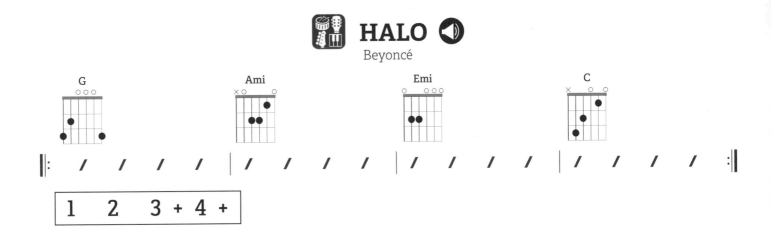

HALO
Beyoncé

Improvisation: Comparing Major and Minor Pentatonic Scales

The major pentatonic scale looks a lot like the minor pentatonic scale. These two scales actually have the exact same notes (A, C, D, E, G). The only difference between the two scales (for now) is which note feels like home, or which is the **tonic**.

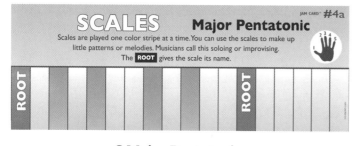

C Major Pentatonic

A Minor Pentatonic

The notes in these two scales are exactly the same. The root is just on a different tonic note.

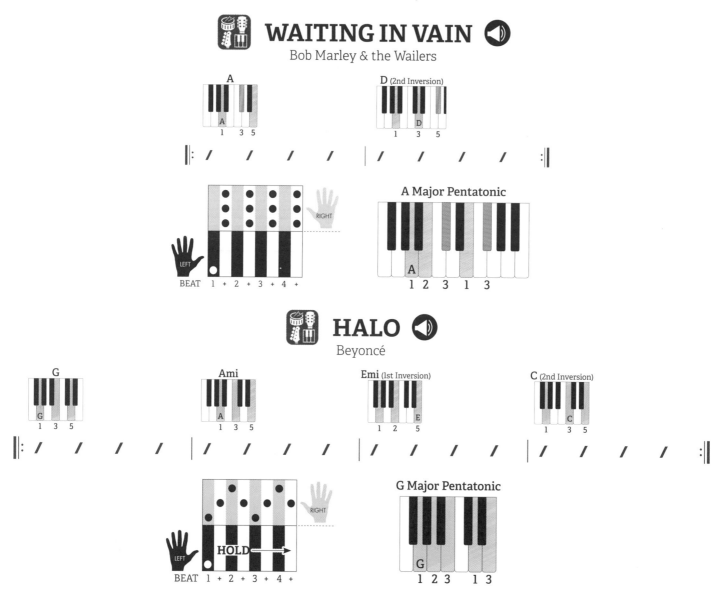

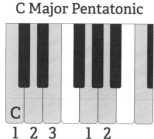

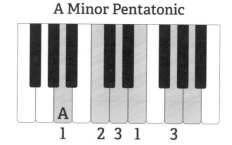

WAITING IN VAIN
Bob Marley & the Wailers

A Major Pentatonic

HALO
Beyoncé

G Major Pentatonic

Improvisation: Major Pentatonic Scale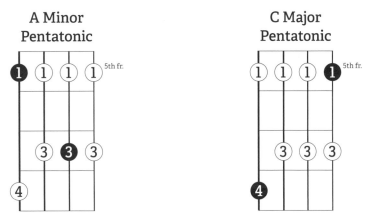

The **major pentatonic scale** looks a lot like the minor pentatonic scale. The only difference between the two scales is which note feels like home, or the **tonic**.

Try this out over a few familiar progressions.

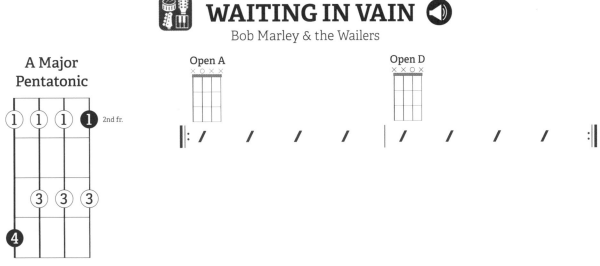

Bob Marley & the Wailers

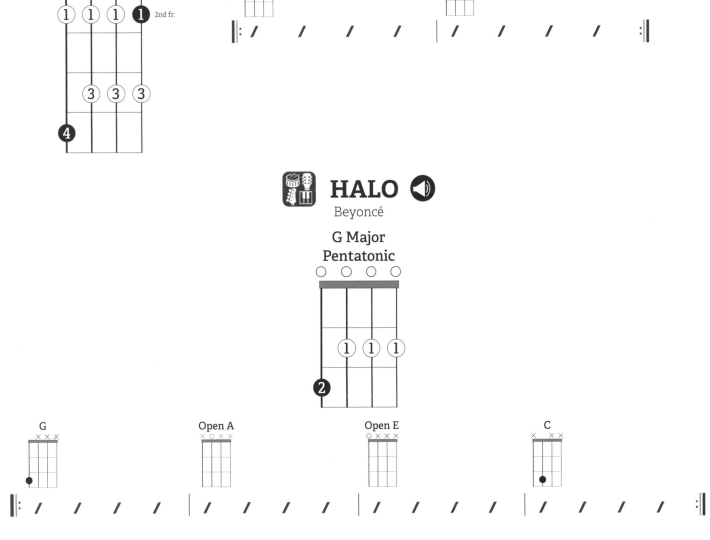

Beyoncé

More Drum Songs

DRUMS

Here are three more songs your bandmates are working on:

 **HALO**
Beyoncé

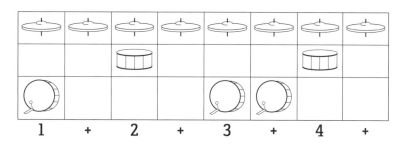

 WAITING IN VAIN
Bob Marley & the Wailers

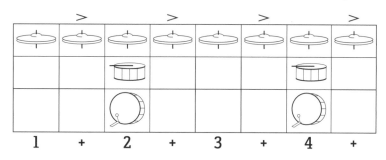
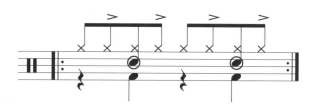

HEY THERE DELILAH
Plain White T's

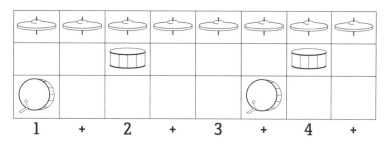

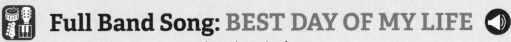 **Full Band Song: BEST DAY OF MY LIFE**

American Authors

 44   42   43   57

MU:Pr5.3.E.5

a) Use self-reflection and peer feedback to refine individual and ensemble performances of a varied repertoire of music.

MU:Pr6.1.E.5

a) Demonstrate attention to technical accuracy and expressive qualities in prepared and improvised performances of a varied repertoire of music.

b) Demonstrate an awareness of the context of the music through prepared and improvised performances.

MU:Re7.2.E.5

a) Identify how knowledge of context and the use of repetition, similarities, and contrasts inform the response to music.

MU:Re8.1.E.5

a) Identify interpretations of the expressive intent and meaning of musical works, referring to the elements of music, contexts, and (when appropriate) the setting of the text.

MU:Pr4.3.E.5

a) Identify expressive qualities in a varied repertoire of music that can be demonstrated through prepared and improvised performances.

MU:Pr5.1.H.5

a) Apply teacher-provided criteria to critique individual performances of a varied repertoire of music that includes melodies, repertoire pieces, and chordal accompaniments selected for performance, and apply practice strategies to address performance challenges and refine the performances.

MU:Pr6.1.H.5

a) Perform with expression and technical accuracy in individual performances of a varied repertoire of music that includes melodies, repertoire pieces, and chordal accompaniments, demonstrating understanding of the audience and the context.

MU:Re7.2.H.5

a) Demonstrate and explain, citing evidence, the use of repetition, similarities, and contrasts in musical selections and how these and knowledge of the context (social or cultural) inform the response.

MU:Cr3.2.2

a) Convey expressive intent for a specific purpose by presenting a final version of personal musical ideas to peers or informal audience.

MU:Pr4.3.2

a) Demonstrate understanding of expressive qualities (such as dynamics and tempo) and how creators use them to convey expressive intent.

MU:Pr5.1.2

b) Rehearse, identify, and apply strategies to address interpretive, performance, and technical challenges of music.

MU:Pr6.1.2

a) Perform music for a specific purpose with expression and technical accuracy.

MU:Cr3.2.2

a) Convey expressive intent for a specific purpose by presenting a final version of personal musical ideas to peers or informal audience.

MU:Pr4.3.2

a) Demonstrate understanding of expressive qualities (such as dynamics and tempo) and how creators use them to convey expressive intent.

211

Performance Notes

- Guitarists have a chance here to play both lead (the riff) and rhythm (the chords). It's important for them to understand the difference and adjust their dynamics accordingly.
- Keyboardists should also be mindful of when they're playing a lead part (like the Intro) and when they're playing a chordal part (like the Verse). This might mean that a keyboardist adjusts their volume to stand out more when playing a melodic line and dials the volume back to play a chordal part, as to blend in with the texture more.
- Bass players should focus on a few different elements in this song: To add motion to some of all of the Choruses, bassists can change their rhythm to quarter or eighth notes. They can also focus on what register to play in. Though the tab says to play the D using the open string, it can also be played on the 5th fret of the A string or the tenth fret of the E string. Each of these strings has a different sound quality to it. Bassists should be challenged to describe the differences in these sound qualities and to come to a decision about which they think is best for this song. Keep in mind, what is best for one section might not be best for another.
- The Bmi chord in the Pre-Chorus can be approximated by having guitarists and keyboardists play D while having bassists play B and having keyboardists use a B in the left hand. The students will be playing a Bmi7 chord, which will sound and function similarly to the Bmi chord.
- The drum part here is simplified from the recording to include only notes that land on an eighth-note subdivision. Drummers should be encouraged to add extra hits in if they are willing and up for the challenge.
- This song offers a chance to get everyone involved in the vocals. The "oh, oh, oh, oh," response sections can be sung by the whole band. Students can practice singing and playing their parts at the same time. An easy way to make any chorus of a song bigger is to have more people sing it. There's only one line of repeated lyrics that the whole band can join in on.

Suggestions for Further Repertoire

- "Ho Hey" by The Lumineers
- "Home" by Edward Sharpe and the Magnetic Zeros
- "Season of the Witch" by Donovan
- "Born in the U.S.A." by Bruce Springsteen
- "Three Little Birds" by Bob Marley & the Wailers
- "For What It's Worth" by Buffalo Springfield

Iconic Score

GUITAR

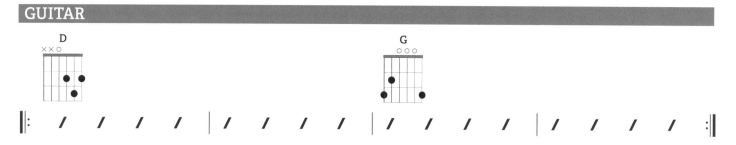

Chorus Riff

KEYBOARD

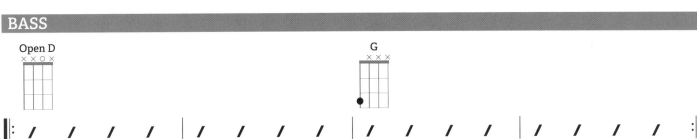

BASS

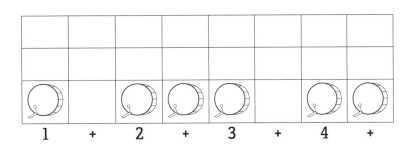

DRUMS

Verse

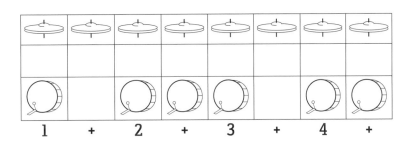

Pre-Chorus

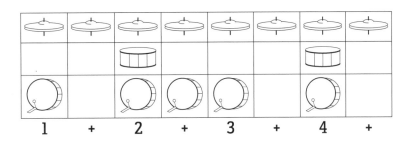

Chorus

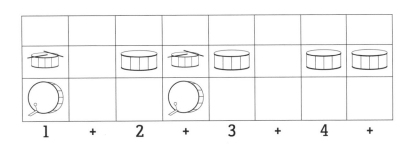

Bridge

Standard Staff Score

Intro Riff (Keyboard Only)

Chorus

Bridge

VERSE

D
I had a dream so big and loud. I jumped so high I touched the clouds.

G
Whoa-o-o-o-o-oh. Whoa-o-o-o-o-oh.

D
I stretched my hands out to the sky. We danced with monsters through the night.

G
Whoa-o-o-o-o-oh. Whoa-o-o-o-o-oh.

PRE-CHORUS

D   **Emi**
I'm never gonna look back, whoa. I'm never gonna give it up, no. Please don't wake me now.

CHORUS

D   **G**
Wo-o-o-o-oo! This is gonna be the best day of my life, my life.

D   **G**
Wo-o-o-o-oo! This is gonna be the best day of my life, my life.

VERSE

D
I howled at the moon with friends. And then the sun came crashing in.

G
Whoa-o-o-o-o-oh. Whoa-o-o-o-o-oh.

   D
But all the possibilities, no limits just epiphanies.

G
Whoa-o-o-o-o-oh. Whoa-o-o-o-o-oh.

BRIDGE

D
I hear it calling outside my window.

I feel it in my soul, soul.

The stars were burning so bright,

The sun was out 'til midnight.

I say we lose control, control.

Skill	4	3	2	1	Next Steps
GUITAR Reading Comprehension Full C and G Chords Major Pentatonic Scale	Student can perform the full C and G open chords in time Student can solo creatively using the major pentatonic scale	Student can perform the full C and G open chords Student can solo using the major pentatonic scale	Student can play the full C and G open chords out of time Student can play the notes of the major pentatonic scale	Student struggles to play C and G open chords Student cannot play the notes of the major pentatonic scale	
KEYBOARD Reading Comprehension Syncopated Comping Patterns Inversions	Student can perform the full C and G open chords in time Student can solo creatively using the major pentatonic scale	Student can perform the full C and G open chords Student can solo using the major pentatonic scale	Student can play the full C and G open chords out of time Student can play the notes of the major pentatonic scale	Student struggles to play C and G open chords Student cannot play the notes of the major pentatonic scale	
BASS Note Length	Student can perform notes with great control over note length	Student can perform notes with control over note length	Student can perform notes with some control over note length	Student has little control over note length	
DRUMS Funk Grooves Choosing the Right Groove	Student can play a variety of funk grooves and smoothly and appropriately transition between them	Student can play a variety of funk grooves	Student can play some of the elements of funk grooves	Student struggles to perform the elements of funk grooves	
DRUMS Right-Hand Independence	Student can perform unique patterns with right-hand hits on any beat of the measure, in time and at a variety of tempos	Student can perform unique patterns with right-hand hits on any beat of the measure in time	Student can perform rehearsed hits on any beat	Student can perform rehearsed hits on some of the beats	

SECTION 10   46 44 45 59

Music Theory: Guitar and keyboard players will practice reading melodies and riffs that use the pentatonic scale. Bass players will play slides and apply them to pentatonic riffs. Drummers will beatbox to transcribe drum parts.

Instrument Technique: Guitar players will perform common variations on open chord. Keyboard players will play bass lines in the left hand. Bass players will apply passing tones to their accompaniments. Drummers will apply heel-up technique to play the more complex kick drum parts. Drummers will also play cross-stick flams and rim shots in the context of hip-hop songs, as well as explore various drum sounds.

Music Theory: Guitarists will read staff and tab notation, focusing on the merits of each. Keyboard players will read ledger lines and the grand staff. Bassists will apply slides to the context of songs. Drummers will keep steady kick drum patterns consistent while soloing with the drums.

Full Band Song: "Kick, Push" by Lupe Fiasco

Music Theory/Instrument Technique: Reading Comprehension

 46   44   45

MU: Cr2.1.E.5

a) Select and develop draft melodic and rhythmic ideas or motives that demonstrate understanding of characteristic(s) of music or text(s) studied in rehearsal.

GUITAR

Instrument Technique: Pentatonic Riffs

Here are a few more pentatonic riffs so you can see the scale in action.

LOVE ON THE WEEKEND
John Mayer

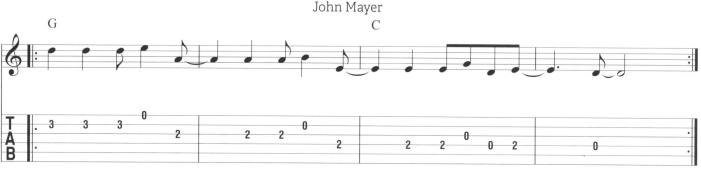

This next riff is played with a **shuffle feel**. This means the eighth notes are played in an uneven rhythm. You've probably heard this popular sound before in countless blues, rock, pop, and jazz songs. Listen to the original recording of this classic blues riff and play with the Jam Track to get a feel for it.

MANNISH BOY

Muddy Waters

A

KEYBOARD

Music Theory: A Pentatonic Melody

Here is an example of a melody that uses the pentatonic scale:

SHAKE IT OFF

Taylor Swift

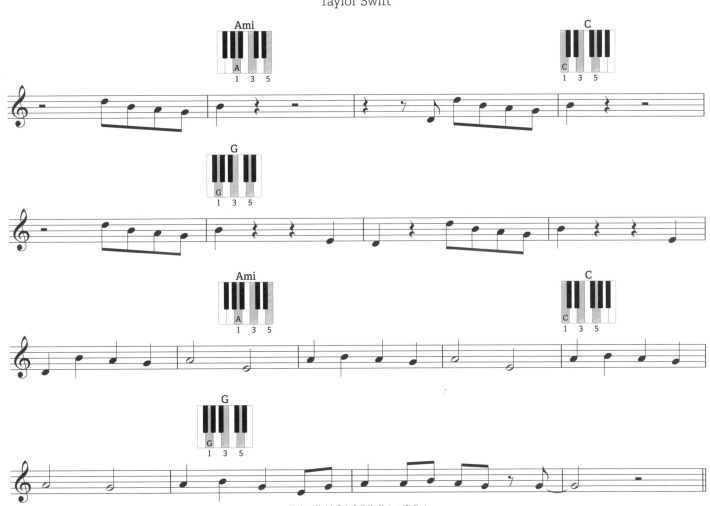

Instrument Technique: Slides

A **slide** is when you move from one note to another by sliding your finger from one fret to another; slides add another form of phrasing.

An example of a bass slide can be found in the appropriately named song, "Slide," by Slave, which starts with a slide up and down the E string. To play this, just play an open E, next apply pressure with a left-hand finger at around the 1st fret and slide your finger up to about the 12th fret, then back down the neck.

Try it in the following situations. All of these examples use the D minor pentatonic scale.

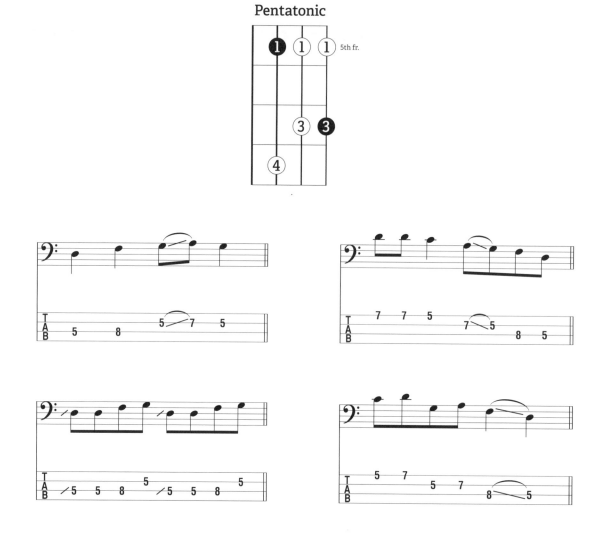

When sliding into a note like in the third example above, start one or two frets lower than the written note and slide into it.

Music Theory: More Notation; Ear Training

MU: Cr1.1.6
a) Generate simple rhythmic, melodic, and harmonic phrases within AB and ABA forms that convey expressive intent.

GUITAR

Music Theory: Tab vs. Notation

Check out the pentatonic riff from the song below. In the first example, try playing it using just staff notation.

One of the difficulties with guitar and notation is that you can play the same notes in multiple places on the fretboard. Here are two ways to play it, this time shown with tab.

The sound quality will change depending on where you choose to play this melody. You can try different ways and listen for which you like best.

KEYBOARD

Music Theory: Ledger Lines and Bass Clef

Here is a pentatonic riff from "Closer" by the Chainsmokers. In this first example, play it using only staff notation:

This sounds higher than the recording, so you can play it down an octave. However, by moving it down an octave, it doesn't fit on the staff, so you'll need to use **ledger lines**. Ledger lines are used to extend the staff with more lines and spaces. Here is what it would look like starting on **middle C**, or the C that lies in the middle of the keyboard:

But perhaps you want to play this with even lower notes, in which case this would be written in the **bass clef**: . The piano is one of the few instruments with a range wide enough to play very low and very high notes, and all those notes can be shown using two clefs and staves, one for lower notes (bass clef) and one for higher notes (treble clef). These two clefs are connected by the middle C:

Here are the notes of the bass clef:

And here's the melody for "Closer" written in the bass clef, starting on the note C:

We will use both clefs a lot more in the future, but for now, just keep in mind that knowing them is another way to be a fluent musician at the keyboard.

BASS

Music Theory: Passing Tones ▶

One application of scales is adding **passing tones** to your performance. It's common for a bassist to play only root notes of chords, but passing tones can be added to create variety. Pick a note from a scale you've learned that is in between the note you are moving from and the note you are moving to. Then, try substituting it for the note on beat 4 of a song you've previously learned.

To add a passing tone to the following song by the Isley Brothers, play the B on fret 2 of string 3 on beat "4+" of each measure.

SHOUT

The Isley Brothers

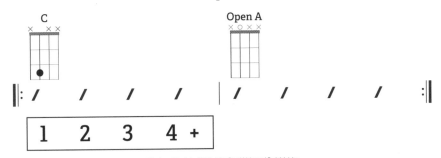

OYE COMO VA

Santana

ZOMBIE

The Cranberries

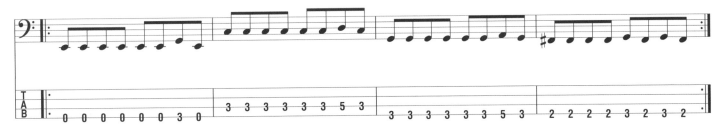

Write a chord progression below. Then, pick appropriate passing tones for the fourth beat of each measure. Remember, the pitch of the passing tone should fall in between the pitches of the root notes being played in each measure.

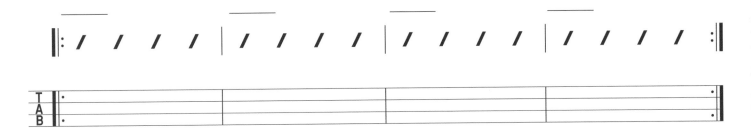

Music Theory: Applying Slides

Here are some more bass lines that contain slides.

For this riff, slide up to the 7th fret on the D string. Then, play the note on the 10th fret of the G string. Finally, play the 12th fret of the D string and slide back down to get your hand in position to play the 5th fret of the A string again.

COME TOGETHER
The Beatles

Here's a similar bass line that also uses slides:

GIVE IT AWAY
Red Hot Chili Peppers

You may be asking, "…but what note do I slide from to play the note on the 14th fret of the D string?" The answer: it doesn't really matter. Don't worry too much about picking a starting note. Instead, aim to land on the 14th fret right in time.

Try this technique in the next song—just don't overdo it. A slide will sound cool every once in a while, but it shouldn't be the main feature of the song.

DRUMS

Section 10 primarily looks at hip-hop music. You can use a lot of the drumbeats that we discussed earlier, but with some modifications to fit the style.

Beatboxing

Try beatboxing the beat below, using a "buh" sound for the bass and a "kah" sound for the snare:

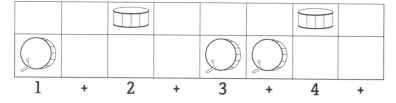

This beat is used in songs such as "Kick, Push" by Lupe Fiasco. We'll cover this Full Band Song later in the section, but here are the isolated drums to get you started:

KICK, PUSH
Lupe Fiasco

Now, try it on the drumset. This drumbeat has a bass drum pattern based from the one you just beatboxed but has additional elements.

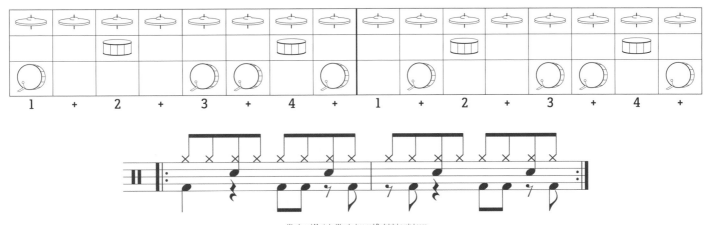

Music History: Sampling

Try playing this beat from "Ham and Eggs" by A Tribe Called Quest:

HAM AND EGGS
A Tribe Called Quest

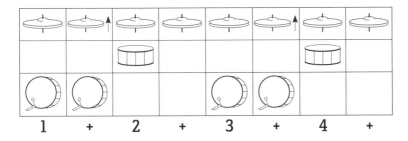

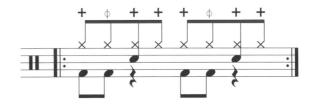

This song uses **sampling** to make the instrumental track. A Tribe Called Quest used parts of three funky tracks from the early 1970s and put them together. Afterwards, they added singing and rapping over the top. The drum part of this tune comes from a song called "We've Gotta Find a Way Back to Love" by Freda Payne. Try playing the same beat over that tune.

Things to notice about the sample:
- You can hear both a drumset and bongos from that track.
- A Tribe Called Quest slightly slowed the drum track down.
- Because A Tribe Called Quest used only a small part of the track, there is less variation in fills, hi-hat openings, and other parts within their song. Hip-hop beats tend to stay very consistent throughout much of the song when they're made using samples.

Instrument Technique: Chord Variations

You can create new chords by adding or removing fingers to add color to chords you already know.

By lifting the first finger from the C chord, you change C to Cmaj7 ("C major seven"):

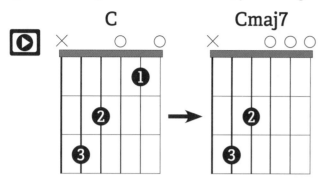
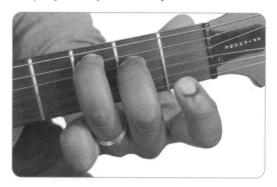

Ami becomes an Ami7 ("A minor seven") when you remove your third finger.

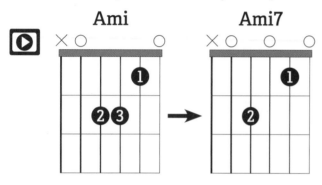

Try switching between them using this song's chord progression:

BULLETPROOF... I WISH I WAS
Radiohead

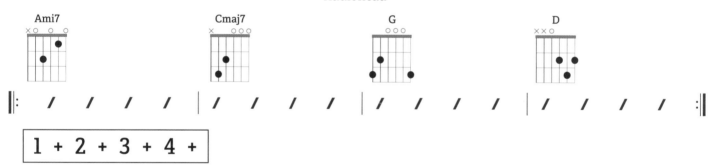

These are just a couple examples of chords you can create with small alterations. Spend some time removing and adding fingers to the chords you already know to make different sounds. Here are a few more examples using the D chord:

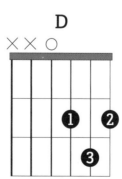

226

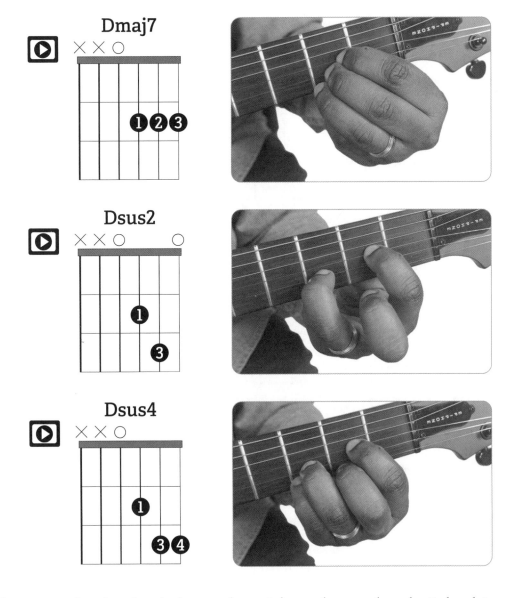

Using this trick, you can also play chords that you haven't learned yet, such as the F chord. Instead, play Fmaj7:

Several of these chords will be used in the next Full Band Song.

Playing Chords: Dmi

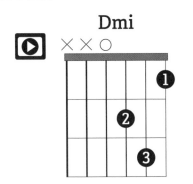

227

Here is a song that uses Dmi:

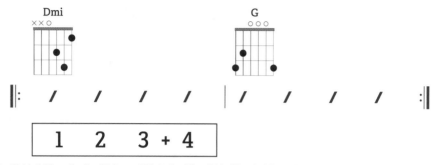

KEYBOARD

Instrument Technique: Playing Bass Lines

We have now introduced the concept of bass clef reading, but how does it relate to the piano itself? For the most part, we have treated the left hand on the piano as part of the comping patterns, but sometimes it can be used to create more interesting and memorable bass lines.

Here are a few examples to try out. First, just play the bass line with your left hand, and then try playing the chords above in your right hand, with whole notes:

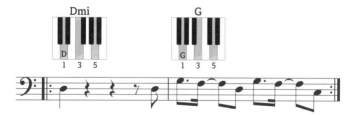

Instrument Technique: Soloing with a Bass Drum Groove

We have spent a lot of time accompanying other instruments while they solo. Drummers can also accompany their own solos. Try keeping a simple bass drum pattern going like this one:

You can also play the bass drum only on beats 1 and 3 for a different sound. Now, try to keep that going while you play some different combinations of quarter notes and eighth notes on the rest of the kit. Start with whatever comes to mind, and then try a few of these patterns, which are similar to the ones you've played before:

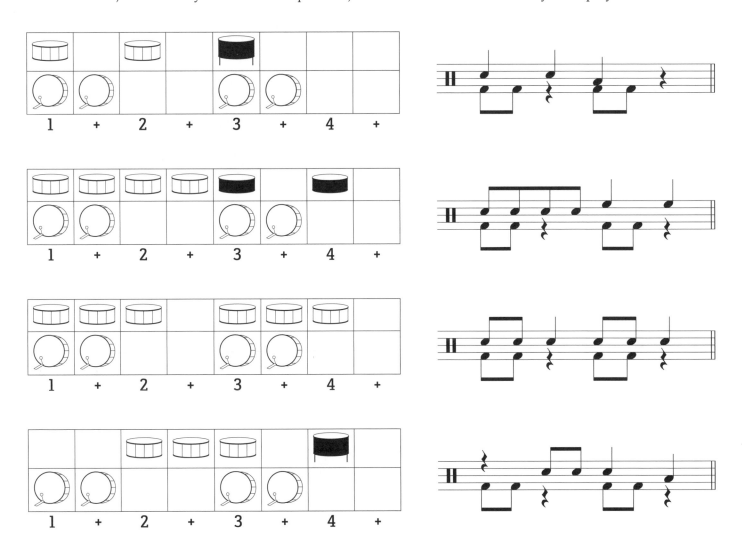

Over the course of a solo, adding these elements in slowly will make it more exciting. Try starting with no bass drum, and then adding it on beats 1 and 3.

Combining a bass drum groove with a solo takes some time, so keep at it. You will have a chance to practice soloing (with or without a bass drum groove) over the next Full Band Song.

Instrument Technique: Exploring More Sounds

Try these sounds out. You can play them on their own, and then put them into a drumbeat.

Cross-Stick Flam

You've played a cross-stick and a flam before. Now, put them together to play a **cross-stick flam**. Here is the symbol we'll use in our drumbeat diagram:

When you play a cross-stick flam, hit the top of the stick you're holding in your left hand with the other stick:

Since you won't be able to play the hi-hat at the same time, your beat might look like this:

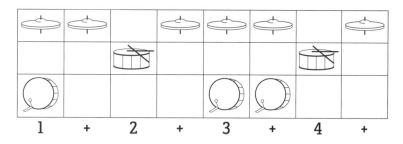

Rimshot

A **rimshot** can produce a very loud sound without using a lot of energy. To play this, hit the rim and the head of the drum at the same time with one stick. It takes a lot of practice to make a rimshot sound consistent each time, so keep practicing it for when you have a chance to be loud.

Cymbal Sounds

Cymbals are one of the most personal things to a drummer, as they can produce a wide variety of tones. All these sounds are very specific, so you probably won't want to use them all the time.

Sizzle Sounds: You can use paper clips, a chain, or even clear tape and a penny/nickel to make the cymbal ring out and "sizzle" for a long time. Make sure you get permission first to do this on any cymbal that doesn't belong to you.

Broken Cymbals: Do you know someone who has a broken cymbal laying around? Don't let them throw it away! Broken cymbals can be great for getting sizzle sounds of their own or stacking with other cymbals. However, don't break a cymbal on purpose! Try some of those sounds on this next drumbeat, which can be played with songs like "My House" by Flo Rida:

MY HOUSE

Flo Rida

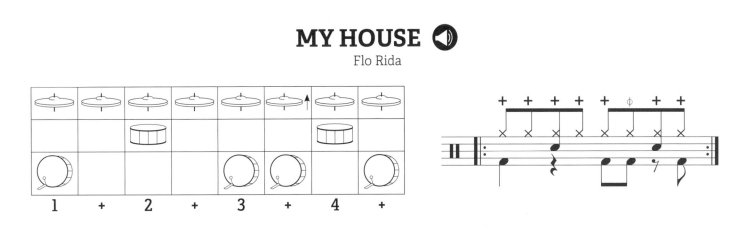

Note—In the original recording, the last bass drum hit happens only sometimes, often at the end of a phrase of four or eight measures. Listen carefully to hear the pattern.

Full Band Song: KICK, PUSH 🔊

Lupe Fiasco

🎸 50 🎹 46 🎸 48 🥁 63

MU: Pr4.2.4

b) When analyzing selected music, read and perform using iconic and/or standard notation.

MU: Pr6.1.5

a) Perform music, alone or with others, with expression, technical accuracy, and appropriate interpretation.

Performance Notes

The next Full Band Song provides opportunities for different instruments to work on the skills they have been practicing so far.

- Guitarists can apply the new chord extensions and modifications they've learned.
- Keyboard players can focus on reading the grand staff and arpeggiating chords.
- Bassists can focus on note lengths and slides in their performance.
- For drummers, the quick pick-up notes in the kick drum take a combination of practice and a good setup. The simplified groove works well as an approximation, but drummers should be challenged to play the more advanced part. Student may want to experiment with the tension on the bass drum pedal to better play these pick-ups. It's also advized that students use a heel-up technique for these quick notes.

Suggestions for Further Repertoire

- "Paper Planes" by M.I.A.
- "Rock Box" by RUN-DMC
- "Gangsta's Paradise" by Coolio

Iconic Score

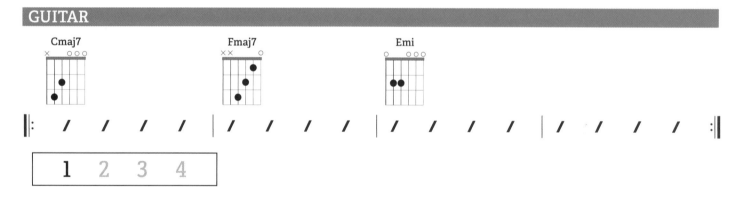

KEYBOARD

We have intentionally left this blank as the Keyboard part relies on specific figures to be played in both the left and right hands.

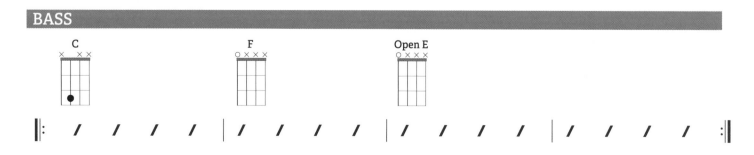

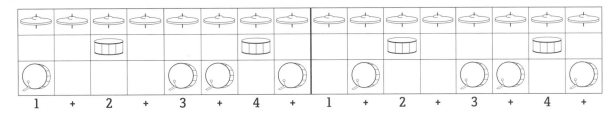

Standard Staff Score

Verse/Chorus

VERSE

First got it when he was six, didn't know any tricks. Matter fact,

First time he got on it he slipped, landed on his hip and bust his lip.

For a week he had to talk with a lisp, like this.

Now we can end the story right here,

But shorty didn't quit, it was something in the air, yea.

He said it was somethin' so appealing. He couldn't fight the feelin'.

Somethin' about it, he knew he couldn't doubt it, couldn't understand it,

Brand it, since the first kickflip he landed, uh. Labeled a misfit, abandoned,

Ca-kunk, ca-kunk, kunk. His neighbors couldn't stand it, so he was banished to the park.

Started in the morning, wouldn't stop till after dark, yea.

When they said "it's getting late in here, so I'm sorry young man, there's no skating here."

CHORUS

So we kick, push, kick, push, kick, push, kick, push, coast.

And the way he roll just a rebel to the world with no place to go.

So we kick, push, kick, push, kick, push, kick, push, coast.

So come and skate with me, just a rebel looking for a place to be.

So let's kick, and push, and coast.

VERSE

Uh, uh, uh. My man got a lil' older, became a better roller (yea).

No helmet, hell-bent on killin' himself, was what his momma said.

But he was feelin' himself, got a lil' more swagger in his style.

Met his girlfriend, she was clappin' in the crowd.

Love is what was happening to him now, uh. He said "I would marry you but I'm engaged to

These aerials and varials, and I don't think this board is strong enough to carry two."

She said "beau, I weigh 120 pounds. Now, lemme make one thing clear, I don't need to ride yours,

I got mine right here." So she took him to a spot he didn't know about,

Somewhere in the apartment parking lot, she said, "I don't normally take dates in here."

Security came and said, "I'm sorry there's no skating here."

CHORUS

So they kick, push, kick, push, kick, push, kick, push, coast.

And the way they roll, just lovers intertwined with no place to go.

And so they kick, push, kick, push, kick, push, kick, push, coast.

So come and skate with me, just a rebel looking for a place to be.

So let's kick, and push, and coast.

VERSE

Yea uh, yea, yea. Before he knew he had a crew that wasn't no punk

In they Spitfire shirts and SB Dunks. They would push, till they couldn't skate no more.

Office buildings, lobbies wasn't safe no more.

And it wasn't like they wasn't getting chased no more,

Just the freedom is better than breathing, they said.

An escape route, they used to escape out when things got crazy they needed to break out.

(They'd head) to any place with stairs, and good grinds the world was theirs, uh.

And they four wheels would take them there,

Until the cops came and said, "There's no skating here."

CHORUS

So they kick, push, kick, push, kick, push, kick, push, coast.

And the way they roll, just rebels without a cause with no place to go.

And so they kick, push, kick, push, kick, push, kick, push, coast.

So come roll with me, just a rebel looking for a place to be.

So let's kick, and push, and coast.

SECTION 10—SAMPLE RUBRIC					
Skill	**4**	**3**	**2**	**1**	**Next Steps**
GUITAR Pentatonic Riffs Chord Variations	Student performs riffs and open chord variations accurately and in time and can play them at stylistically appropriate moments	Student can perform riffs and open chord variations accurately and in time	Student sometimes performs riffs and open chord variations accurately and in time	Student rarely performs riffs and open chord variations accurately and in time	
KEYBOARD Pentatonic Melodies Ledger Lines Full Staff Playing Bass Lines	Student performs melodies and bass lines accurately and in time and plays them at stylistically appropriate musical moments	Student performs melodies and bass lines accurately and in time and can read the notes on the grand staff	Student sometimes performs melodies and bass lines accurately and in time and can read most of the notes on the grand staff	Student rarely performs melodies and bass lines accurately and in time and can read some of the notes on the grand staff	
BASS Slides Passing Tones	Student performs slides and passing tones in time and adds them at stylistically appropriate musical moments	Student performs rehearsed slides and passing tones in time	Student sometimes performs rehearsed slides and passing tones in time	Student rarely performs rehearsed slides and passing tones in time	
DRUMS Hip-Hop Grooves Cross-Stick Flam Rim Shot Cymbal Sounds	Student performs various drumset techniques accurately, in time, and at stylistically appropriate moments	Student performs various drumset techniques accurately and in time	Student sometimes performs various drumset techniques accurately and in time	Student rarely performs various drumset techniques accurately and in time	

SECTION 11

 52   49   50   🥁 65

Music Theory: Guitar, keyboard, and bass players will play riffs that use the blues scale and apply it to soloing. Guitar players will play two- and three-note power chords. Keyboard players will expand the performance of inversions by using more complex comping patterns. Bass players will play riffs that derive from power chord shapes. Drummers will focus on which instruments are best used to accompany various types of music.

Instrument Technique: Drummers will perform patterns to that focus on isolating kick and snare drum to build independence.

Composition: Composing with power chords. Guitars and bassists can use fret numbers to compose with power chords. Instructors can help translate those to note names for keyboard players if they want to work together. Drummers can work on composing original grooves to go with the other musicians.

Full Band Song: "Umbrella" by Rihanna. Students will apply various techniques, such as power chords, chords as riffs, inversions, and fills to the performance of this song.

Music Theory: Blues Scale

 52   49   50

MU:Cr1.1.E.5

a) Compose and improvise melodic and rhythmic ideas or motives that reflect characteristic(s) of music or text(s) studied in rehearsal.

GUITAR

Music Theory: Blues Scale

BAD 🔊
Michael Jackson

SUNSHINE OF YOUR LOVE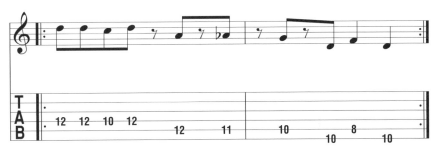

Cream

Both of these riffs use the **blues scale**. You can use this scale to write riffs or play solos. The blues scale is similar to the minor pentatonic scale with an added "blue" note. There is no fret reference number shown here because this scale shape can be moved up and down the neck of the guitar, just like the pentatonic scales.

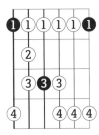

Try writing a riff using notes in the blues scale:

Instrument Technique: Slides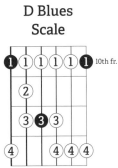

There are several different types of **slides** you can play on the guitar. We will focus on a common slide that moves from one note to another on the same string without lifting off the fretboard. Similar to hammer-ons and pull-offs, the slur in the notation tells you not to pick the second note. Try these examples using the D blues scale:

D Blues Scale

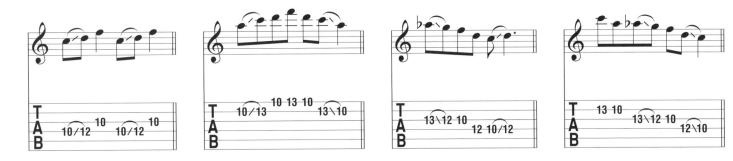

Play a solo over the next song using the D blues scale and add some slides to it, along with hammer-ons and pull-offs. If you find something cool, write in the tab below!

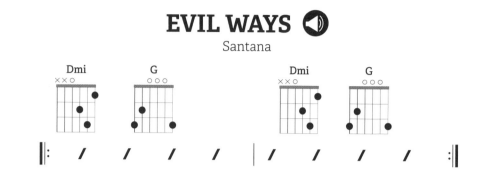

EVIL WAYS
Santana

KEYBOARD

Music Theory: The Blues Scale

Both of these riffs use the **blues scale**; it simply adds a passing note between the third and fourth notes of the minor pentatonic scale:

BAD
Michael Jackson

Words and Music by Michael Jackson
Copyright © 1987 Mijac Music
All Rights Administered by Sony Music Publishing LLC, 424 Church Street, Suite 1200, Nashville, TN 37219
International Copyright Secured All Rights Reserved

SUNSHINE OF YOUR LOVE
Cream

Words and Music by Eric Clapton, Jack Bruce and Pete Brown
Copyright © 1967, 1973 E.C. Music Ltd. and Dratleaf Music, Ltd.
Copyright Renewed
International Copyright Secured All Rights Reserved

Here is the blues scale on a Jam Card:

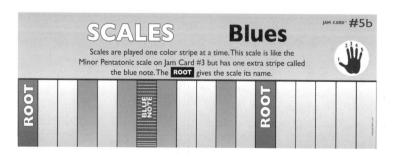

238

Try this scale with this next song, which also uses the Dmi chord from the last section:

EVIL WAYS
Santana

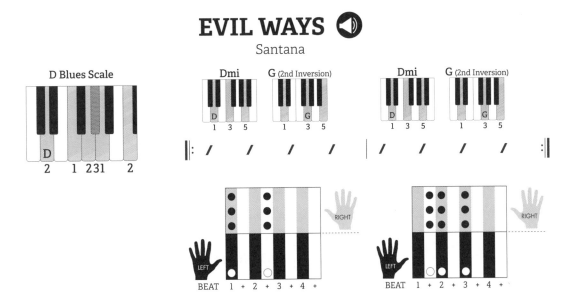

BASS

Music Theory: Blues Scale

BAD
Michael Jackson

SUNSHINE OF YOUR LOVE
Cream

Both of the preceding examples use the **blues scale**. You can use this scale to write riffs or play solos. The blues scale is the minor pentatonic scale with an added "blue" note. There is no fret reference number shown on the scale grid on the next page, because this scale shape can be moved up and down the neck of the bass, just like the pentatonic scales.

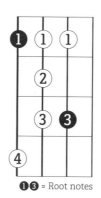

= Root notes

Let's try the blues scale with "Evil Ways" by Santana, transposed to D minor (originally in G minor). Also try playing the blues scale over earlier Jam Tracks.

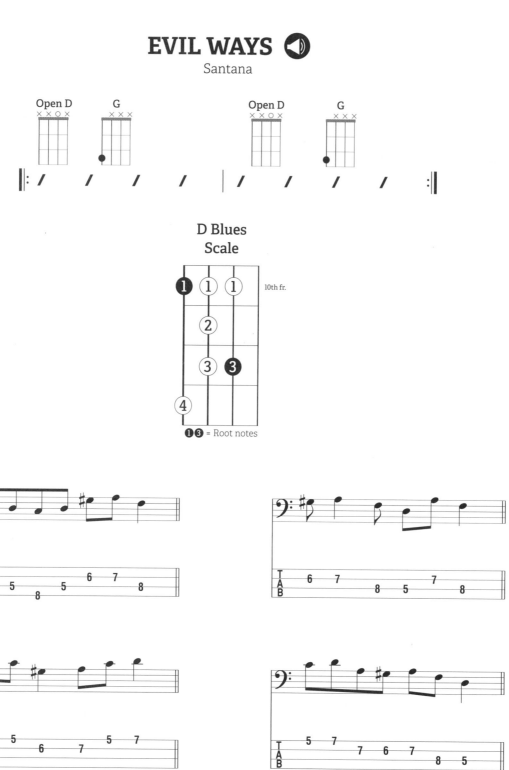

Instrument Technique

 65

Instrument Technique: Combining Bass and Snare Drum Freedom

Here are some exercises that combine the snare and bass drum in different patterns along with a constant eighth-note rhythm played on the hi-hat:

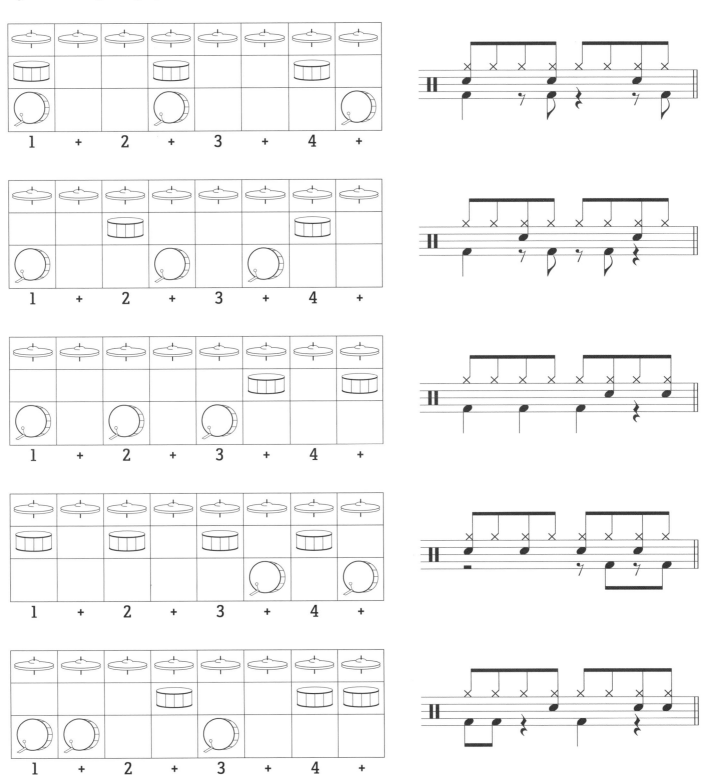

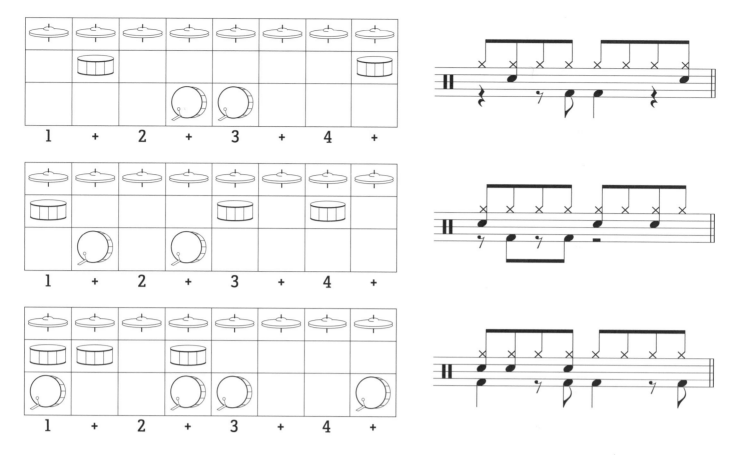

Make up some more combinations on your own, and write them in the diagrams below:

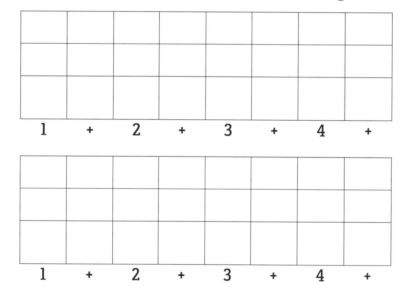

Music Theory: Choosing the Right Drum Groove

Here are a few more songs to transcribe and create beats for:

GIVE ME ONE REASON 🔊
Tracy Chapman

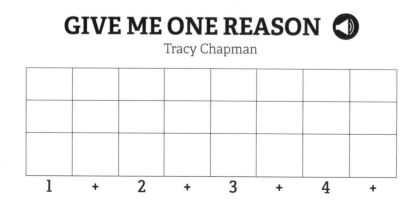

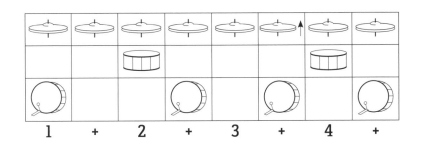

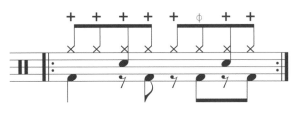

SÚBEME LA RADIO

Enrique Iglesias ft. Descemer Bueno, Zion & Lennox

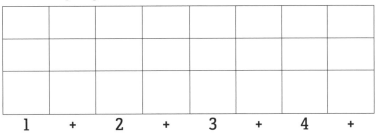

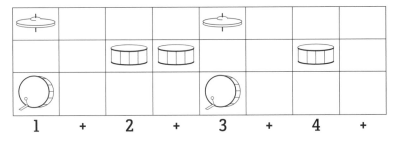

This last example does not feature a typical backbeat, so carefully count along:

WILD THING

The Troggs

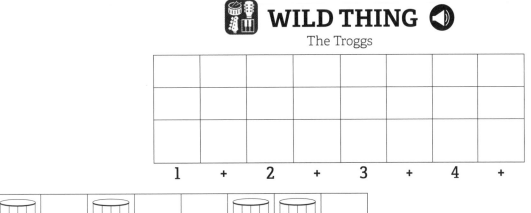

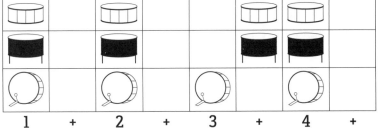

THE EDGE OF GLORY

Lady Gaga

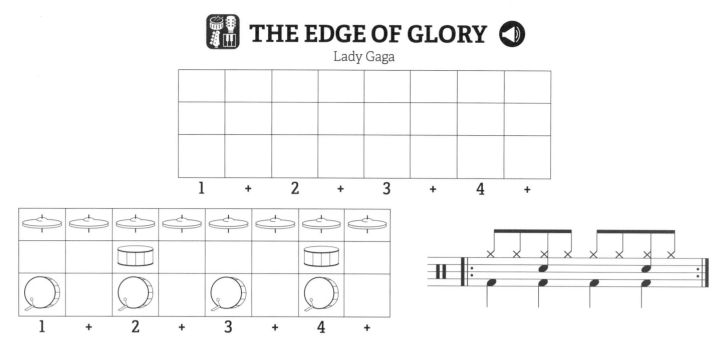

Music Theory: Power Chords, Inversions, and Common Tones

MU: Cr2.1.E.5

a) Select and develop draft melodic and rhythmic ideas or motives that demonstrate understanding of characteristic(s) of music or text(s) studied in rehearsal.

GUITAR

Instrument Technique: Power Chords

Power chords will allow you to play even more songs. Every power chord has the same shape that can be moved up or down the guitar. Start with a two-note power chord, A5:

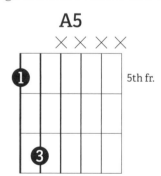

You can also play a power chord with three fingers. Try them with the next song.

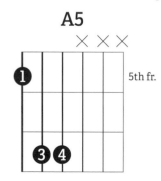

STRAY CAT STRUT

Stray Cats

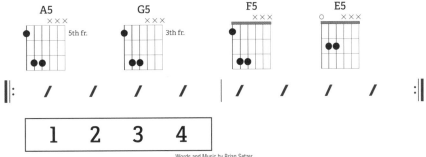

Power chords can be played on the 5th string as well:

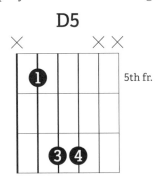

You can also finger the three-note power chords using a **barre**, in which you fret two notes with one finger. In this case, you can use your ring or pinky finger to lay flat across the two higher notes in the chord, holding them both down with one finger.

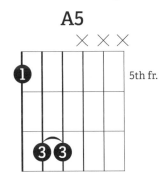

Here is a song that uses power chords on both the 6th and 5th strings:

SMELLS LIKE TEEN SPIRIT

Nirvana

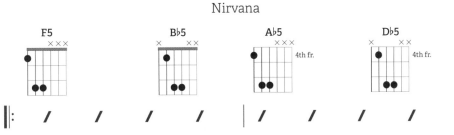

Music Theory: Common Tones ▶️

Look at the chord progression C–Ami, which is used in the Intro to "Hey There Delilah":

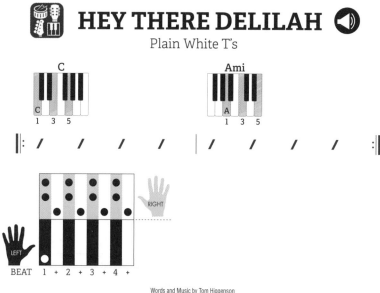

HEY THERE DELILAH 🔊

Plain White T's

Words and Music by Tom Higgenson
© 2005 WC MUSIC CORP., FEARMORE MUSIC and SO HAPPY PUBLISHING
All Rights Administered by WC MUSIC CORP.
All Rights Reserved Used by Permission

What are the notes in each chord? Answer: **C–E–G** and **A–C–E**. Now, which notes are in common? Answer: C and E, which are called **common tones**. To move easily between chords, keep the common tones and only move the changing note. You can play these three different ways:

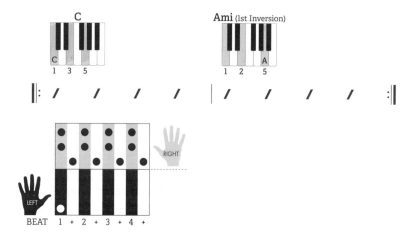

You may find that starting with an inverted chord is the easiest way to play a progression:

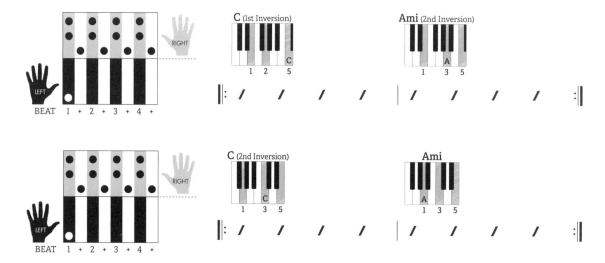

246

Try playing the root of each chord with your left hand while playing the inverted chords with your right:

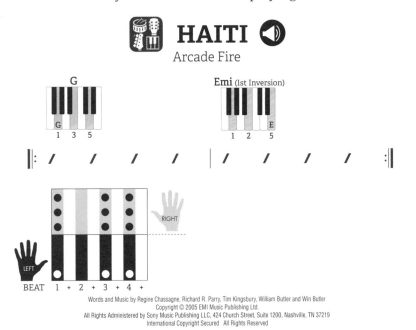

HAITI
Arcade Fire

BASS

Music Theory: Chords as Riffs

While many songs have chords that last a whole bar, some songs change chords quickly. This can make the chords sound more melodic, like riffs. Many of these chords as riffs are instantly recognizable, even before someone starts singing. Bassists can play root notes of those chords along with the guitar or keyboard player to emphasize the changing chords. This is extremely popular in classic rock music. Here are a couple examples:

STRAY CAT STRUT
Stray Cats

SMELLS LIKE TEEN SPIRIT
Nirvana

Composition

🎸 55   **🎹 51**   **🎸 52**

MU:Cr2.1.6

b) Use standard and/or iconic notation and/or audio/video recording to document personal simple rhythmic phrases, melodic phrases, and two-chord harmonic musical ideas.

GUITAR

Composition: Composing with Power Chords 🔈 ▶️

To write a song with power chords, pick a string number (5 or 6) and a fret number (1–10). Play a power chord at that location with your first finger on that fret and string. Pick four chords this way and write a rhythm to play them with.

$$\|: \quad / \quad / \quad / \quad / \quad | \quad / \quad / \quad / \quad / \quad | \quad / \quad / \quad / \quad / \quad | \quad / \quad / \quad / \quad / \quad :\|$$

KEYBOARD

Composition: Composing with Inversions

Now it's your turn to make up a song based on inversions:

4. Using this Jam Card, choose four chords, in any key you'd like. We've picked D, Bmi, G, and Emi in the key of D as an example:

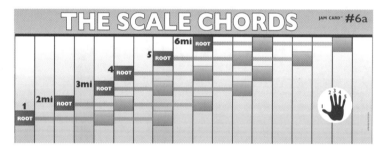

5. Write the notes of each chord above the chord name, and then figure out the common tones between them:

D: D–F♯–A
Bmi: B–D–F♯
G: G–B–D
Emi: E–G–D

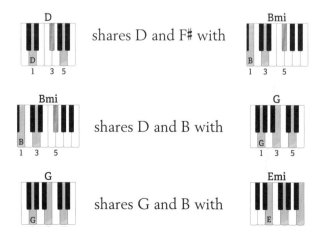

D   shares D and F♯ with   Bmi

Bmi   shares D and B with   G

G   shares G and B with   Emi

6. Write in the inversions you could use that keep the most common tones from chord to chord. Here is an example solution:

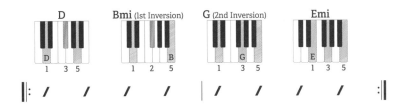

Composition: Composing with Power Chords 🔊 ▶

Rock guitarists use simple two-note "chords" called **power chords**. As a bass player, you can often just play the root note of the power chord. Compare the diagrams below:

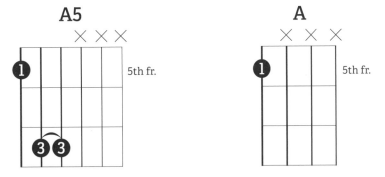

To write a song with power chords, pick a string number (3 or 4) and a fret number (1–10). Play the root of the power chord at that location with your first finger on that fret and string. Pick four power chords (notes) this way and write a rhythm to play them with.

249

Full Band Song: UMBRELLA

Rihanna

| | 56 | | 52 | | 53 | | 68 |

MU:Pr6.1.5

a) Perform music, alone or with others, with expression, technical accuracy, and appropriate interpretation.

Performance Notes

This song is an opportunity to use a few new musical concepts and start fleshing out the score into something more than a single repeating chord progression. Here are some key things:

Guitar: This song uses mostly power chords for the guitar. This is an opportunity for students to practice playing power chords based on the A and E strings. It also allows students to focus on note length, as the Verse chords should be chord and the chorus and bridge chords should be held out. In the first Verse, the guitar is playing an ostinato riff originally played on a keyboard. This ostinato can continue in the Choruses and second Verse if performers want to create multiple guitar parts to be played simultaneously. Notice the two different places the B♭5 chord can be played. Depending on the chords that lead and follow another chord, a different fingering or placement might be appropriate. These suggestions are provided as they don't require as much movement.

Keyboard: The keyboard plays three different parts in this song. The first is an eighth-note riff that outlines the chords used. This can be played in the Intro and Verses. The block chords can be played in the Chorus and Bridge section using inversions to make the voicings smoother and easier to play. The power chords in the second Verse do not have 3rds and are an opportunity for students to explore different chord sounds on their instruments as well as different tones on their keyboard.

Bass: The bass part covers mostly root notes throughout this song. In the second Verse there are a couple fills that help change up the instrumental accompaniment between the first and second Verse. Students should feel free to play those fills or create their own, as long as it still fits in with the rest of the music.

Drums: The drums for this song are mostly consistent. The beat provided approximates what is played in the recording, with many of the 16th-note hits removed. Students should be encouraged to either simplify or make the beat more complex based on their own skill level. They may also want to switch up which instruments they play in each section to change the texture. They can also compose transitional fills.

Voice: A great challenge for any instrumentalists is to play while simultaneously singing. Encourage singers to try to sing the chorus and play their parts at the same time. This doesn't necessarily have to be done for a final performance, but students who are successful at doing both could join in on the vocals during the chorus to fill out the vocal part.

Improvisation: A blues scale solo works well over a power chord-based song like this. Guitarists should be encouraged to include bends, hammer-ons, and pull-offs.

Similar Repertoire

- "New Kids in School" by The Donnas
- "Vertigo" by U2
- "All the Small Things" by Blink-182
- "You Really Got Me" by The Kinks
- "Iron Man" by Black Sabbath
- "Hit Me with Your Best Shot" by Pat Benatar

Iconic Score—Chord and Groove Bank

Because this song is so riff-based, its iconic score appears different than those of the other Full Band Songs. Below is a bank of chords and scale choices that occur within the song; there are also two groove options for drummers.

GUITAR

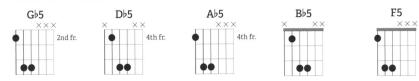

KEYBOARD

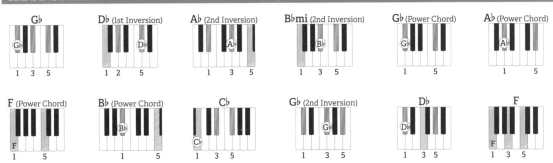

BASS

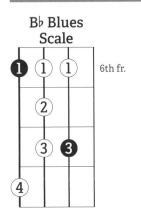

DRUMS

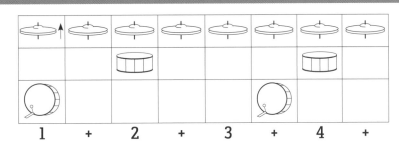

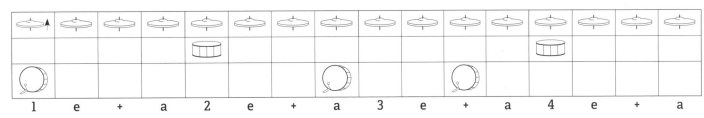

Standard Staff Score

Verse 1

Chorus

Verse 2

Bridge

VERSE

G♭5   A♭5
You have my heart, and we'll never be worlds apart.

          F5   B♭5
Maybe in magazines, but you'll still be my star.

              G♭5   A♭5
Baby, 'cause in the dark you can't see shiny cars.

                    F5   B♭5
And that's when you need me there, with you I'll always share, because...

CHORUS

G♭5   D♭5   A♭5
When the sun shines, we'll shine together. Told you I'd be here forever.

                      B♭5
Said I'll always be your friend. Took an oath, I'mma stick it out 'til the end.

G♭5   D♭5   A♭5
Now that it's raining more than ever, know that we'll still have each other.

                      B♭5   G♭5
You can stand under my umbrella. You can stand under my umbrella.

          D♭5   A♭5
(Ella, ella, eh, eh, eh.) Under my umbrella.

          B♭5   G♭5
(Ella, ella, eh, eh, eh.) Under my umbrella.

          D♭5   A♭5
(Ella, ella, eh, eh, eh.) Under my umbrella.

          B♭5
(Ella, ella, eh, eh, eh, eh, eh, eh.)

VERSE

              G♭5   A♭5
These fancy things, will never come in between.

                    F5   B♭5
You're part of my entity, here for infinity.

                    G♭5   A♭5
When the war has took its part, when the world has dealt its cards,

      F5   B♭5
If the hand is hard, together we'll mend your heart.

BRIDGE

C♭5   G♭5
You can run into my arms. It's OK, don't be alarmed.

          D♭5   A♭5
Come here to me. There's no distance in between our love.

C♭5   G♭5
So go on and let the rain pour.

                            F5
I'll be all you need and more, because...

Words and Music by Shawn Carter, Thaddis L. Harrell, Christopher Stewart and Terius Nash
© 2007 WC MUSIC CORP., CARTER BOYS PUBLISHING, 2082 MUSIC PUBLISHING, SONY MUSIC PUBLISHING UK LTD., SONGS OF PEER, LTD. and MARCH NINTH MUSIC PUBLISHING
All Rights for CARTER BOYS PUBLISHING and 2082 MUSIC PUBLISHING Administered by WC MUSIC CORP.
All Rights for SONY MUSIC PUBLISHING UK LTD. Administered by SONY MUSIC PUBLISHING LLC, 424 Church Street, Suite 1200, Nashville, TN 37219
All Rights for MARCH NINTH MUSIC PUBLISHING Controlled and Administered by SONGS OF PEER, LTD.
All Rights Reserved   Used by Permission

Skill	4	3	2	1	Next Steps
GUITAR Slides Power Chords	Student can improvise using slides in time Student can perform three-string power chord riffs in time	Student can perform rehearsed slides in time Student can perform two-string power chord riffs in time	Student can perform rehearsed slides Student can perform two-string power chords	Student struggles to perform slides Student cannot perform two-string power chords	
GUITAR/ KEYBOARD/ BASS Blues Scale	Student can perform unique solos using all the notes of the blues scale	Student can perform short phrases using the notes of the blues scale	Student can play the notes of the blues scale	Student cannot play the notes in the blues scale	
KEYBOARD Common Tones	Student can determine and perform appropriate inversions based on common tones and near tones for a four-chord progression	Student can determine and create appropriate inversions between two chords	Student can identify the common tones between two chords	Student cannot identify common tones between chords	
BASS Chords as Riffs	Student can perform riffs with accuracy of pitch, time, note length, and style	Student can perform riffs with mostly accurate pitch, time, note length, and style	Student inconsistently perform riffs with accurate pitch, time, note length, and style	Student cannot perform riffs	
DRUM Bass and Snare Drum Freedom	Student can perform unique patterns with bass/snare hand hits on any beat of the measure, in time and at a variety of tempos	Student can perform patterns unique patterns with bass/snare hits on any beat of the measure, in time	Student can perform rehearsed bass/snare hits on any beat	Student can perform bass/snare hits on some beats	

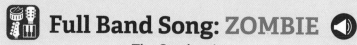
 59   55   55   70

MU:Pr6.1.5

a) Perform music, alone or with others, with expression, technical accuracy, and appropriate interpretation.

MU: Pr4.2.4

b) When analyzing selected music, read and perform using iconic and/or standard notation.

Performance Notes

This final Full Band Song combines many of the elements that have been covered throughout the book.

- **Guitar:** Guitarists should use open chords for the Verses of the song and power chords for the heavier Chorus. The riff that occurs in the Intro and after the Chorus of the song combines hammer-ons, pull-offs, and tab reading. If students are playing electric guitars, and have access to distortion, they should add it when playing power chords.

- **Keyboard:** Keyboardists can play inversions during the Verse of the song. You can also expand the performance by having students play open 5ths (power chords) during the chorus. The riff is stylistically similar to the guitarist part, so keyboardists will have to focus on when to play smooth and connected and when to play detached.

- **Bass:** Bassists can play just root notes at quarter or eighth notes. But if they're looking to play a more authentic rendition of the song, they can play the straight eighth notes with the passing notes. Over the D chord, the bass plays an F♯, putting the whole chord in 1st inversion.

- **Drums:** This drum part combines fills, varying a basic backbeat, open vs. closed hi-hat, and using different cymbals and drums.

- This song has a Verse and Chorus that use the same chord progression throughout. Because the harmonic material never changes, this gives student a good opportunity to examine the form and decide how to differentiate between song sections:

  - Changing the tone of the instruments, such as adding distortion in guitar.

  - Changing the texture, such as only having keyboards in the Verse and having guitars come in at the Chorus.

- The original form of the song is listed throughout, and you can follow the form exactly or create new sections, such as a guitar or keyboard solo or sections highlighting just the bass and drums.

- The vocal range moves from low to high from the Verse, Pre-Chorus, and Chorus, and then back down again at the end of the Chorus. This is an opportunity to utilize different vocalists with different ranges for each section.

Iconic Score

GUITAR

Verse

 Emi

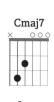 Cmaj7

 G

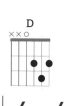 D

‖: / / / / | / / / / | / / / / | / / / / :‖

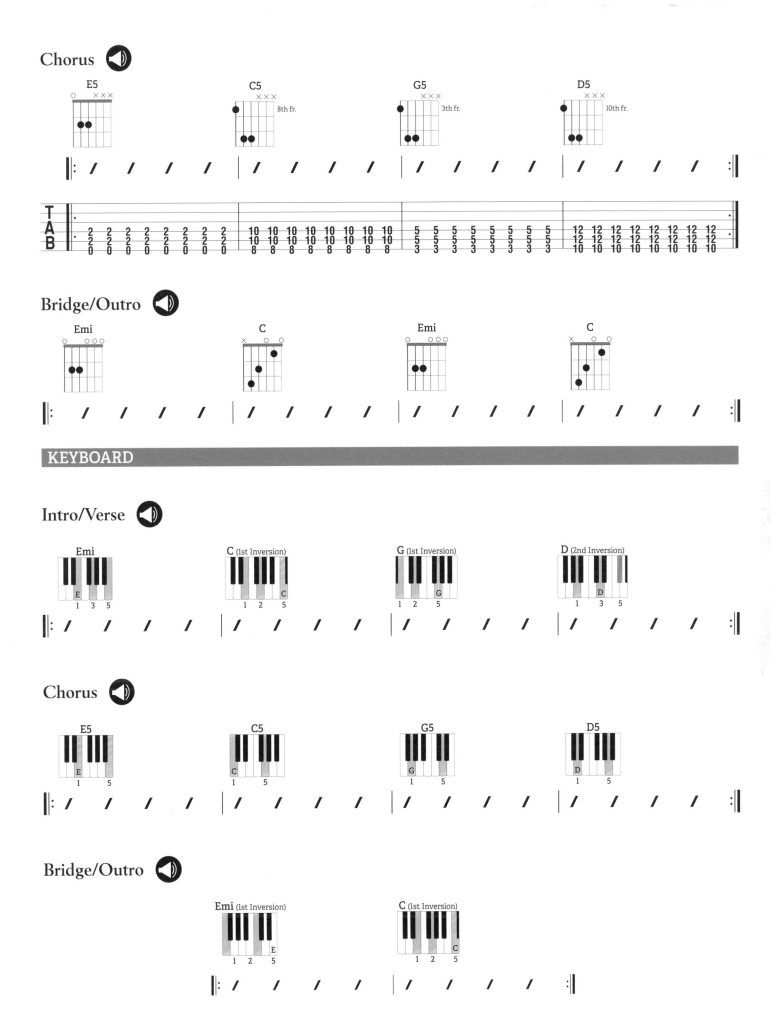

BASS

This space has been intentionally left blank.

DRUMS

Intro Fill

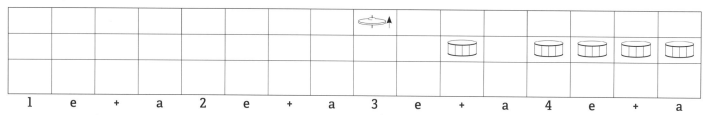

Play this drumbeat eight times:

Verse

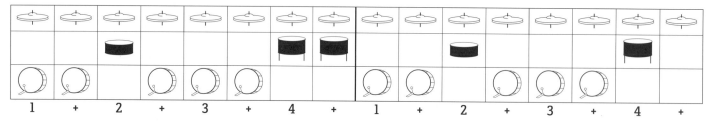

Then play this pattern, with the fill starting on beat 3:

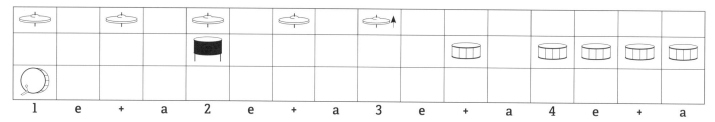

The Chorus is a repeated two-measure drumbeat. Play the hi-hat open:

Chorus

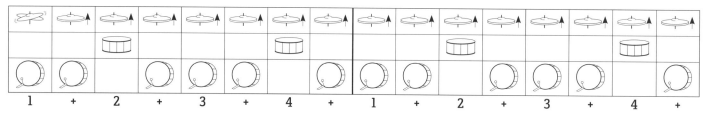

Bridge/Outro

You can use the same pattern that you played on the Verse for the Outro.

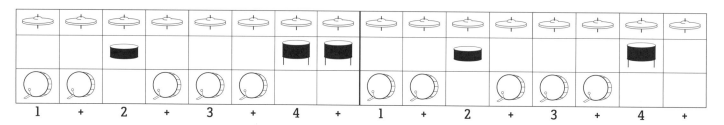

Standard Staff Score

Main Riff

Intro

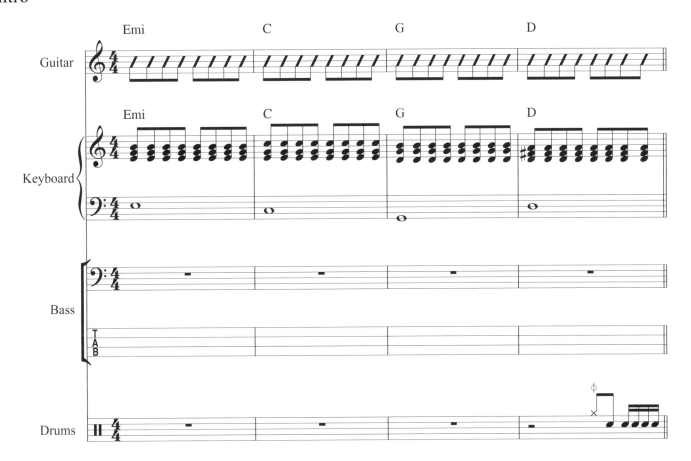

Verse

Chorus

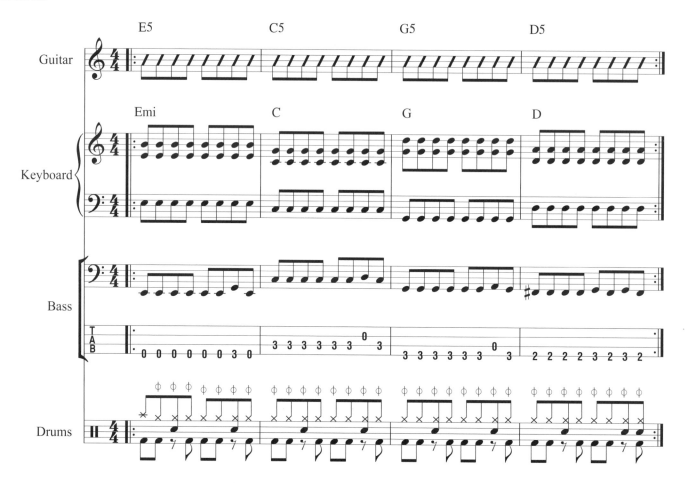

Bridge

VERSE

Emi   Cmaj7   G   D
Another head hangs lowly, child is slowly taken.

Emi   Cmaj7   G   D
And the violence caused such silence. Who are we mistaken?

      Emi   Cmaj7   G   D
But you see it's not me, it's not my family. In your head, in your head they are fighting,

        Emi   Cmaj7
With their tanks, and their bombs, and their bombs, and their guns.

      G   D
In your head, in your head they are crying.

CHORUS

        E5   C5   G5   D5
In your head, in your head, zombie, zombie, zombie, hey, hey.

          E5   C5   G5   D5
What's in your head, in your head, zombie, zombie, zombie, hey, hey, hey?

VERSE

Emi   Cmaj7   G   D
Another mother's breakin' heart is taking over.

Emi   Cmaj7   G   D
When the violence causes silence, we must be mistaken.

      Emi   Cmaj7   G   D
It's the same old theme since nineteen-sixteen. In your head, in your head they're still fighting,

       Emi   Cmaj7
With their tanks, and their bombs, and their bombs, and their guns.

   G   D
In your head, in your head they are dying.

CHORUS

     E5   C5   G5   D5
In your head, in your head, zombie, zombie, zombie, hey, hey.

             E5   C5   G5   D5
What's in your head, in your head, zombie, zombie, zombie. Hey, hey, hey?

SECTION 12—SAMPLE RUBRIC					
Skill	**4**	**3**	**2**	**1**	**Next Steps**
ENSEMBLE Group Playing	Student can play consistently in time with rest of band	Student can play mostly in time with rest of band	Student can play sometimes in time with rest of band	Student cannot play in time with the band	
ENSEMBLE Individual Performance	Student plays their part with consistently rhythmic and harmonic/melodic accuracy	Student plays their part with few rhythmic and harmonic/melodic mistakes	Student plays their part with several rhythmic and harmonic/melodic mistakes	Student cannot play their part	
ENSEMBLE Responding	Student responds consistently and quickly to changes in tempo, dynamics, and style in live performances	Student responds to most changes in tempo, dynamics, and style in live performances	Student responds to some changes in tempo, dynamics, and style in live performances	Student does not respond to changes in tempo, dynamics, and style in live performance	

APPENDIX A

Songs with Common Chord Progressions

These are songs with useful chord progressions for working on with your Modern Band. However, it is important to check the lyrical content of each song to determine what is appropriate for your students, as many of them have themes and language that may be inappropriate for your classroom.

SONG TITLE	ARTIST	YEAR	CHORD PROGRESSION
All This Love	Robin Schulz	2021	vi–IV–I–V
Love Not War (Tampa Beat)	Jason Derulo x Nuka	2020	vi–IV–I–V
Nightlight	Illenium	2020	vi–IV–I–V
Play	Alan Walker ft. K-391, Tungevaeg, Mangoo	2019	vi–IV–I–V
She Got Me	Luca Hänni	2019	vi–IV–I–V
Despacito	Luis Fonsi ft. Daddy Yankee	2017	vi–IV–I–V
No Vacancy	OneRepublic	2017	vi–IV–I–V
Ain't Your Mama	Jennifer Lopez	2016	vi–IV–I–V
Cheap Thrills	Sia	2016	vi–IV–I–V
Messin' Around	Pitbull with Enrique Iglesias	2016	I–IV–V
Play That Song	Train	2016	I–IV–vi–V
Dear Future Husband	Meghan Trainor	2015	I–vi–IV–V
Hello	Adele	2015	vi–IV–I–V
Marvin Gaye	Charlie Puth ft. Meghan Trainor	2015	I–vi–IV–V
Bailando	Enrique Iglesias ft. Descemer Bueno, Gente De Zona	2014	vi–IV–I–V
Thinking Out Loud	Ed Sheeran	2014	I–IV–V
All of Me	John Legend	2013	vi–IV–I–V
Contact	Daft Punk	2013	vi–IV–I–V
Hey Brother	Avicii	2013	vi–IV–I–V
Say Something	A Great Big World ft. Christina Aguilera	2013	vi–IV–I–V
Vivir Mi Vida	Marc Anthony	2013	vi–IV–I–V
Drive By	Train	2012	vi–IV–I–V
Hall of Fame	The Script ft. will.i.am	2012	vi–IV–I–V
The Light Behind Your Eyes	My Chemical Romance	2012	vi–I–IV–V
Marilyn Monroe	Nicki Minaj	2012	vi–IV–I–V
Stronger (What Doesn't Kill You)	Kelly Clarkson	2012	vi–IV–I–V
Brighter Than the Sun	Colbie Caillat	2011	I–IV–vi–V
Friday	Rebecca Black	2011	I–vi–IV–V
International Love	Pitbull ft. Chris Brown	2011	vi–IV–I–V
I Was Here	Beyoncé	2011	vi–IV–I–V
Little Talks	Of Monsters and Men	2011	vi–IV–I–V
Skyscraper	Demi Lovato	2011	vi–IV–I–V
Sparks Fly	Taylor Swift	2011	vi–IV–I–V
We Found Love	Rihanna ft. Calvin Harris	2011	vi–IV–I–V

What Makes You Beautiful	One Direction	2011	I–IV–V
Airplanes	B.o.B ft. Hayley Williams	2010	vi–IV–I
Baby	Justin Bieber ft. Ludacris	2010	I–vi–IV–V
Good Life	OneRepublic	2010	I–IV–vi–V
Just a Dream	Nelly	2010	vi–IV–I–V
Love the Way You Lie	Eminem ft. Rihanna	2010	vi–IV–I–V
21 Guns	Green Day	2009	vi–IV–I–V
Beautiful	Akon ft. Colin O'Donis, Kardinal Offishall	2009	vi–IV–I–V
Hey, Soul Sister	Train	2009	I–V–vi–IV
In My Head	Jason Derulo	2009	vi–IV–I–V
Love Me	Justin Bieber	2009	vi–IV–I–V
Hero of War	Rise Against	2008	vi–IV–I–V
I'm Yours	Jason Mraz	2008	I–V–vi–IV
Kids	MGMT	2008	vi–IV–I–V
If I Were a Boy	Beyoncé	2008	vi–IV–I–V
Poker Face	Lady Gaga	2008	vi–IV–I–V
What About Now	Daughtry	2008	I–vi–IV–V
Apologize	Timbaland ft. OneRepublic	2007	vi–IV–I–V
Confusion and Frustration in Modern Times	Sum 41	2007	vi–IV–I–V
Flightless Bird, American Mouth	Iron & Wine	2007	I–vi–IV–V
Happy Ending	MIKA	2007	I–V–vi–IV
No One	Alicia Keys	2007	I–V–vi–IV
Nobody's Perfect	Miley Cyrus/Hannah Montana	2007	vi–IV–I–V
So Small	Carrie Underwood	2007	vi–IV–I–V
Stand	Rascal Flatts	2006	vi–IV–I–V
Jesus of Suburbia	Green Day	2004	I–vi–IV–V
Holiday	Green Day	2004	vi–IV–I–V
Wagon Wheel	Old Crow Medicine Show	2004	I–V–vi–IV
Numb	Linkin Park	2003	vi–IV–I–V
Think Twice	Eve 6	2003	vi–IV–I–V
A New Day Has Come	Céline Dion	2002	vi–IV–I–V
Complicated	Avril Lavigne	2002	vi–IV–I–V
Don't Forget Me	Red Hot Chili Peppers	2002	vi–IV–I–V
Electrical Storm	U2	2002	vi–IV–I–V
Great Romances of the 20th Century	Taking Back Sunday	2002	vi–IV–I–V
Here Without You	3 Doors Down	2002	I–V–vi–IV
The Scientist	Coldplay	2002	vi–IV–I–V
Angel	Shaggy ft. Rayvon	2001	I–IV–V–IV
Hotel Yorba	The White Stripes	2001	I–IV–V
I Wanna Talk About Me	Toby Keith	2001	I–V–vi–IV
It's My Life	Bon Jovi	2000	vi–IV–I–V
Born to Make You Happy	Britney Spears	1999	vi–IV–I–V
In the Aeroplane Over the Sea	Neutral Milk Hotel	1998	I–vi–IV–V

Save Tonight	Eagle-Eye Cherry	1998	vi–IV–I–V
Good Riddance (Time of Your Life)	Green Day	1997	I–IV–V
Bidi Bidi Bom Bom	Selena	1994	I–IV–V–IV
Glycerine	Bush	1994	I–V–vi–IV
I'll Make Love to You	Boyz II Men	1994	I–vi–IV–V
Self Esteem	The Offspring	1994	vi–IV–I–V
Cryin'	Aerosmith	1993	I–V–vi–IV
Mr. Jones	Counting Crows	1993	I–IV–V
Zombie	The Cranberries	1993	vi–IV–I–V
My Name Is Jonas	Weezer	1992	I–V–vi–IV
Eternal Flame	The Bangles	1988	I–vi–IV–V
Alone	Heart	1987	vi–IV–I–V
I Still Haven't Found What I'm Looking For	U2	1987	I-IV-V
Nothing's Gonna Stop Us Now	Starship	1987	I–vi–IV–V
With or Without You	U2	1987	I–V–vi–IV
True Blue	Madonna	1986	I–vi–IV–V
I'm Goin' Down	Bruce Springsteen	1985	I–V–vi–IV
Forever Young	Alphaville	1984	I–V–vi–IV
Every Breath You Take	The Police	1983	I–vi–IV–V
Africa	Toto	1982	vi–IV–I–V
Here I Go Again	Whitesnake	1982	I–IV–V–IV–V
Down Under	Men at Work	1981	I–V–vi–IV
The Thin Ice	Pink Floyd	1979	I–vi–IV–V
Beast of Burden	The Rolling Stones	1978	I–V–vi–IV
Old Time Rock and Roll	Bob Seger	1978	I–IV–V
So Lonely	The Police	1978	I–V–vi–IV
The Passenger	Iggy Pop	1977	vi–IV–I–V
Blitzkrieg Bop	The Ramones	1976	I–IV–V
The Big Ship	Brian Eno	1975	vi-IV-I-V
Born to Run	Bruce Springsteen	1975	I–IV–V
No Woman, No Cry	Bob Marley	1974	I–V–vi–IV
D'yer Mak'er	Led Zeppelin	1973	I–vi–IV–V
Tuesday's Gone	Lynyrd Skynrd	1973	I–V–vi–IV
Crocodile Rock	Elton John	1972	I–vi–IV–V
I Can See Clearly Now	Johnny Nash	1972	I-IV-V
Angel from Montgomery	John Prine	1971	I-IV-V
Take Me Home, Country Roads	John Denver	1971	I–V–vi–IV
Those Magic Changes	Grease	1971	I–vi–IV–V
Let It Be	The Beatles	1970	I–V–vi–IV
Here Comes the Sun	The Beatles	1969	I–IV–V
Baby Baby Baby	Aretha Franklin	1967	I–vi–IV–V
San Francisco	Scott McKenzie	1967	vi–IV–I–V
Wild Thing	The Troggs	1966	I–IV–V–IV

Unchained Melody	The Righteous Brothers	1965	I–vi–IV–V
Monster Mash	Bobby Pickett	1962	I–vi–IV–V
Return to Sender	Elvis Presley	1962	I–vi–IV–V
Blue Moon	The Marcels	1961	I–vi–IV–V
Duke of Earl	Gene Chandler	1961	I–vi–IV–V
Runaround Sue	Dion	1961	I–vi–IV–V
Stand by Me	Ben E. King	1961	I–vi–IV–V
We Belong Together	Ritchie Valens	1959	I–vi–IV–V
La Bamba	Ritchie Valens	1958	I–IV–V–IV
Lollipop	Ronald & Ruby	1958	I–vi–IV–V
Loveable	Sam Cooke	1958	I–vi–IV–V

APPENDIX B
Tips for Curating Student-Centered Repertoire

Getting student suggestions is both helpful and challenging, as it will provide you with many ideas for songs to play, but you must also consider which of these song ideas are appropriate for the level of students that you teach. Here are a few teacher-tested tips you can use:

Share Out
- Letting each student pick one or two songs to share with the group (and even to play a short clip) can be a fun way for students to get to know each other better and find classmates with common interests.

Use Anonymity
- On the flip side, some students (especially those who might have more niche musical tastes) might be nervous about sharing their favorite music. Having them write down some favorites is a good and quick way to get song ideas.
- Technology can be a helpful aid for song submissions as well. You can use an online survey or form to let students submit anonymously (or not). Some teachers have given students specific guidelines for submissions such as: "Songs with a female singer," "Songs about the weather," "Songs that have a guitar solo," "Songs from the '90s," etc. Give each student some time to explore options for themselves before submitting.

Teacher Guidance
The teacher has two main options for final repertoire selection. We would suggested that you use both methods depending on the circumstances.
- Pick several songs that you know are playable for your students, and allow them to pick between them. This is especially helpful for new programs or younger students, some of whom may not have a wide musical knowledge. It is also an opportunity for you to share songs with students that may not be as familiar to them, as you see fit, all while providing them with choice.
- Use student-suggested material and filter through it to find songs that are at an appropriate music level and choose among them. There is nothing so special to a student as the opportunity to play a song that has a connection to their life. It allows them to express themselves safely and build social currency in a fun and healthy way!

Areas of Flexibility for Arrangement
- Approximate and differentiate difficult riffs, chords, rhythms, etc.
- *Lyrics can be changed.*
  - It is up to you to determine what types of lyrics make a song acceptable or not, regardless of them being changed. That being said, re-writing lyrics can make songs even more personal to students and is a vehicle for teaching them how to write their own material.

- *Don't limit yourself to songs with chord progressions that all your students know.*
  - A song with four chords can look intimidating if a student is just picking up an instrument for the first time. However, if four students (or four groups of students) all learn ONE new and different chord, those students can instantly combine their skills to play a four-chord song. For further clarification on this idea, see the end of Section 1.
  - If there is a section (a chorus, for example) of a song your students can play and a more challenging one they can work towards, have them start with the doable section and add players to the challenge sections as you progress! Students can start to learn new chords/riffs little by little in the new sections.

Tips for Rehearsing a Band

There are many correct ways to rehearse a Modern Band, depending on your circumstances. Here are a few considerations to take when starting a Modern Band.

Large Group vs. Small Group

- Large group rehearsals allow teachers to model strong rehearsal techniques and keep the class on task. In contrast, small group rehearsals allow students to learn leadership skills and take ownership of their musicianship. Most teachers do some combination of both.

Sound Considerations

- Modern Bands can be loud, especially when students are working informally or in small groups. It is valuable to teach students quiet ways of practicing, such as:
  - Using acoustic versions of their instrument (or practice pads for drummers).
  - Teaching appropriate amp volume levels when practicing alone, as well as when playing with a large ensemble.
  - Using headphone adapters so that students can hear themselves when isolated. Some technology exists, such as Jam Hubs, that allow multiple students to plug in and hear themselves in a small group through headphones.
- It is recommended to have the school or students invest in ear protection.

Teacher Directed vs. Peer-to-Peer Guided Instruction

- In a successful Modern Band program, there will be times where the teacher directs instruction and other times where students work individually on their independent skills, in small groups, as leaders of the ensemble.

Pacing

- It is important to infuse new ideas and material into rehearsals. It can be tempting to work relentlessly on a single song in an effort to perfect it. However, in popular music, quantity can lead to quality. Learning many songs will lead to students learning more skills and hearing a wider variety of musical sounds, which in turn allows them to play all songs at a higher level. Teachers are encouraged to use parts of student-centered songs as warm-ups, play-alongs, sing-alongs, and just for fun to keep students engaged while simultaneously tackling challenging material.

Instrument Variety

- While studying any instrument can become a lifelong endeavor, Modern Band allows for the opportunity to explore multiple instruments even at the early stages of musical fluency. In order to develop your class's overall musicianship, it is a strategy to allow your students to switch instruments while learning new repertoire and skills. This process takes on many forms, so it is important to develop classroom management systems that make the most sense for your population of students and frequency of class meetings.

Tips for Vocal Health

Singing in popular music is no different than singing in other genres when it comes to vocal health. It is important that you properly warm up your voice prior to singing to ensure a healthy voice throughout your entire life. Here are some suggestions to follow:

- **Warm up your voice with hums:** A good way to warm up your voice is by humming along to your favorite songs. This can be done for a few minutes at a time and is a great way to begin to wake up your vocal chords.

- **Drink plenty of water:** It is important for singers to stay hydrated, so drink water regularly to keep your voice hydrated.

- **Drink water at room temperature:** Drinking cold liquids will tighten up your vocal chords and make it difficult to sing, especially higher in your vocal range. The best thing to do is drink water at room temperature so that your voice remains hydrated and relaxed.

- **Avoid sugary drinks:** Soda, juice, and other sugary drinks take a toll on your voice. It is best to avoid them as much as possible, especially before singing.

- **Avoid yelling or screaming:** Although many of our favorite singers in popular music might belt or scream from time to time, it is really important that young singers avoid doing this unless they are working with a professional who can teach them to do it safely. The best approach is to try and reach a similar effect while properly supporting your voice and vocal muscles. If you begin to experience any type of pain or discomfort, stop the activity and allow your voice to rest and recuperate.

- **Avoid yelling or screaming altogether:** While this might also seem obvious, it is really important that singers avoid screaming in their everyday lives. This might happen during a sporting event when cheering on a team or at school after they announce the winners of the school decathlon. Whatever the case may be, it is important that singers avoid screaming entirely in order to preserve good vocal health.

- **Avoid talking when you are sick or have a sore throat:** While you might be tempted to continue going about your daily routine, it is important that you minimize talking as much as possible when you are under the weather. Your voice will thank you for it later!

- **Avoid throat clearing:** While singing, you might be tempted to clear your throat of any excess phlegm. However, keep in mind that clearing your throat will only create more phlegm, causing you to enter into a vicious cycle of constantly needing to clear your throat. In these cases, the best thing to do is to swallow as best you can to remove the phlegm and drink plenty of water to clean it out.

- **Stop singing if your voice is tired:** If you've been singing for a while and you begin to experience vocal fatigue, it is very important that you stop and allow your voice to rest. Powering through this type of fatigue could lead to a more serious vocal injury and should be avoided as much as possible.

General Vocal Health Tips

- If it hurts, DON'T DO IT! There is no reason for any type of healthy vocalization to cause you pain.

- Keep your warm-ups to about 15-minute increments within a couple of hours of your performance, as over-singing can cause unnecessary fatigue.

- When you're done singing, always give yourself a cool down to stretch and relax the tired muscles. Try a low hum or lip trill for a few minutes; some yawning and low sighing can help too!

- Try getting your blood pumping on the day of a performance—it will help to open your lungs and loosen up your singing muscles. It's also good for stress, tension, and performance anxiety.

- Breathe! Practice taking quick, quiet, and wide (spreading the rib cage/back out to the sides) breaths while you sing. And only breathe when you need to, so if you want to take a breath before a big phrase but haven't used all the air in your lungs yet, try exhaling quickly before inhaling again. (avoids stack breathing, stacking new air on top of the old).

- Always try to inhale through the mouth, and not the nose!

- Having trouble with high notes? Sing in the mirror and look for signs of tension. Is your neck looking strained? Is there a lot of space between the front of your tongue and the back of your bottom teeth? (Practice singing while keeping the tip of the tongue touching the back of your bottom teeth) Are your shoulders rising?

- If you're still having trouble, try making things silly to reduce stiff muscles. Lip trill the whole song, or sing it while skipping around the room!

- Hydrate as much as you comfortably can before the performance. Sipping water throughout a performance to "wet your whistle" is fine, but over hydration while performing could strip your throat of the good mucus that lubricates naturally and much more efficiently than water. Avoiding caffeinated drinks, as these are considered diuretics and astringents that could dry you out.

- If you can sing through a sore throat or cold without mentholated cough drops, that is best! Menthol creates a numbing sensation which effects pain receptors in your throat while you sing, this could cause more damage that you would feel once the menthol wears off.

- Don't forget to eat within a few hours before a performance. Everyone is different, but a normal diet will keep your mind and body happy.

- Always make sure you can hear yourself by proper placement/volume of front monitors, you may even consider wearing in-ear monitors or ear plugs to protect your hearing and prevent over-singing to hear yourself. (This also means avoiding placement directly in front of separate amplifiers for guitar and bass.)

Chord/Scale Diagrams & Drum Legend

GUITAR

Ab5 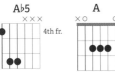	A	A5	Easy Ami	Ami	Ami7	Bb5	Easy B	Easy C
C	C5	Cmaj7	Db5	D	D5	D5 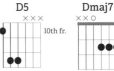	Dmaj7	Dsus2
Dsus4	Dmi	Easy E	E	E5	Easy Emi	Emi	F5	Fmaj7
Gb5	Easy G	G	G5					

A Major Pentatonic	A Minor Pentatonic	C Major Pentatonic	D Major Pentatonic	G Major Pentatonic
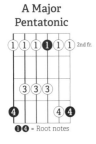	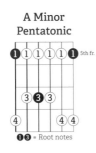	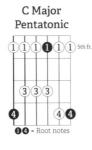	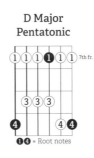	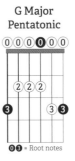

Blues Scale	Bb Blues Scale	D Blues Scale
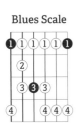	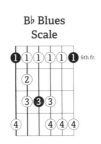	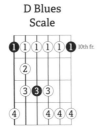

A♭ (2nd Inversion)

1 3 5

A♭ (Power Chord)

1   5

A

1 3 5

Ami

1 3 5

Ami (1st Inversion)

1 2   5

Ami (2nd Inversion)

1 3 5

B♭

1 3 5

B♭ (Power Chord)

1   5

B♭mi (2nd Inversion)

1 3 5

B

1 3 5

Bmi

1 3 5

Bmi (1st Inversion)

1 2   5

C♭

1 3 5

C

1 3 5

C (1st Inversion)

1 2   5

C (2nd Inversion)

1 3 5

C5

1   5

D♭

1 3 5

D♭ (1st Inversion)

1 2   5

D

1 3 5

D (1st Inversion)

1 2   5

D (2nd Inversion)

1 3 5

D5

1   5

Dmi

1 3 5

E♭

1 3 5

E

1 3 5

E5

1   5

Emi

1 3 5

Emi (1st Inversion)

1 2   5

F

1 3 5

F (Power Chord)

1   5

G♭

1 3 5

G♭ (2nd Inversion)

1 3 5

G♭ (Power Chord)

1   5

G

1 3 5

G (1st Inversion)

1 2   5

G (2nd Inversion)

1 3 5

G5

1   5

Gmi

1 3 5

A Major Pentatonic
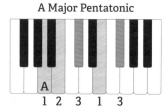
1 2 3 1 3

A Minor Pentatonic
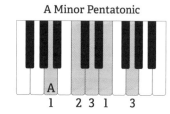
1 2 3 1 3

C Major Pentatonic
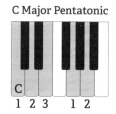
1 2 3 1 2

D Major Pentatonic

1 2 3 1 3

G Major Pentatonic
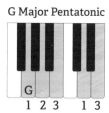
1 2 3 1 3

B♭ Blues Scale
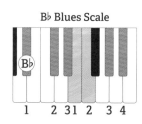
1 2 31 2 3 4

D Blues Scale
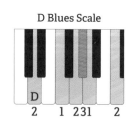
2 1 231 2

BASS

Open A	B	C	Open D	Open E	F#	G

A Major Pentatonic	A Minor Pentatonic	C Major Pentatonic	D Minor Pentatonic	D Major Pentatonic	G Major Pentatonic
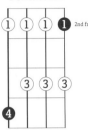	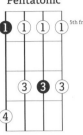	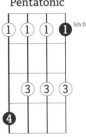	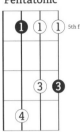	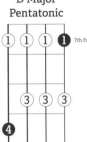	

Blues Scale	D Blues Scale	B♭ Blues Scale
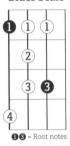	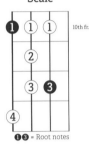	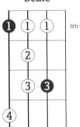
❶❸ = Root notes	❶❸ = Root notes	

DRUMS

 Hi-hat cymbal

 Snare drum

 Kick drum

 Ride cymbal

 Floor tom

 Crash cymbal

 Open hi-hat cymbal

 Rack tom

 Hi-hat pedal

 Rim click

 Claves

 Guiro

 Flam

 Cross-stick

 Cross-stick flam

Anchor Finger	A fretting finger that stays on the same fret and string between two or more chords
Arpeggio	Playing a chord one note at a time
Backbeat	A drumbeat played with snare hits on beats 2 and 4
Barre	Fretting multiple strings with the same finger
Bass Note	The lowest note in a chord
Beat	A single musical pulse
Beatboxing	Imitating percussion sounds with the mouth
Bend	To pull a string up or down with the fretting hand to raise the pitch
Blues Scale	A scale with an added "blue" note, often used in blues and rock music
Bridge	The section of a song that often happens just once and introduces new musical and/or lyrical material
Chord	A group of two or more notes
Chorus	The section of a song that has the same lyrics each time
Clave	A repeating, rhythmic pattern from Afro-Cuban music
Comping	Accompanying a musician, often a singer or soloist, on an instrument
Composition	Creating and writing music
Cross-Stick	A note played with the drum stick laying on the drum head with the shoulder striking the rim
Cross-Stick Flam	A combination of flam and cross-stick technique in which the stick laying horizontal plays the first stroke and the second note is played by striking the horizontal stick
Dot	A dot added to a note that adds half the original note's value
Double-Stroke Roll	Playing an alternating drum stick pattern during which each stick strikes twice, such as RRLLRRLL
Down Strum/Stroke	Strumming/plucking the strings of the guitar/bass with a downward motion
Dynamics	The volume of music
Fills	A short passage played by the drummer to transition to a new section or emphasize a musical phrase
Finger Style	Playing with the fingers of the picking hand, as opposed to a pick
Flam	Two taps, played close together; typically, a softer note followed by a louder note played in the opposite hand
Guiro	A Latin American percussion instrument consisting of a hollow gourd with notches carved into one side and played with a stick or tines
Hammer-On	To play a note and then play a second by forcefully placing another finger down on the fretboard on the same string
Heel Down	Playing the hi-hat or kick pedal with the heel of your foot on the pedal

Heel Up	Playing the hi-hat or kick pedal with the heel of your foot up
Improvise	To spontaneously make musical choices
Introduction	The section of a song at the beginning of a song before a verse or chorus
Lead Sheet	A diagram that shows the chords and outline of a song
Ledger Lines	Musical lines placed above or below the five lines of the staff
Legato	To play notes smooth and connected
Major Chord	A chord that uses the root, 5th, and major 3rd
Match Grip	A way of holding drum sticks where the top of both hands are parallel to the drum head
Measure	A single bar of music, usually consisting of four beats
Minor Chord	A chord that uses the root, 5th, and minor 3rd
Note	A single musical pitch
Paradiddle	A drum rudiment, or sticking combination, played either RLRR or LRLL
Pentatonic Scale	A scale with five different notes
Picking	Plucking one string at a time
Power Chord	A chord that uses just the root, 5th, and sometimes the octave
Pull-Off	To play a note and then play a second by plucking the fretting finger down off of the string
Repeat	Two vertical dots at the end of a phrase that tell the performer to play the phrase again
Rest	A musical symbol that tells the performer to stop playing for a certain number of beats
Riff	A melodic figure played on an instrument in a song
Root Note	The note a chord is named after
Sampling	Using a piece of pre-recorded music in a new composition
Scale	A collection of notes used to play/compose riffs, melodies, and solos
Single-Stroke Roll	Playing an alternating drum stick pattern during which each stick strikes once, such as RLRL
Slide	Playing a note and then moving your finger up or down the fretboard without lifting it off the fretboard
Slur	Connect two or more notes with hammer-ons, pull-offs, or slides
Song Form	The order of sections in a song (e.g., Verse, Chorus, Verse, Chorus, Bridge, Chorus)
Staccato	To play notes short and separated
Strumming	Playing more than one string of the guitar at a time with an up-and-down motion of the strumming hand
Syncopation	Emphasis on the upbeats of music
Tablature	Notation that shows which strings and frets to play in order to play music on the guitar and bass
Tie	An arched line that connects the values of two notes

Tonic	The first note in a scale, which the scale is named after
Transpose	To change the key of a song
Up Strum/Stroke	Strumming/plucking the strings of the guitar with an upward motion
Verse	The section of a song that often changes lyrics each time
Walking	Playing the bass by lightly pulling and releasing the strings with the fingertips

NOTES

NOTES